FOREWORD BY SHEILA WALSH

BOUND TO A
PROMISE

A TRUE STORY OF LOVE, MURDER, AND REDEMPTION

Bonnie Floyd
ZEPH 3:17

BONNIE FLOYD

CREATIVE ENTERPRISES STUDIO

BEDFORD, TEXAS

Published in association with Creative Enterprises Studio, PO Box 224, Bedford, TX 76022. CreativeEnterprisesStudio.com

Unless otherwise noted, Scripture quotations are from the New King James Version (NKJV), copyright © 1979, 1980, 1982, Thomas Nelson, Inc., Publishers.

Quotations designated NIV are from The Holy Bible, New International Version. Copyright © 1973, 1978, 1984, 2011, International Bible Society. Used by permission of Zondervan Bible Publishers.

Quotations designated NLT are from the Holy Bible, New Living Translation, copyright © 1996, 2004. Used by permission of Tyndale House Publishers, Inc., Carol Stream, Illinois 60188. All rights reserved.

All quotations from the trial are from *The Queen v. Melanson Harris, Marvin Joseph, and Donaldson Samuelson*, case no. 62 1995, in the Antigua and Barbuda High Court of Justice in the Eastern Caribbean Court of Appeal (Criminal).

ISBN: 978-0-9890521-5-3

Library of Congress Control Number: 2013944986

Interior Design: Inside Out Design & Typesetting
Interior Art: www.istockphoto.com
Cover Design: Dugan Design Group

Printed in the United States of America
13 14 15 16 17   MG   6 5 4 3 2 1

To Billy Bean Soup and his First Mate Kate,
you knew me as a sweet little girl,
as a spiteful teenager, and then
as a spirited woman,
and you loved me through it all.
Your adventurous life has taught me to live
every day to the fullest . . . as if it could be my last.
I will love you forever,
Bean

Contents

CONTENTS

Foreword

$\mathcal{I}$ am often asked to endorse books, and every now and then I am asked to write a foreword. I try to say yes as often as possible, for I remember the days of writing and wondering if anyone would ever want to publish or read what I had written. A well-written endorsement from someone who already has a loyal following can open doors to a new author or someone who is just beginning the painstaking discipline of telling their story.

Most of the time I have met the person who sends the request. Occasionally the name is new to me, but I find the depth and quality of what they have written compelling. Then there are rare situations when before I am even asked to look at a manuscript, I step up and volunteer to stand beside the book before it's even written. This is one of those occasions.

Bonnie is my office-manager and my friend. We have significant history together. We have walked through dark days leaning solely on the cross of Christ and the mercy and grace of our Redeemer. We have watched God make the impossible possible, showering us with His goodness over and over again. We have traveled together and have shared war stories to tell. We have wept together and laughed until tears were streaming down our faces. All of that to say, I love and trust Bonnie. But it was only when I was finally able to pry the manuscript of this book out of her hands and read it cover to cover that I began to realize the depth of what she has lived through.

I took the manuscript with me on a trip and couldn't put it down.

This is a heartbreaking story of intrigue, murder, and betrayal with more twists and turns than the wildest rollercoaster ride. But it is so much more.

This is a story of redemption!

This is a story of grace!

This is a story of forgiveness at a depth few of us will ever have to know so personally.

This is a story that profoundly illustrates that God and only God can bring the most radiant beauty from the most devastatingly evil places.

Bonnie's faith is rock solid because she has walked through the darkest nights and found God faithful.

Just like that young shepherd boy who fought lions and bears, never knowing that God was preparing him to lead His people, Bonnie, in Christ's strength has slain the dragons that threatened to devour her. I cannot wait to see what lies ahead!

> The Lord is my shepherd; I shall not want. He makes me to lie down in green pastures; He leads me beside the still waters. He restores my soul; He leads me in the paths of righteousness for His name's sake. Yea, though I walk through the valley of the shadow of death, I will fear no evil; for You are with me; Your rod and Your staff, they comfort me. You prepare a table before me in the presence of my enemies; You anoint my head with oil; my cup runs over. Surely goodness and mercy shall follow me all the days of my life; and I will dwell in the house of the Lord forever. (Psalm 23)

Sheila Walsh
Award-Winning and Best-Selling Author
Speaker and Recording Artist

Acknowledgments

$\mathcal{T}$he first person I must thank has to be the one who relentlessly encouraged me to write this book. My Donnie, you knew from the beginning that one day *Bound to a Promise* would come to fruition, and you never gave up spurring me on. I use the word *spur* intentionally because like a stubborn horse I needed to be poked in the side to get going. You are the love of my life and God's greatest blessing. You have filled the last twenty-six years with more protecting, caring, and adoring love than I would have thought to ask God for.

Over the years there have been other relentless encouragers. I dare not begin to name names, but you know who you are. You are the parent, the aunt, the sister, the longtime friend from Peoples Church, and the shorter-time friend from Genesis Metro Church. I would also be remiss not to mention the ones who I only met briefly at a retreat, yet you encouraged me as though we had been friends for a lifetime.

Kimberly Noelle, a.k.a. the Comma Queen. You have been by my side since the day I got *the call*. We have wept together, healed together, laughed together, and created this book together. From the prologue to the epilogue and then, from the inside flaps to the back cover, there isn't a word you haven't been a part of or a comma you haven't placed! Your persistence to strive for nothing less than excellence (regardless of the deadline) has helped me to make *Bound to a Promise* what it is today. It will never cease to amaze me how you can take what I think is a perfectly worded sentence, change it around, and make it eloquently say so much more, and say it so much better! How do you do that? Our friendship has been proven by the test of time and distance. You, Mark, and the girls mean more to Donnie and me than words could ever begin to express. Your love and support in countless ways over the years will never be forgotten. I love you, My Friend, forever!

Dianna, a.k.a. Rachael Reread. After moving to Texas it took me two years to find you, but you were worth the wait! If I were to write a dictionary (and you know I'd love to), the definition for *faithful friend* would be "Dianna Golata." You are *always* there for me, and the proof of that is in the countless hours you have spent reading, rereading, and then reading my manuscript again. You have an uncanny way of correcting something and making it feel like an encouragement. How do you do that? Thank you for loving me the way you do; I love you right back forever!

Carrie, a.k.a. Harriett Hatchet. It's interesting to me the order God brought you into my life. You could easily be termed *new blood*, for the definition of that is "new people in an organization who will provide new ideas and energy," and God knew we needed that! You definitely brought something new to the "organization," and that was the ability to hack out, oh I'm sorry I mean, edit out literally pages and pages of what I thought was necessary to the story and could never be removed. There were times I wanted to squirt crazy glue down into your delete key and permanently disable it! One of your other amazing abilities was to delete a ten-page story and rewrite the whole thing in a powerful paragraph. How do you that? Though I jest, my love for you is real and runs very deep. I simply can't imagine my life without you in it. You have become so much more than a friend—we have become family forever!

ACKNOWLEDGMENTS

The publishing world, I have come to find out, is brutal. I have dealt with multiple publishers in the process of getting my book published and struggled tremendously to find one I could trust, until I met Mary Hollingsworth. Her company and team, Creative Enterprises Studio, can only be described as a godsend, literally. I would be hard-pressed to meet a woman in publishing with more knowledge, expertise, and integrity than Miss Mary. From editing to typesetting and interior design to the brilliant creations from her cover designers, the whole experience has been nothing but an absolute thrill for me. I trust you completely, Miss Mary, because from the beginning you took my hand and held it tightly, and you have yet to let it go. I thank God every day for not allowing me to veer off the path for too long that led me to you!

Victoria, I have used the world *relentless* when acknowledging My Donnie and others, but honestly, most pale in comparison to you. The day I got *the call*, you appeared at my door to encourage me that the faith you had observed in me would now see me through. Some might think your coming over so soon, without being a close friend, was inappropriate, but I didn't. Your unexpectedly showing up spoke volumes, telling me God was sending His people to help me endure that earth-shattering experience, and I would make it to the other side of pain. From that day forward our friendship grew exponentially, and you became my Barnabas. You pushed me—sometimes literally—to meet key people who God then used to change the course of my ministry. When I was certain I could hunt and peck fast enough to write a book, you forced me—literally—to learn how to type. And now, nineteen years later, you are cheering me on from the finish line, because the finish line is where you have always stood. I love you Toria, forever!

Introduction

Bound to a Promise is a true story, as fictional and fascinating as it may seem. I have lived every terrible and triumphant moment of it and have finally made it to the other side of pain. As I continue to walk this journey, I have learned the secret of being content and finding perfect peace in any situation.

I have often been asked why I haven't written this book sooner, since the tragic part of the story happened years ago. I have told my story over and over through the years and have always known in my heart I needed to put it into print. But somehow the story never truly felt finished to me. As I attempted the daunting task of writing this book, I always felt there should be more—more *something*—but I did not know what . . . until now.

What I eventually found is astonishing because a key part of the story had been hidden for more than ten years. When it was finally unveiled to me, it unlocked a treasure I would have never dreamed possible, propelling this unfinished story from the past into the present.

The truth is this story is too big for an ordinary book. There's so much more to tell—so many other adventures to experience and wonderful places to describe. If you'd like to live this extended story with me, several Quick

Reader (QR) codes are included throughout the book to provide additional and interesting information. When you come to a QR code, scan it with your smart phone, and you'll be whisked away to the historic places and exotic islands where this story took place. (The same information can be accessed at www.bonniefloyd.com/btap)

Bound to a Promise is my story. It has changed me dramatically . . . and it may well continue to unfold for years to come.

BONNIE FLOYD

Prologue

Then the Phone Rang . . .

February 1, 1994: It was six o'clock in the morning on what seemed a normal, cold, foggy day in Fresno, California. Then the phone rang. Donnie was already up and in the shower, so I sprang up in bed, cleared my throat, and answered the phone with my cheery, "Good morning!" as though I had been up for hours.

"Is this Mrs. Bonnie Clever-Floyd?"

I suddenly froze as a cold chill of fear crawled up my spine.

The voice on the other end of the phone was unfamiliar, his question strange, and it sent a shiver through me. For the first time in my thirty-three years, the last person I wanted to be was Bill Clever's daughter.

"Mrs. Floyd, my name is Paul Howard, and I'm calling from the United States embassy in Antigua. I'm sorry, ma'am, but I need to ask you again, are you Bonnie Clever-Floyd?"

I stood motionless, still confused about why I was afraid to admit to this man who I was. I knew his question must pertain to my dad. Why else would he have been asking if I was Bonnie Clever-Floyd? I had never hyphenated my name, and as hard as it was to give up the name Clever, when I married Don Floyd, I became a Floyd through and through.

After a long pause, I firmly replied with a cracking voice, "No!"

By that time, I was sure Mr. Howard had discerned that the phone call was not going to go well. But then again, do those types of calls ever go well?

"Mrs. Clever-Floyd, are you the daughter of William Norman Clever?" he asked for the third time.

I simply could not reply. I was pacing the floor; dread had filled the room, fear had taken up residency, and confusion had consumed my mind. I heard Mr. Howard say, "Mrs. Floyd, Mrs. Floyd, are you still there?"

I knew I had to answer this Mr. Howard. I could not hang up and pretend the phone had never rung; it was far too late for that now.

"Yes, Mr. Howard, I am still here."

With relief in his voice, he asked for the last time, "Mrs. Floyd, are you the daughter of William Norman Clever?"

After a long silence, I answered solemnly, "Yes, Mr. Howard, I am."

So now the inevitable was about to be spoken. My life was about to change in ways no one in their wildest imaginations could have ever dreamed. But it was not a dream; it was a nightmare, and I was wide awake!

chapter**One**

Growing Up in Two Different Eras

$\mathcal{A}$s I stood paralyzed in time by the dread of what was coming next, highlights of my life that led to this terrifying moment played through my mind like a B-rated movie trailer in the old theater on a Saturday afternoon.

I grew up in Columbia, California, which is a historic state park in the Mother Lode Country. Columbia was founded during the gold rush days back in 1850 by a small party of prospectors who discovered the lode or main vein of gold in that region, the mother lode. News of their discovery spread, and a flood of miners soon joined them.

Scan this code for information about Columbia, CA

Unlike many settlements that have changed with the times, Columbia seems to be frozen in the 1800s. Growing up there was wonderful! How many kids get to grow up in two different eras at the same time?

Within the state park my family owned two popular saloons and the Columbia House restaurant, which was opened by my grandpop in 1958. Then in 1960 Dad took it over after moving to California from New Jersey with Mom and my two sisters, Susan and Linda. I came along in December of 1961, so unlike the rest of my family, I am a native Californian.

The Columbia House was a favorite place among the locals as well as visiting tourists. Everything on the menu was scrumptious, and all our recipes were originals and made from scratch. Dad's navy bean soup actually made him a local celebrity—so much so that the townspeople called him "Billy Bean Soup."

Dad began calling me "Bonnie Bean Soup" after himself, and eventually I became just "Bean." I loved being called Bean better than Bonnie. Every time Dad called me Bean, I heard him say, "I love you." Since it was my dad who nicknamed me Bean, it was the same honor to me as a son who is named after his father. After all, I secretly wished I had been born a boy so I could be even more like my daddy!

One of my favorite spots in town was the stagecoach. You could always find me at the counter selling tickets, riding shotgun with the driver or on horseback with the stagecoach bandit. Robbing those unsuspecting tourists was so much fun. It's a good thing I had to wear a bandana over my face because I couldn't keep myself from laughing.

I had a great life as a child, and I cherish my memories of those days. I would not trade one moment of my childhood. I felt secure in my parents' love for me and for each other. But the climate soon began to change.

To think their fighting could possibly lead to a divorce was definitely not a place I wanted to go in my mind. I had seen too many of my friends go through that, and the end result was always the same—the parents hated each other, and my friends wound up spending every other weekend with their dads. I was determined that was not going to happen to this "daddy's girl."

Don't get me wrong; I love my mom. She is a wonderful mother who was always about her family and found her fulfillment in just being Mom. There has never been a time when Mom was not there for my two sisters and me.

My dad was adventurous, handsome, intelligent, and successful. He was determined to live life to the fullest, and unlike my mom, he didn't seem content with just being a dad. He was eternally yearning, trying new things.

To keep himself content, Dad began accumulating businesses. He also started buying "toys," such as boats and motorcycles. His first purchase was a ski boat, and then a twenty-four-foot pleasure boat he and Mom named the *Bonnie Sue Lin*. One thing was becoming apparent—Dad was never content for long. Soon the *Bonnie Sue Lin* was not enough. He had to go for something bigger.

The *Sarsaparilla* was a beautiful, thirty-six-foot Grand Banks yacht, and because it was an ocean-going vessel, Dad started making plans for the big trip he always talked about taking. His dream was to go out hundreds, even thousands of miles beyond the Golden Gate Bridge. And what he really wanted to do was stay out for a few months, instead of a few days. His plan was to sail the coast of California into Baja, Mexico, down and around the tip of Cabo San Lucas, and up to La Paz into the Sea of Cortez.

And that is exactly what we did.

Our Mexico trip was more wonderful than any of us could have imagined. Even my sister Linda, who was in the prime of her teens and not one bit happy about taking an extended vacation, had the time of her life. We grew close as a family in ways we had never experienced before. All we had was each other, and we found that each other was all we needed. Laughter always filled the sea life air. I believe one of the greatest things children can experience is watching their parents laugh together and love on each other.

Within just a few short months after returning home, our close-knit family started unraveling. How I wish we could have just returned to the sea.

chapter Two

The "D" Word

*E*ven though I didn't know who God was, He knew me. He knew I was about to have one of the toughest years of my life. So I believe He gave me two very close friends my sixth-grade year, Shelley and Kathy.

Poor Shelley! That year, her parents had begun the process of divorce. My heart was breaking for her, and I was so curious how they had gotten to that point. I asked Shelley about her parents and told her I feared the same for mine. I was a worried and scared twelve-year-old, trying hard to understand adult problems with the mind of a child. Susan and Linda had both married and moved on with their lives, away from me. I felt so alone and had no one who could understand what I feared, except Shelley.

That conversation turned out to be a very big mistake! I remember vividly the day I got into trouble for asking Shelley questions.

I was playing at Kathy's house when my mom showed up early to take me home. As soon as I got into the car, I knew something was wrong. I repeatedly asked Mom, "Why did you have to pick me up so early? Am I in trouble?"

My stomach hit rock bottom when we crested the top of our long, steep driveway, and I saw Dad's truck in the carport. That was not a good sign; it was much too early for him to be home from work.

The three of us sat down, and Dad talked as Mom remained silent. "Bonnie, why would you tell Shelley that your mom and I have been fighting all the time? You know better than to air family business with other people! Do you know that because of what you've done, people are saying your mom and I are getting a divorce?"

He said it; he actually said the "D" word!

I'd never heard either of them say the actual word.

I looked up at him and said, "I asked Shelley because I've been worried that you and Mom are going to get a divorce. I figured she would know the signs. I didn't think she would tell her mom. I'm sorry, Dad. "

He interrupted with the all-too-familiar, "Yes, that's right, you didn't think! How many times do I have to tell you to think before you speak?"

With my head down I quietly asked, "But just tell me, Dad, are you and Mom getting a divorce?"

Without hesitation, he replied, "Married people argue, that's just what they do, but it doesn't always mean they are *getting* a divorce. From now on you do not discuss what goes on in this house with anyone. Do you understand?"

With a blank stare I trembled, "Yes, Dad, I understand, and I'm sorry for airing family business."

I slowly got up and went to my room. I felt sick and desperately wanted to bawl my eyes out, but there was no way I was going to let that happen. If Mom came in, she would be all lovey and mushy, and if Dad came in, there was no way I was going to let him see me cry. So I sat on my bed thinking about the day's events. I actually mustered up the courage to ask the divorce question, and the answer I got from Dad was, "Fighting doesn't *always* mean married people are getting a divorce," which was really no answer at all.

So what category do we fall into—"always" or "not always," for crying out loud?

One night after I had gone to bed, I heard my parents start to argue again. It became pretty heated, and after a while it became so loud that I turned the volume way up on my little TV to drown out their voices. The next morning, I awoke to find that my mom had left during the night and was headed for St. Louis, Missouri.

It happened; it finally happened. Now what?

I was numb and so unsure of what my life would be like then. All I knew was, no matter what, this daddy's girl was going to live with her dad, *period!* I loved my mom, but being with Dad was my whole life.

Something's Up

It was quite different without Mom around, but we adjusted quickly. Dad and I were getting along just fine. One day he picked me up early from school, which normally would have concerned me, but since Mom had left, life was anything but normal

"Bean," he said, "I spoke to your mother today. She's coming home from St. Louis soon, and she wants you to live with her."

The shock of his words stung me like a bee. "What? *No!* I don't want to live with her. I mean, it's not that I don't want to ever be with Mom; I just want to live with you. Don't make me do this, Dad, please!"

He calmly assured me that I would not have to live with Mom and that I could stay with him. I loved my mom and didn't want to ever hurt her, but the thought of leaving my home and leaving my dad was more than I could handle.

One night, as Dad and I were having dinner, the phone rang. I jumped to answer it.

"Hello?"

"Hi, Bonnie, is your dad there?"

I knew that voice; it was the nice waitress who worked in our restaurant. *Why is she calling my dad?*

"Hi, Kathy, we're eating dinner right now."

"It's okay, Bean, I'll take it," Dad said.

What? Taking a call in the middle of dinner? That was never allowed in our home, and I knew it wasn't one of Mom's rules. *Something's up!*

My dad had hired Kathy about five years earlier as a waitress at the Columbia House. She was the nicest waitress we had ever had at the restaurant, at least to me. I would describe her as a pretty lady with a sweet, tiny voice, blond hair, and a funny eye. It didn't go sideways or anything, but her pupil was crooked.

I asked her one time why her eye looked funny, and I immediately got "Look #27" from Dad. He had forty-nine looks, and I knew what each of them meant in detail. Look #27 clearly meant "inappropriate question!"

Kathy gave Dad her own look and then explained to me that when she was a little girl she was chipping rocks outside when a rock flew up into her eye and damaged the pupil. I asked her if she was blind, which invoked Look #27 again! Kathy kindly answered, "No, Bonnie, I'm not blind. I still have one good eye, but with the other I can only make out shades of light and dark."

When Dad got off the phone with Kathy that night, I had to ask why she would be calling us at home.

"Well, Bean, she was just calling to say hello and to see how we were doing. Is that okay with you?"

"I guess?" I replied reluctantly.

"That's good, because Kathy will probably be calling me more often."

Are you kidding me? Why would the waitress be calling more often to check on us? We don't need checking on! I don't have a good feeling about this!

True to his words, Kathy did call more. She also started showing up in more places than just the restaurant. It seemed on her days off she was always with my dad. I didn't mind it much at first, but when Dad started letting her ride my motorcycle and use my water skis, I minded. Then he went even further—he invited her to go riding and go to the lake without me. I was not sure how I felt about all that or where it was leading, but I did know waitress Kathy was starting to get on my nerves.

It wasn't long before Kathy had moved in with Dad and me. There was never an actual move-in day; it just happened over time. Dad had filed for a divorce from Mom by then, and the whole situation seemed awful. I was on a mission to oust the intruder from our house on the hill. She was *so* not my mom. She once did something I believed was so unjust that my dad would kick her out on the street the instant he learned of it.

I had a bad habit of leaving the bath water in the tub and not draining it. Kathy would remind me every day after school that I had not drained the tub. What really ticked me off was that when she discovered I had forgotten to drain the tub, she didn't just bend over and pull the plug. Instead, she annoyingly left it for me to do. My mom would have never done that.

One particular day, I came home once again to have Kathy tell me to drain the bathtub. When I walked into the bathroom, I could not believe my eyes! The bathwater I had left that morning was now a muddy brown color. In it were varying sizes of rocks, leaves, and sticks that were a disgusting mess. As I stood there in complete shock, a big toad frog jumped from one big rock to another!

I was absolutely appalled. I could not believe she had made such a mess in the tub, and if she thought for one minute I was going to clean up that disaster, she needed to think again!

You just wait until Dad sees what you've done and the mess you have made. He is going to be so mad. I . . . can't . . . wait.

Much to my dismay, Dad did not react at all as I had imagined. As a matter of fact, he found it to be one of the most hysterical things he'd ever seen. As he walked out of the bathroom, he said with laughter, "Well, Bean, after you finish cleaning up that mess, I bet you never forget to drain the tub again!"

Dumbfounded, I stood in my bathroom, just the toad frog and me . . .

chapter Three

He Leaves Me

$\mathcal{I}$ honestly believed, as all children of divorced parents believe, that if push came to shove and there was a choice to be made, my dad would most certainly choose me over Kathy. I viewed her as an unnecessary intruder. Dad and I had no need for her, and the longer she stayed, the more confused and difficult I became.

The air was always thick in the house, never feeling peaceful, and I was primarily to blame. It had to be hard for Kathy to live in my mom's house with me, the constant thorn in her side. I didn't really care how Kathy felt about our home; I just wanted her to leave.

When a shiny new Airstream trailer showed up alongside the house, I had convinced myself that it was for Kathy so she didn't have to live in my mom's house anymore. But I really should have seen it coming . . .

Dad dropped the bomb one night. He had put the house up for sale.

For sale! Why?

He was explaining why they didn't need a big house anymore when I blurted out, "You're never coming back, are you?"

He gave me Look #17, which meant, "You're not going to like my answer, Bean." I knew that look all too well; it had just never hurt like that before.

Inevitably, the day arrived when I would actually move in permanently with my mom. The ride over to her apartment was quiet. What was there to say? Nothing I could say would change his mind, and I knew it. There would be no tears this time either. I rarely cried anymore, simply because it hurt too much when I did, and it never changed anything anyway.

We pulled up to the building that had come to be my mom's new home. It occurred to me that Mom and I were going from living in one of the largest houses in Columbia to living in a tiny space above a florist shop. Life as I knew it was changing drastically again. No, on second thought, it was being turned completely upside down.

My dad and I said our good-byes, which were short but certainly not sweet. In an anticlimactic fashion, he drove away to avoid drawing this moment out to a full drama situation.

I worked up my nerve and entered the small apartment. I sat in the quiet alone, waiting for Mom to get home from work. She finally came home and found me in solitude with a blank stare draped across my face. She tried hard to console me, to convince me that my being with her full time would be a good thing.

Her boyfriend soon stopped in (on his way to the bar, I'm sure). I didn't look at him or speak a word in his direction. I heard him tell Mom I would "get over it" in no time. "Kids are resilient," he said, "and she'll be fine."

I looked up at him with hatred in my eyes and defiance in my voice, "I will *never* be fine, and I will *never* get over this!"

At that he blurted out to me, "If you think your dad is so great, why don't you just get in my truck, and I'll take you back to that dirty good-for-nothing sucker!" Incensed I stood right up, looked him dead in the eye, and dared him to take me back.

By that time I was crying and continued all the way back to Dad. I committed right then and there to tell my dad how I would change: I would be good and promise to treat Kathy nicely. I would beg him to let me stay with them.

The truck roared up the hill to the house, and Dad jumped out of the Airstream to see who had come barreling up the driveway. Before the truck even came to a stop, the man I despised reached across me and threw open the door. *"Get out!"* he yelled as he spun out and drove away.

I ran into Dad's familiar, safe, and secure arms sobbing. Promising. Begging. Pleading. But all to no avail.

I saw pain in his eyes, and I heard in his voice the sorrow he felt for what this was doing to me, but he couldn't take me back, not now. He and Kathy had made too many plans. They had made the decision to leave her two young sons and me behind. He couldn't take me and ask Kathy to leave her children. I would have to go back to Mom. There was no other choice.

The second drive back to Mom's that day was pure agony and torture for me. Mom was relieved when Dad brought me back, but in her heart she knew it was only a matter of time. She knew Dad was moving forward to pursue his lifelong dream, and nothing, not even his daughter, was going to stop him.

Dad never made a secret of his plans to one day sell everything and live at sea. That's why he opened one business after another in Columbia—to financially be able to retire in his forties and travel the world. All the while, Mom made it clear that her plans were never to leave her daughters and grandchildren. She wasn't going anywhere!

Dad wasted no time "gettin' outta Dodge." Within days, Dad, Kathy, and the Airstream had left Columbia for good.

I reluctantly settled into Mom's, and it wasn't nearly as awful as I had anticipated. How could it be with a mom like mine? She spoiled me rotten and loved me as only a mom can. That awful boyfriend never stepped foot in our apartment again. We never talked about it, but I knew in my heart that she wasn't about to be with a man who would treat her baby girl that way.

I began to enjoy the whole high school experience and meet new friends, who introduced me to the world of partying. I found getting high or being drunk helped to ease the pain of the divorce and Dad's leaving me. For the first time in a long time, I thought I was happy.

chapter**Four**

Life Redirected

I heard from Dad occasionally through my mom, but rarely talked to him personally. I didn't realize it at the time, but my mom had become a filter. A year later she reluctantly informed me I would be going on a vacation with my dad. I hadn't seen him at all since he and Kathy left Columbia in the Airstream. I was so excited to spend a few weeks with him I could hardly stand it. To my disappointment, however, I discovered our vacation included Kathy and her two boys. My days of having Dad all to myself were long gone, and the sooner I came to terms with that, the better off I would be. I did get some alone time with Dad in the truck as we drove from one destination to another, while Kathy and the boys rode together in the Airstream.

We vacationed in the Northwest (Oregon mostly), and I had a surprisingly great time. I got to know Steven and Aaron much better, and they really were two terrific boys. They were both very funny—Steve with his antics, and Aaron continually cracking us up with his contagious laughter.

One particular evening as we settled into the RV park, Steve, Aaron, and I hopped onto our bikes for a ride. As usual the boys found new friends right away, and I rode around scoping out the place. I quickly noticed all the campers seemed upset about something. Ladies were crying and others were gathering together in huddles.

I rode back to our campsite and ran into the Airstream yelling, "Dad, Dad, something bad has happened, and the whole park is acting weird about it!"

He asked Kathy to turn on the radio, and just as she did, the DJ declared, "The King is dead."

"What king?" I asked.

Dad and Kathy looked at each other in disbelief and then back at me. "Elvis, Bean! Elvis Presley, the king of rock and roll."

Now I was in disbelief. You might think our evening was going to be a real downer with such shocking news, but not when Kathy was around. She broke out all their Elvis cassettes and poured champagne for Dad and her and sparkling cider for the kids. She decided to have a party to celebrate the life of Elvis Presley, the king of rock and roll.

The Journals

All in all we had a great vacation, and a new school year was about to begin. Mom's career began taking off, and we were able to move out of her tiny apartment above the florist shop and into the most beautiful duplex in town.

Dad and Kathy had been traveling all over the United States in the Airstream and began sending me Kathy's journals that told all about their grand adventures. On two different occasions they even settled down for a few months in one place. One place was Ogden, Utah, where my grandpop lived.

Dad's and Grandpop's relationship always puzzled me. They loved each other but never showed it. I know Dad admired Grandpop's intelligence and wise business sense, the same way I admired Dad for his. Grandpop left Dad and my grandma—who I never met—when my dad was about the same age I was when he left me. I believe Dad resented Grandpop for leaving him, but loved him and didn't hold it against him. I guess it was much the same way I felt about Dad leaving me.

The second time they settled down was on a beautiful beach on the gulf side of Baja, Mexico. I'll never forget the summer I spent there with Kathy's boys and her niece, Virginia. It was another great summer spent with Dad and Kathy. With Virginia added to the mix, it was perfect. Don't get me wrong, Kathy still bugged the heck out of me, but I have to admit, she was beginning to grow on me . . . a little.

Good News

My senior year of high school started with exciting news. My mom had met a wonderful man. His name was Wayne, and I really liked him. Mom thought he was so handsome, and she radiated with a big smile when he was around. His visits became more and more frequent, and soon they married. I couldn't have been more pleased for them.

Soon after Mom and Wayne married, they moved to his old stomping grounds in the Northwest. As soon as I graduated, I was set to leave Sonora and move to Oregon to live with them. Before moving I decided to spend a few weeks with my sister, Susan, and her family in Fresno. Little did I know a visit to Fresno would become permanent and change my life forever.

It didn't take long for me to find a great job with a new optometrist in town, which actually turned into a professional career. My full-time job and my private life were polar opposites. During the day I was surrounded by wonderful coworkers whose whole lives revolved around Jesus—something that was completely unfamiliar to me. I was drawn to these Christian people, and I thoroughly enjoyed getting to know them. However, in the evenings and on the weekends I was surrounded by people who knew nothing about God; their entire existence revolved around partying. It was as if I lived a double life. I would no more smoke a joint before work or at lunch than fly to the moon, but at home I would hardly do anything without getting high first.

TURNING POINT

One day I picked up a business card I had found lying around that read, "Dial a Bible Message." I had no idea where I had even found it. It sparked my curiosity, and I wondered what it was, but I didn't dial the number. I didn't throw the card away either; I just put it on my dresser. Eventually, after seeing that card day after day, curiosity got the best of me, and I finally called the number. What I heard was a recorded message from an older gentleman with a very kind voice. He first spoke a phrase of encouragement and then quoted a scripture from the Bible.

Mr. Dial-a-Bible-Message Man, whoever he was, became part of my daily routine, and I looked forward to coming home every night after work and calling him to hear his message and scripture. I always did that before I sparked up a joint because, come on, I would not want to call a man of God while I was high, right?

While I was feeling a pull toward spiritual things, I was also involved with Jerry, a man twelve years my senior. We dated and lived together for six years, even after I learned that he was a married man. I was desperate for companionship, to love and be loved. I longed for the security that type of relationship brought to my life and hoped one day he would want to marry me. I later realized that my deep dysfunctional need stemmed from my being left by my dad as an early adolescent. I spent my teen and young adult years searching for anything to fill the hole that was created by my parents' divorce.

That long-standing relationship ended, and in less than a year he was married to another woman. Security evaded me once again. Instead of focusing on my career and learning how to live on my own, I neglected both to be with Bob, the new man in my life. I let him spoil me with gifts and take me on trips; I was swept away—the wrong way!

Moving On

I became friends with Bob's brother and sister-in-law, Danny and Laura. I liked these two people from the instant I met them. I quickly came to realize why I liked Danny and Laura so much. They were Christians and were wonderful to me, just like the people I worked with and the Dial-a-Bible-Message Man. Danny and Laura were not the only ones telling me about Jesus at that time. My sister, Susan, had become a Christian after she met her new husband, Teddy. Teddy knew Jesus, and because of his faith in Christ, Susan's whole life had received an extreme makeover. My makeover was coming too; I just didn't know it yet.

Danny and Laura loved Jesus; they were extremely knowledgeable about the Bible. Danny told the most jaw-dropping, awe-inspiring God stories I had ever heard. Often I would lose all track of time when at their house because I was captivated by what they were telling and teaching me.

Over the years it wasn't only Christians who were sharing their faith with me; there were people of other religions who were strongly trying to influence my life. To me, the all-important question was, if they all claim to be right, how can I possibly know who's telling me the truth? Even after all my research, I still did not have a clear answer to that question.

One day I knelt down on my knees—something I was not accustomed to doing but seemed right at the time—and prayed out loud to whoever was the one true God:

> *God, I don't know which one You are, but one thing I know for certain is that there can only be one true God. I can't figure this out on my own because they all sound right, and they all claim to be right. So I am asking You, begging You, please don't let me make a mistake. Don't let me choose the wrong religion and follow a false god. Amen!*

When I first met Bob, we spent countless hours weighing the pros and cons of many different religions. However, this became a dividing point in our relationship and proved to be a fatal chasm for us.

The day before Thanksgiving, Bob decided he was going a different direction, so once again my heart was broken. I had become attached to his family and had plans to spend the holiday with them. Clearly my plans were shattered.

With literally nowhere to go, I called my sister, Susan, crying as I told her what had transpired. Susan is one who overflows with love and compassion; I had no doubt she would take me in. She insisted I drive straight to her house and stay with her and Teddy as long as I needed. She also informed me that they were going to their church's Thanksgiving communion service that evening, and I would be going with them.

It was on that night, November 26, 1986, at Northwest Church in Fresno, California, that I received the answer to the prayer I had just recently prayed: *the God of the Bible—the God of Abraham, Isaac, and Jacob—is the one true God. This God is the One who sent His only Son, Jesus, into the world as an atoning sacrifice for my sins. Jesus made a way that I could live eternally through Him by offering me His free gift of salvation.* And I accepted His gift that November night.

My search was over, my sins were forgiven, and I had a feeling my life would never be the same.

After finding the truth for which I had been searching, I was going in a new direction; a new course had been set for my life. The same could be said of Dad and Kathy. After traveling the country in the Airstream and working as captain and first mate on various luxury yachts, they made a purchase that would finally put them on the course my dad had always dreamed. It was a beautiful thirty-eight-foot Alajuela, a solid teakwood sailboat, and they endearingly named it *Silver Heels*. Plans were set in motion to sail around the world, fulfilling my dad's lifelong dream. It took months of preparation for them to finally set a westward course that would take them off the Pacific Coast and out to open sea.

Dad would never set out to sea until he was completely confidant that his crew (which consisted only of Kathy and him) and his vessel, *Silver*

Heels, were thoroughly equipped and all kinks had been worked out. So before they made the crossing to Hawaii and then on to Palmyra Island, they had a *shakedown sail* (the nautical term for when the performance of a ship is tested).

These tales would be best told through their eyes.

The Journals of Silver Heels

April 16, 1985

I had to pinch myself to see if it had really happened. We had cast our dock lines off dock C2 Marina Village Alameda for the last time, "Look out world, here we come!" I heard Willie (Dad) increase both his and the engine's rpms when I yelled as we were leaving the dock, "Wait! I forgot to buy another bottle of Clorox." The last few days—or has it been months—had been rather exhausting. After crossing off ten full pages of "Things to Do," we decided it was time to break the pencil and go for it.

The first thing Billy had to do was take off one hundred feet of chain to raise the water line due to my thorough job of stocking the ship's stores. After all, what could a few plum puddings, a gross of Jujubes candy, or a few cases of champagne and sake weigh? Silly Billy!

Though we had been living aboard Silver Heels *and sailing it for quite some time, we decided to make a shakedown sail up into the sloughs of the San Joaquin Delta.*

What had started out as a picturesque day turned into a day of thirty-knot winds. When we finally reached Mayberry Slough, it took us two hours to anchor, if you can call all that rope work anchoring. Wild Bill lassoed every available tree! "Well, Bucka-

roo, if we don't hold tonight, we're taking the whole damn bank with us!" he declared.

The next morning we went fishing, and I caught a beautiful striper. It was so big that I had to tie a chicken breast to it to make lunch. Seems like I'm going to have to get luckier fishing or put a chicken coop on board!

࿇

April 22, it was Billy Bean Soup's birthday, and we found an available slip at the Outrigger Marina & Café, a quaint and tranquil place to spend a day or two. It was a beautiful morning, and all was peaceful until a fisherman came and asked if Billy Bean Soup was aboard, and if so, he had a phone call. As we walked down the dock to answer the call, there on the patio of the café appeared the Carney gang, our dear friends Betty and Larry. They were singing out a wonderful "Happy Birthday" song to "Old Ancient Age" (a.k.a. Bill). In true Carney fashion, they brought a party with them, everything from hot dogs and champagne to quail eggs. They even brought their daughter and son-in-law, Terry and Jim. Somehow Larry has always managed to track down his best friend on his birthday.

It is hard to know what to buy a fifty-year-old spoiled man for his birthday, but I knew what Bill would miss most while circumnavigating—his best friend, Larry! So I made a Carney caftan (Larry told me I could not call it a dress). Betty tied a pillow around Bill's belly, placed the curly black wig on his head, and presto, we had a Larry Carney twin. Now when Bill is missing Larry, he can dress up and pretend!

It was a blissful few days with our dearest friends, full of non-stop laughter, shenanigans, and plenty of bubbly!

After a tearful good-bye to the Carneys, it was time to rest up, or should I say recover, because the next day it was time to say farewell to the Outrigger and move on.

෧෨

After popping a bottle of champagne while passing under the Golden Gate, we enjoyed a beautiful sail watching several whales spout us a passing greeting . . . Hawaii, here we come!

෧෨

It has taken us three days to acclimate ourselves to the continuous motion and our new sleeping pattern. We both had the zombie stare and headaches the first days out, but now we seem to be growing accustomed to the "bulkhead bounce." We have gotten ourselves into somewhat of a system—I refrain from using the word routine, *because that is one thing sailing is not! We run both the ship's and our own biological clocks on a twenty-four-hour period. Sail changes can't wait until the sun comes up, and the eyelids can't close just because the sun went down.*

෧෨

One day after a lunch of drippy burgers, I felt large and lethargic, so Billy hung a tow line over the side so I could go for a swim to bathe off my burger fallout. Somehow it was hard to relax and enjoy the coolness of the water when "chatter cheeks" kept on about trolling for sharks and saying two knots is the perfect speed to catch the big one!

The evenings have become delightfully warm, and we love sitting out and watching the sun go down while it changes the clouds and sky into a mural of colors. We have enjoyed the solitude of the ocean and the isolation from land.

⁓

It was right after the sun came up one morning when Barnum, a baby seal, came over to visit. He was so excited to see us; we thought the poor thing was going to wear himself out performing for us. He especially enjoyed playing with my red sweatshirt that I hung out over the water with the deck brush. We had to say good-bye when we felt a nice beam wind refreshing. He tried to follow us for a while but finally had to give up—spunky little guy! It wasn't long though before the supper show was about to start. Barnum, our baby seal, would be a tough act to follow!

We were not disappointed. A pod of sperm whales crossed right under our bow. They were so close I felt as if I could reach out and touch those dear square heads. We didn't think the last one in the pod was going to cross over in time. I braced myself for the big thud, but he dove down and broke clear. This was an amazing day!

⁓

The seas are really rough today as we are sailing dead downwind after doing the midnight shuffle on deck; we were up the whole night chasing the wind and making sail changes. The last twelve hours of pounding has made Bill's back sore (he broke it a few years ago), and he has put his brace back on. I'm feeling ragged around the edges myself. It seems the closer we get to Hawaii, the cloudier it gets. Did we make a wrong turn somewhere?

∾

This week the sea has been doing its bump-and-grind routine, and it makes it difficult to walk or do anything easily. Now I know what it would be like to sleep in a cement mixer! Silver Heels *is holding up well, and our spirits are high. We are having a super time.*

Every new day brings surprises! It looks as if someone turned on the bubble machine during the night. What looked like millions of transparent bubbles in the water were really baby man-of-wars (Portuguese jellyfish). Bill picked some up in a bucket; it's hard to imagine that something so fragile could be carrying such a deadly poison.

∾

Today will mark our halfway point. It is very difficult to plan a surprise party on a thirty-eight-foot boat. Bill thought I had a severe case of dysentery when I spent a good part of the morning in the head making toilet paper flowers for our luau outfits. It took me half a roll just trying to remember how to make them.

As we approached the 1100-mile mark, we watched the numbers on the log click away. 1098 . . . 1099 . . . 1100. We're halfway there!

I ran back down to the head to change into my sarong and toilet-paper-flower bra top (Oops! Spring is busting out all over). Guess I should have made it out of paper towels! My captain loved my Wahine transformation. After hanging up the halfway banner

25

I made, we popped the champagne I had on ice and indulged in my freshly baked apple pie and Tillamook cheese. What a wonderful day for us! Until the halfway point, we were always leaving California behind, but now we are on our way to Hawaii.

༒

The next few days were spent running with twenty to twenty-five knots of apparent wind; we seem to be making great time. The closer we get, the more excited we get. I just can't believe it—one more night and we will be in Honolulu! Now that we were making landfall, we will stand watches all night. We should spot the Makapuu Point Light about 3:00 a.m. I was so excited, I spent the afternoon cleaning.

Billy asked, "Are you expecting the mayor to come down to the dock to greet us? I'm sure he doesn't expect us this soon, but surely the hula girls with leis of orchids will be waiting for me!"

༒

"Landfall!" Wish I could tell you all about the long-awaited moment, but I can't . . .

Luckily the big event was recorded in Bill's log. He wrote, "Well folks, after 2,200 miles to get to Hawaii, Kathy is . . . asleep! There it is—the island of Oahu. Wahoo! We hit it right on the button. The compass course we have been sailing on for eighteen days is right down Kawai Channel. Hey, there's Diamond Head, and look, there's Waikiki Beach. Wake up, Kathy! But 'Zzzzz' is all I hear from her."

༒

We arrived at Ali Wai Harbor with sixty-nine Transpac race boats. Not only were there no hula girls; we were told there was no room at the inn. After we tied off at the fuel dock, we started calling around the island. Every call ended the same, "Call back next week when the Transpac Race is over." I felt as if I was in a fog as I watched people hustling and bustling all about us. After so many days of solitude at sea, it felt as though someone had pushed our fast-forward buttons.

We finally landed a guest pass at Kaneohe Yacht Club, and it would be available to us tomorrow. So we decided to sail over to Waikiki Beach, anchor out, and watch the boat races.

After the anchor was down, the champagne was flowing. We felt so happy; I think we both popped right along with that cork. We toasted Hawaii; we toasted Silver Heels, *and we toasted the captain and his first mate, Kate!*

I was sure nothing would keep me awake that night, but I was wrong. After about an hour of sleep, I was wide awake. I sat up all night in the cockpit mesmerized by the lights off Waikiki Beach. What a beautiful site! I suppose I should have found the high-rises offensive after sailing across the Pacific, but not so! It's such a gorgeous site and made me want to raise the flag while singing out, "I'm proud to be an American!"

Scan this code
for more entries
in Mom's
Journals

chapter Five

The Cute Guy on the Wall

$\mathscr{M}$y newfound faith in Jesus continued to grow, and so did my friendship with Danny and Laura. Even though I began my new life as a Christian at the church where Susan and Teddy went, I seemed to be more drawn to Peoples Church, where Danny and Laura attended.

The Sunday before Christmas, I walked into Peoples Church for the nine o'clock service as I normally did. I turned to look for Danny and Laura, and there, right before my eyes, was the most gorgeous male specimen I had ever seen. He had a full head of wavy brown hair—not too long, not too short. He leaned against the wall with both hands slightly tucked into the front pockets of a pressed pair of new Wranglers, a brown tweed blazer, and the "baddest" pair of boa cowboy boots I had ever seen.

Scan this code for information on Peoples Church.

I slipped around the corner to adjust any hair that might be out of place. I steadied myself, worked up my nerve, and headed straight for him. Much to my delight, he looked right at me and gave me a smile. I thought I was going to melt right then and there. I gave him a smile back, and as I walked past him, he said, "Merry Christmas."

"Well, Merry Christmas to you too," I said as I continued on my way over to the balcony staircase, casually strolling past as if he didn't matter. I was sure I felt his eyes watch me go up the stairs, but just to be sure, I glanced back to catch a peek. With all the poise I could muster, I let my gaze hold for a moment and caught him nonchalantly looking up at me. This told me exactly what I wanted to know; I'd caught his attention.

For the next few weeks, whenever the church doors were open, I was there, coolly standing at that spot on the wall where I had first seen him, but he never showed. I had almost given up all hope of ever seeing the mystery man again. Then one Sunday I walked down the aisle and was startled when a guy with his back to me whipped around and said, "Hi!"

It's him! It's really him! Breathe, Bonnie, just breathe.

My first thought was to grab him by the shoulders and violently shake him to ask, "Where have you been?" Instead, I gave him a sweet smile and said, "Hi" and calmly continued to my seat beside Danny and Laura.

By the time I said my good-byes to them after the service, the sanctuary had cleared out, and much to my dismay, so had the cute guy. I made my way to the exit, and as I looked up, there in the doorway he stood. A silhouette of a man standing with his legs slightly apart, hands tucked casually into his front pockets, was waiting for me. I knew that stance; I'd been envisioning it for the last month. His face broke into a soft grin as he spoke, "Hi, my name is Don. What's yours?" Unable to breathe and hoping not to faint from a lack of oxygen to the brain, I was able to open my mouth and say, "Bonnie; my name is Bonnie."

He held his gaze on my breathless face for a moment, then broke the silence by asking, "Are you hungry?"

"I could eat, why?"

Dinner with him went by quickly. I could have sat and talked with him all night. He was fascinating and adventurous, much like my dad. He had recently returned from an ironman-type training in England in preparation for a four-wheel-drive competition in which he was about to compete. The competition was called the Camel Trophy, and it was to be held in Madagascar, of all places.

This Don Floyd was unreal!

We saw each other several times over the next few weeks. I had come to the conclusion that he was perfect; yes, perfect in every way. One of our dates was a casual Sunday afternoon spent at his parents' place.

We headed east into the country toward the foothills of the Sierra Nevada Mountains. It was a gorgeous day, and the bright blue sky was a beautiful backdrop for the big, billowy white clouds that were dancing overhead. It was no wonder Clovis was called the "Gateway to the Sierras," because I certainly felt as if I were entering somewhere beautiful.

Don's parents lived on five acres, three of which were beautifully landscaped. I knew immediately that Mrs. Floyd was a lady with a green thumb. When you walked through the gate, it opened up to a wonderland of botanical beauty. This was too much for one lady to handle, green thumb or not! She had to be married to Mr. Green Jeans.

We walked up to the sliding glass door on the back patio and were met by Mrs. Floyd, who insisted I call her Patsy. She was such a pretty lady. She could not have been more than five feet tall with slightly graying hair and friendly eyes that sparkled when she looked at me.

"Come on in, you two. I've been waiting to finally meet this mystery girl," she said with a smile.

Within a few minutes, into the kitchen walked Mr. Floyd (a.k.a. Mr. Green Jeans.) He wore a pair of faded overalls and an old favorite plaid shirt. I immediately knew I was standing in the presence of one of the kindest men who would ever shake my hand.

Like Patsy, he insisted I call him Carl. He wasn't tall in stature, but I instinctively knew he was a great and mighty man in the ways that mattered. I thought they were the cutest couple I had ever met.

After about an hour Don slipped on a pair of old, worn overalls, and he and his dad headed for the shop outside. As they walked away I thought they looked like Mike and Ike, so very cute and so all-American.

Later that afternoon one of Don's sisters, Sandy, brought her two young sons out to visit PoPo and Grandma. When she walked in the door, I thought she looked a little familiar but quickly dismissed the thought. There was no way the "Polly Purebreds" raised in this house could have been anywhere I ever hung out.

Sandy was very pretty and looked very much like Don; they could have easily been twins. She was nice to me, but there was a coldness about her. Shortly after she arrived, PoPo and Uncle Donnie came in from the shop to love on the boys. We sat around the kitchen for a long while until I offered to take one of the boys outside to swing. Jason was the cutest and most affectionate little guy and loved to swing; it seemed we were out there for hours.

As I walked back into the house, I noticed the strangest look on Don's face. There was a cold, awkward air in the room that made me feel very uncomfortable. I tried to understand what had happened in the time I had been outside with Jason, but I remained a bit perplexed.

Don headed back outside to the shop, and the rest of my day was spent with Patsy, which I loved. She knew as much about the Lord as Danny and Laura. She asked me about how I became a Christian, and she seemed to hang on every detail I revealed.

As Patsy and I got to know each other, Don and his dad stayed outside the rest of the day. I began to fear the cold air I felt from him earlier was more than just a feeling. When it was time to say goodnight, I hugged this special couple good-bye. Crushed inside, I felt it might be the last time I ever saw them. Don did not say a word on the long, agonizing drive home, and neither did I. What was there to say?

When we pulled into Susan's driveway, he leaned across the seat in front of me and threw open the door. I looked his way, desperate for him to tell me what I had done, but he was looking straight ahead just waiting for me to get out. Without a word I slipped down out of the truck and closed the door. He backed out of the driveway and roared off.

I stood there for a long time, numb. I knew this pain—the pain of being left all alone while my heart asked a thousand questions—questions that caused a longing ache deep within my heart.

I looked up at the sky, the same sky that had been so beautifully filled with billowy clouds earlier in the day. It was now a black canvas, dotted with tiny stars. It was a good analogy of the condition of my heart. What was once bright, beautiful, and full of hope was now dark, empty, and full of despair.

I thought, *will true love ever find me? Anything that seems too good to be true usually is.*

It was so hard to put on a happy face. I didn't want to talk about it, and I didn't want anyone to know I was broken inside. I wanted to bury the whole thing; I had no idea what happened and why he dumped me with literally no explanation. All I wanted to do was cry, but crying was something I had learned to control a long time ago.

I didn't have the slightest hope he'd ever call again. It was a good thing because my phone surely wasn't ringing. I had experienced this before; I didn't dwell on it. It was obvious, when people leave me, they don't come back. I'd given up trying to figure it out, though I knew it had something to do with his sister Sandy.

My days consisted of going to work, reading my Bible, and going to church. I thought a lot about Patsy and wished there was some way to see her again. As I read my Bible, I desperately hoped it would help me make sense out of what had happened.

Danny had told me once that the Bible was the answer book to life, and I was definitely in need of answers. I went searching and never found the answer as to why Don had dumped me. Dad had left me to sail around the world, and Mom left for Oregon after marrying Wayne. I had experienced heartache in friendships with my dearest childhood friends. Every boy or man I had ever loved had broken my heart. With a track record like that, I was in desperate need for an unconditional love that would never leave me.

In my search for answers, I actually found a scripture in Hebrews 5 that said God would never leave me or forsake me! And Romans 8:38–39 says,

> I am convinced that nothing can ever separate us from God's love. Neither death nor life, neither angels nor demons, neither our fears for today nor our worries about tomorrow—not even the powers of hell can separate us from God's love. No power in the sky above or in the earth below—indeed, nothing in all creation will ever be able to separate us from the love of God that is revealed in Christ Jesus our Lord. (NLT)

I then knew the assurance of Jesus' unconditional love for me. I had never known that kind of love, so it was wonderful to experience it and know it then.

Almost a month had gone by since that dreadful Sunday Don left me standing at the curb, and I was finally doing all right. I would survive that heartbreak as I had all the rest, but it was different that time. I didn't get high or drunk to ease the pain; I went to church and spent time reading my Bible.

Late one night I got a call from my friend Diana. She had become my closest friend while I was living with Jerry. When she became engaged I was a part of her wedding shower, her wedding, and when she got pregnant with her first baby, I attended her baby shower. We had stayed close friends even though she and her new little family had moved to Sacramento.

When I answered the phone, Diana's first words were, "*Soooo*, I hear you're dating Donnie Floyd these days."

"What did you say?" I said in shock, as my mind went reeling. *So that is why Sandy looked familiar to me; she's Diana's childhood best friend!*

"Donnie Floyd! I was talking to Sandy today, and she told me Donnie brought you out to the Floyds' last Sunday after church. How on earth did you meet and start dating? Tell me all about it!"

"Uh . . . well . . . first, why are you calling him Donnie?"

"What do you mean? That's his name."

"Oh, he introduced himself as Don, and that's all I've ever called him. As for dating him, I'm not."

"What do you mean? Sandy said you are, and trust me, if Donnie Floyd brings a girl home to meet his parents, he's serious about her."

"Well, he might have been last week, but not so much this week," I sarcastically replied.

"Huh?"

"Diana, he dumped me, okay?"

"What happened?"

"I have no idea what happened. One minute we were as happy and serious as any new dating couple could be, and then, *bam!* He dumped me with no explanation at all."

"Okay, back up. Start over from the beginning and tell me everything that happened."

After telling her how we had met and all that had transpired up to that fateful Sunday, she asked me if at any point Sandy and Donnie had been alone without me in the room. When I told her about taking little Jason out to the swing, she became quiet and said, "Oh Bonnie, I'm sorry. I know exactly what happened now."

"Would you mind filling me in?"

"Sandy is Donnie's middle sister, and they are *very* close. She has always been the filter that girls who date Donnie have to go through. Hardly any of them meet her standards. If Sandy doesn't like them, Donnie doesn't date them. I know Sandy; she's been my best friend for many years, and as much as I love you, Bonnie, I know your past of living in sin, smoking pot, and being a party girl just doesn't measure up to her standards."

"I thought she looked familiar, but I couldn't place where I had known her, so I dismissed the thought. So she remembered me from your showers and wedding and told Don."

"Yep, that's Sandy!"

"I told him the first night we went out that I was a new Christian and there were some things about me he should know. He told me he didn't need to know, that the past was the past, I was forgiven and that was all that mattered. What a joke! He sure fed me a mouthful of baloney."

"I'm so sorry, Bon Bon. Obviously Sandy doesn't know he dumped you yet, or she wouldn't have told me you guys were dating. Hang in there; you'll find someone else really soon. I know you will."

"Thanks, Diana, but I'm finished with men for a while . . . a long while."

That night I laid in my bed contemplating things: why wasn't the forgiveness I received from Jesus when I repented of my sins enough for Don and Sandy? Why did he say my past didn't matter when clearly it did? I wondered if Patsy thought I wasn't good enough for her son now that she knew about my past. I had a hard time believing that one, but why wouldn't she? Two of her kids did.

I came home from work one day and had just sat down on the end of my bed when the phone rang. I answered it and it was *him*.

I didn't panic; I didn't need to tell myself to breathe; I wasn't elated; I was pretty much emotionless.

What does he want? Hasn't he done enough damage? Does he really think I want to hear from him? I have nothing to say, and don't care a thing about what he might have to say to me.

"Where are you?" he asked.

"I think you know where I am, since you're the one who called me."

"I mean where are you in the house? Are you alone?"

"I'm in my room! Was there something you needed?"

"Yes, I want to talk to you about something."

"Okay, talk."

"I am calling to say I'm sorry and to ask for your forgiveness."

Silence filled the phone line, and I truly didn't know what to say or how to react.

Breaking the silence he continued, "I haven't been able to get you out of my head. You are all I think about every day. I told you it didn't matter what you did in the past, and at the time, I didn't think it did until Sandy filled me in on the details. Sandy knew a lot about you, Bonnie. She knew about your past and told me all about it, but that was *before* you met Jesus. The Bible says you are a new creation; the old has gone, the new has come! Who am I to hold your sins against you? Jesus' forgiveness is all you or anyone else ever needs."

Silence filled the air again; I simply had no idea how to respond to him. No man had ever apologized to me, much less asked for forgiveness.

Is this for real?

"Bonnie, if you could find it in your heart to forgive me, I'd like to ask if we could start seeing each other again."

I paused for a moment, unsure if I should open myself up to this again but humbled that he would ask for my forgiveness. "Okay, I guess," I replied.

"Okay, you guess you *forgive* me?"

"I mean I guess we can go out again."

"But do you forgive me?"

I did forgive him, but that was a foreign concept to me; I don't think I had ever said the words "I forgive you" to someone before that. The feeling was strange, as if my forgiving him somehow placed me above him. I did manage to finally say, "Yes, I forgive you."

We ended our conversation by making a date for Friday night. His parting words were, "Get decked out."

When he came to the door on Friday, he was wearing those boa boots again but had traded his tweed blazer for a long, herringbone topcoat.

GQ had come to my door.

It was a good thing I took him seriously when he told me to get decked out. Don had made reservations for dinner and then surprised me with tickets to a play at a local theatre. Needless to say, it was a perfect evening. He treated me as a princess all night. Whether he was helping me out of the car, into the restaurant or the theatre, his hand was always right there on my back to escort me. After the most amazing kiss goodnight, I looked up into the sky. It was black with tiny stars just as it had been the night he broke my heart, but this time it wasn't the agonizing darkness that illustrated my heart, it was the promising brightness of the stars that filled the sky.

As he got in his truck to leave, he asked if I would like to spend the next day with him. Of course, my answer was yes.

"Do you own a pair of hiking boots?" he asked.

"Yes I do. Why?"

His parting words were, "Good, wear them with some old jeans and a sweatshirt."

I'd never been woodcutting before, but there I was in the midst of the breathtaking Sierra Nevada Mountains. I was learning many things about Don. He was not only a carpenter by trade, but also a mechanic and a welder, a hunter, an avid four-wheeler, and now a lumberjack!

Is there no end to this guy?

We spent the day with Don's family (his dad, sister Deanna, and her fiancé, Ron) in that picturesque setting, then we headed off the mountain around three o'clock in the afternoon. The plan was to go out to the Floyds' house, unload the truck, and have dinner. I was learning that they were one very close-knit family who spent a lot of time together.

I was excited about seeing the Floyds again, hoping his mean sister, Sandy, Donnie's Dating Dictator, wouldn't be there.

Much to my disappointment, when we turned onto the lengthy driveway leading to the house, Sandy's car was parked in front of the garage.

Donnie could sense me tensing up and tried to assure me by taking his hand off the gearshift, putting it on my knee, and giving it a squeeze.

When we walked into the house, I was a wreck, thinking about all Diana had told me about Sandy.

Breathe, Bonnie, just breathe!

Patsy wasted no time in greeting me, and she quickly offered a much-needed, warm and comforting hug. The next one to greet me was little Jason. He ran right up to me, gave me a hug, and said, "You wanna go push me on the swing?"

I almost laughed out loud.

Kid, if you think for one minute I'm going to leave Don alone with your mother, you are sorely mistaken!

As I walked farther into the house, there she was. I felt like a Dalmatian puppy about to encounter Cruella de Vil. To my surprise, when she looked up at me, she smiled.

Don't buy into it, keep your distance, and whatever you do, Bonnie, watch your back!

I smiled at her—a small, halfhearted smile.

Surprisingly, Sandy was nice to me, and after a while my nerves settled down a bit. The evening was going very well, and once again I loved being in the Floyds' peaceful, loving home.

Later that day Sandy pulled me aside. "Bonnie, I want to apologize for just blurting out everything I knew about you to Donnie. I was trying to protect my brother; I've been that way with him my whole life. I didn't know you had become a Christian until Mom let me have it last week, and I had no idea he had broken it off with you."

Wow! Is she really saying this to me? I can't believe it, but way to go, Patsy!

Sandy went on to say, "I felt terrible when I found out, and I tried talking to Donnie, but he had made up his mind, and there was no talking him out of it. Mom also tried talking to him, but all he would do was get mad and walk out. One day Dad had had enough and tore into him."

Sandy told me exactly what Carl had said to Donnie:

Son, your problem is, you can't accept that she's been forgiven, and you can't get over the fact that she's lived with a guy. Well, what about you, bud? What about all you've done? While she was with one guy, how many different girls were you with? And you knew better, son! You've been a Christian your whole life, and that girl just got saved, which means you are without excuse, and she has been forgiven.

I sat there for a moment in stunned silence. I could not believe she was confessing that to me. I also could not get over what Carl had said to Donnie. Never in my life had I known a family like that. I didn't know what my future held with Donnie, but I could only hope it was becoming a member of his remarkable family.

chapter**Six**

Sunrise, Sunset

$\mathcal{I}$t wasn't long until it was time for Donnie to leave for Madagascar. He was gone for close to month, and I spent quite a bit of time out at the Floyds' house while he was away. I knew I had fallen in love with him, and I couldn't wait for his return.

There was much fanfare when Donnie returned to California after his adventure competition in Madagascar. His U.S. two-man team tied for first place, and his entire family and all his friends, along with the local television stations, were there to greet him at the airport. But I was by far the most excited!

To my disappointment, Donnie was ill upon his return home. He had contracted malaria. If that wasn't enough, he was lamenting over the Camel Trophy competition, in which the U.S. had been wrongfully accused of cheating in their victory over Italy.

When Donnie's 105-degree malaria temperature broke, so did his grimness, and just over a month later, Donnie presented me with the most beautiful engagement ring and asked me to be his wife. Eleven weeks later, on August 22, 1987, we became Mr. and Mrs. Don Floyd.

Our wedding was everything I ever wanted it to be. But as the big day approached, there was still something missing. As much as I had tried to convince myself that my wedding was going to be perfect in every way, there was no way it could be without my dad.

I had sent Dad letters telling him all about Donnie and that we were to be married. To my dismay I never heard a word from him. Most likely they had sailed on from their last address.

Marrying Donnie without my dad there was not at all how I had envisioned my wedding day. I missed Dad so much that my heart hurt, and I was getting married without him to walk me down the aisle. So much had changed in the years since he and Kathy set off to sail around the world. The biggest change was in me. I wanted him to meet the "new me" and, of course, My Donnie.

Our rehearsal dinner was at Donnie's parents' house, and during dinner the phone rang. Dad Carl came up to me and said in my ear, "Honey, the phone is for you, and I think you might want to take it in our bedroom."

When I picked up the phone, my dad was on the other end. I let out a squeal of joy, sat back on the bed, and started to cry. "Dad, how on earth did you find me?"

"Come on, Bean, you know I've always been able to track you down. Did you think I was going to let my little girl get married without hearing from me? So tell me all about your wedding tomorrow."

Dad had received my letters all at once, and when he couldn't get an answer at Susan's, he went on a quest to find me. He said he had enough information from my letters about Donnie and his family to know how to find me. He was calling me on a ham radio from the Solomon Islands, so of course he was not calling to say he was on his way. But knowing he went on a quest to track me down and talk with me before I said "I do" was really enough for me. I loved my dad so much, and that day he showed me how much he loved me the best way he knew how. What I didn't know then was that he had a little something else up his sleeve.

My wedding day arrived and I could not believe it was really happening. Waiting outside the chapel door to walk me down the aisle was my stepdad, Wayne, looking very handsome in his black tuxedo. I had grown to love him, and he had more than earned the honor of walking me down the aisle. As we approached the foyer that led to the church sanctuary, there stood two people I was not expecting to see at all—Larry and Betty Carney. Larry was looking at me endearingly with his arms outstretched. With big tears in his eyes, he said, "Your dad sent me, since he couldn't be here himself."

I know my daddy loves me . . . Larry Carney tells me so!

After long hugs and big tears, Betty and Larry slipped in the side door of the sanctuary to take a seat, and I took Wayne's arm as we headed down the aisle.

During the reception Larry came to the head table and handed me a big cardboard box from Dad and Kathy. Inside we found island treasures and the biggest, most beautiful seashell I'd ever seen. Larry looked down at me with fatherly eyes and a genuine love and asked if it would be all right to sing a song from my dad. Gazing down at me as he held his belly with both hands, he started to sing in his deep, beautiful, baritone voice, "Is this the little girl I carried, I don't remember her growing older, when did she? Sunrise, sunset . . ."

As Larry ended *his* beautiful rendition of that most beloved song from the great musical *Fiddler on the Roof,* he leaned down, kissed me on my cheek and told me my dad loved me. My wedding day was perfect in every way!

For our honeymoon Donnie insisted we get away for two weeks. He planned a trip up the coast of Northern California. We would take his truck, fitted with the largest luxury truck camper made. Some brides might not think that was a dream honeymoon, but I did. I loved his big Chevy dually; I loved the coast; and most of all I loved being with My Donnie. It was perfect!

Settling In

We settled into married life well, but in his job Donnie did not seem to be fulfilled. He mentioned when we were dating that his dream was to become a licensed general contractor and own his own construction company.

With my encouragement, within our first year of marriage, Donnie was able to permanently leave his job and become the general contractor and owner of Floyd Construction. Within two years of breaking ground on our first speculation home, Floyd Construction had grown to the point that I was able to quit my job as well. Our dream had come true—Donnie and I would work together, running our own business.

chapter Seven

He's Coming Home!

*O*ur first years of marriage were full of many experiences, and I loved being Mrs. Don Floyd. We shared a great love for the Lord and a remarkable love for each other.

One void never seemed to go away, though—I missed my dad. The longer I was married, the more I longed for Dad to come home and meet Donnie. He and Kathy had been gone for so long that I started to wonder if they would ever come back, even though Kathy was so good about staying in touch and filling us in on all their adventures through her journals.

She even sent the nicest gift that I know took many days for her to make for me, and it arrived on our first wedding anniversary. It was a handmade cookbook put together in what we would call a "scrapbooking" project today. The entire thing was handwritten and full of pictures that went along with each recipe and many wonderful stories interjected along the way. It was a true act of motherly love, and I knew it from the moment I read her opening letter on the first page.

Dear Bonnie,

Bon appétit! I do hope you enjoy this book and all the recipes as much as we did creating these dishes and memorable times.

I have two very real passions in my life, Bonnie. One is food and the other is your father! Fortunately they both go together so well. Whenever you hear the saying "The way to a man's heart is through his stomach," believe it! Now I didn't say we didn't have an alternate route, but we will save that for dessert. What nicer way is there to say "I love you" than a meal prepared with tender loving care, good music, candlelight, and each other.

The real joy of magical food is in the sharing. We treasure our time together, making each meal a ritual. However, we do enjoy breaking bread with friends, especially after discovering some new tasty delight!

The more we travel the more we know that there are no limits to food horizons. There's always a new adventure to be found in *Silver Heels'* galley.

All these recipes are tried and true and have your dad's smile of approval. Hopefully I have included all the pinches of this and dashes of that to make these dishes successful for you.

Preparation is only half the trick to gourmet delights . . . *presentation* is so important!

Your dad always says that I can even make a can of Spam look good! Looks aren't everything, but they sure help.

Make these dishes pretty . . .

Make yourself proud!

All My Love,
Kathy

For the first time, after reading her letter and turning page after page of that cookbook, I perceived Kathy as a mom, something I would have never believed could happen.

Finally the time arrived for the man so precious to me to come home to California! The day I had longed for, prayed for, and imagined a thousand times—Dad and Kathy would be with us in person very soon!

We got the news through Betty and Larry that they would be flying into San Francisco International Airport in three weeks.

I could hardly concentrate on anything else; I must have driven Donnie just about nuts with my dad stories.

"Babe, have I ever told you that my dad dove for Jacques Cousteau?"

"Yes, honey, you have."

"Can you believe he can speak three foreign languages fluently?"

"I know! French, Spanish, and Japanese; it's amazing, honey!" he'd say with a smile.

Donnie knew how excited I was, and he was so patient with me. I do believe, though, if I had told him one more dad story, he might just have put a sock in my mouth.

All the family had gathered at the airport with balloon bouquets and welcome home signs the day they were set to arrive. We filled the air with excitement as we anxiously waited at the gate near the immigration door.

Every time that door slid open, we would all get wound up, hoping it was them waltzing through next. It was getting to be a ridiculously long wait, and I was actually starting to get irritated. Donnie had to reel me in a little.

At one point the door, for what seemed like the hundredth time, released to make way for more passengers arriving, and an elderly couple walked through. I quickly noticed the elderly man looked much like Grandpop. I couldn't get over the resemblance, and then instantly it dawned on me: *that's not an old man, that's my dad!*

I grabbed Donnie, who was still looking through the immigration door, and said, "That old man is Dad!"

"No, it isn't, Bonnie. It can't be; he's an old man."

"I'm telling you, that's my dad!"

Donnie, who of course had never met the man, tried to calm me down and rationalize with me. I broke loose of his hold and headed for the old geezer.

The old guy seemed to hunker down even more and lean into the old woman as if he needed her support to put one foot in front of the other. For an elderly couple they sure managed to pick up their pace. When I caught up to them, I stepped in front of them and stopped them dead in their tracks. The old guy would not make eye contact, so I bent way down and looked up into his eyes. When I did, I was looking into the eyes of my father. I screamed, "I knew it was you!" and tackled him.

Because they had been gone for so long, they thought it would be funny to don disguises before they emerged from customs. Their plan was to successfully bypass all of us and then slip up from behind for the big revelation. My dad was so much fun, and I had missed him terribly.

During their two-month visit, their top priority was to spend quality time with their closest friends and family. I can honestly say I had never been so happy in all my life. I had my dad and My Donnie together. I knew they would hit it off; how could they not? They shared several great qualities—they were brilliant, adventurous, and intriguing men.

Kathy and I grew closer with each passing day. She enjoyed sharing her love of cooking with me, and I was learning so much and loving every minute of it.

Something I was most excited about was the one-on-one time Donnie and I would have with them. Up to that point I had not had an opportunity to talk to them about Jesus and what He had done for me. When opportunities arose, I seized them, and to my frustration every conversation ended with Dad saying, "Honey, it has obviously made a positive change in your life, but I'm doing just fine the way I am."

I was disappointed that I was failing to get through to them, but I wouldn't let myself get discouraged and was determined to never give up. After all, Jesus, Danny, and Laura never gave up on me, so Jesus, Donnie, and I were certainly not going to give up on them.

Donnie and Dad were inseparable during the weekdays. Dad couldn't get enough of learning all about our custom home construction business, and he eagerly shared his expertise in business management.

After a few weeks with us in Fresno, it was time to visit my stepbrother Steve. We loaded up the RV we had borrowed from our friends and headed for San Diego. That trip to "America's Finest City" proved to be a monumental time for my relationship with Kathy. We enjoyed ourselves immensely, laughed until we cried, and bonded in ways I could have never imagined.

The whole experience gave cause for me to recognize that Kathy was a fun-loving, nutty lady, and I liked it! No, I *loved* it! And I loved *her*—everything about her. How could someone I had disliked so intensely and labeled an intruder in my life turn out to be someone so dear?

Kathy wanted to be a mom to me, yet she wasn't trying to replace my mother. As a matter of fact, I never heard her utter an ill word about my mom. The lingering feelings from my teen years toward Kathy were beginning to shift. So much so, that calling her Kathy began feeling disrespectful. Not wanting to make a grand announcement that I had indeed had an epiphany, I decided it best to ease them into this transition slowly. Anything more than that would have thrown both Dad and Kathy into cardiac arrest.

I will always treasure the look on her face the first time I introduced her to my friends as "my mom, Kathy." That evening I overheard her telling Dad what I had done; she was delighted! As I stood outside their door, my heart grew. I couldn't help but think how much I resembled the Grinch.

Every person I knew liked Kathy a lot,
But I did not . . .
So what happened to me then? Well, in Whoville they say,
That my small heart must have grown three sizes that day!

The day for them to leave came all too soon, and I spent the entire day with a perpetual lump in my throat. I would not let my dad see me cry; I'd mastered that a long time ago, but keeping myself from crying didn't keep my heart from splitting in two.

I loved that man more than any daughter could ever love her father; there was no question of that in my mind. I wanted to hold on to him so tightly and beg him not to leave me again. Why did loving him always have to hurt so much?

chapter Eight

Always Topping the Thing He Did Last

$\mathcal{L}$ess than two weeks after their return to *Silver Heels*, I received the first of many letters that were to come on a very regular basis. My favorite part of it was where Mom wrote, "Just to let you know . . . your dad has been very good lately. He is saying things like 'gosh darn,' 'golly ding,' and 'shoot-a-rootie-toot,' rather than the naughty alternatives. He even suggests we say grace occasionally at dinner."

My heart warmed at the thought of sharing the Lord with them and that they left with Jesus on their minds.

All the letters and phone calls kept us connected, and we were so much a part of their lives, and they, ours. They discussed with us how shortly after their return to *Silver Heels* they hashed and rehashed their present lifestyle and plans for the future. They decided it was time to sail *Silver Heels* to France and for them to start replenishing their bank account by working on a charter yacht again.

"Why France?" we asked.

"Because we've never toured the *Cote d'Azur*, and there's always new scenery to explore!"

As soon as they made their decision, they began busily sending out resumes and collecting charts, all in preparation for their new adventure. But before they got a chance to cast off their lines and set sail, they were offered a job as captain and first mate on the motor yacht *Sportsman*, effective immediately.

No time for sailing to France, they had only time enough to put *Silver Heels* on the hard and jump on a plane. *Sportsman* was a sixty-three-foot Riva made by Ferrari—a luxury yacht—and it was gorgeous!

In all the excitement of their new adventure, I did ponder a thought: how was it that the man who had always managed to top the thing he had done last, now appeared to have topped out? He certainly wasn't topping what he had done last by going from owning his own boat and sailing around the world to being an employee on someone else's boat, or so I thought. When I began receiving Mom's journals, I knew I was wrong.

Their journals consisted of all sorts of intriguing tales about those who chartered *Sportsman*—an Iraqi billionaire, the king of Spain, the prince of Monaco, and even Lady Diana was onboard for a day! Needless to say, my thought that Dad had possibly "topped out" by taking this job on *Sportsman* was far from accurate. That was another unbelievable experience in my dad's long list of adventures, and they were having the time of their lives. My admiration and love for my father was as yeast is to dough—it just kept growing and growing.

There was another very important guest who chartered *Sportsman*, not once but twice. His name was Peter Ogden. He was a British Harvard graduate who, along with a partner, formed Computacenter, Europe's leading independent provider of IT infrastructure services.

Peter was one of Dad and Mom's favorite charters. They often spoke of what a wonderful and generous man he was. He had even been knighted for founding the Ogden Trust, which encourages and sponsors students from deprived backgrounds in teaching and learning physics.

One article written about this humble gentleman quotes him as saying,

I'd have to say this knighthood is all about the work of the Ogden Trust, which I was delighted to set up. I'm very fortunate to have earned a significant amount of money, and it gives you choices in life. So it seemed logical to me that I had an obligation to give it back."[1]

Learning of the interesting experiences and people who Dad and Kathy were fortunate enough to meet was so intriguing to Donnie and me. One of their favorite adventures was Kathy's opportunity to attend the Roger Verges Gourmet Chef School in France and become a certified *Le Cordon Bleu* chef. I was so proud of her!

A Personal Discovery

One morning as I was reading my Bible and praying, my mind wandered to thoughts of Dad. All of sudden, a thought came into my head that I didn't like at all: *Bonnie, you love your dad more than you love Me.*

I sat there in silence for a long time, contemplating that thought. I believed God was speaking to me. The Bible says that anything we love, admire, or are devoted to above God is an idol. I began to argue with the Lord, telling Him that I most definitely had my priorities straight, and He was number one in my life, not my dad. I could have argued with God all day long, but I would have never won, because He was right—He is always right.

I quickly came to realize that my dad had become an idol in my life, and you don't have to be a Christian to know that one of the Ten Commandments is, "You shall not make an idol for yourself."

So, I asked the Lord, *How can I possibly ever learn to love my dad less?*

God quickly let me know that I didn't have to learn to love my dad less; I needed to love Him *more*. That was easy for me to understand. Love comes when you spend time with a person and get to know him, even if that person is Jesus Christ.

Summer was over and the leaves were beginning to change colors when I received an exciting fax from Mom: "Put on your dancing shoes; we're coming home for Christmas!" I was so excited that I started dancing right then. I needed to get busy! There would be places to go, people to see, and lots of parties to plan.

To say it was a whirlwind two months would be putting it mildly. We picked them up at the San Francisco airport with a warm welcome. And at the risk of sounding horribly materialistic, one of the first things I noticed about Mom was her Christian Dior designer handbag. When we got into the car, I asked her if I could just pet her gorgeous purse. She replied, "I love you, Bean, but you're not getting my purse." We laughed and then she told me all about how she had persuaded Dad to buy it for her.

We had an incredible time being together for Christmas and in the days that followed. One thing Mom wanted to be sure to fit into the schedule was for her to have some quality time with her boys in San Diego and get to know Steve's new girlfriend, Cyndi. Dad stayed in Fresno to have his own quality time with Susan, Linda, and me. Mom's time with Steven, Cyndi, and Aaron was just what her mother's heart needed.

Something my heart looked for was another opportunity to share Jesus with my dad. I got that opportunity one night when Donnie and I were having dinner with Dad.

We got a little insight into why Dad was so cynical toward Christianity. He told us stories about things he and Mom had encountered on some far-off islands while sailing around the world. On one occasion, the islanders were walking around in dirty white bras along with their custom native dress. Apparently Christian missionaries had come there, and they told these women that not covering their breasts was a sin and distributed white bras to them.

On a different island, in another part of the world, Christian missionaries had told the natives that eating shellfish was a sin, and as a result of that ill-given advice, the people there were literally starving to death.

I know Dad was hoping for a little debate, but I wasn't going to engage because there was nothing to debate. I agreed with him and thought it was ridiculous.

"You know what, Dad? You are absolutely right! If all those missionaries did was give those poor people a religious list of "dos and don'ts" and then left them, they did more harm than good."

Now Dad was the one who was dumbfounded; he never thought I'd agree with him.

He told me that though he often played the devil's advocate with me, he believed Christianity was the true and right religion and Jesus was the Son of God. I looked right at Dad and tried to explain that it took so much more than that. I told him he needed a Savior and His name was Jesus! He would just look at me, and I knew exactly what he was thinking, *I don't need anyone, Bean, I've always done a fine job taking care of myself.* I purposed in my heart never to get discouraged, because all God asks of us is to share Jesus; saving my dad was His job.

Once again their trip home sailed by, and before we knew it, we were back at the airport saying good-bye. I was dealing with the all-too-familiar please-don't-go lump in my throat. Both Donnie and Dad knew how hard these good-byes were on me, so this time they secretly planned a quick getaway to try and make it easier. As we walked them to their gate, Donnie distracted me for a moment, and when I turned back around, they were gone. I panicked for a minute, frantically looking everywhere for them and finally spotted them in line to board the plane. Dad was looking at me with Looks #1—I love you; #43—This is going according to plan, and #20— Don't follow me. Obediently I stood still, trying to tell him with my eyes how desperately I loved him. He looked backed with Look #3—I know what you're thinking.

Mom, who was incapable of standing back and letting anyone be sad for long, started waving her purse in the air and called out, "Hey, Bean, I love you with all my heart!" And with perfect aim, she hurled her Christian Dior purse through the air right into my arms. "Take care of my purse!"

With smiles on all of our faces and joy in our hearts, they walked through the gate and out of sight.

chapter**Nine**

From Years at Sea to Living on Land

The year 1992 was very good for Floyd Construction and for the motor yacht *Sportsman*. If it were not for the invention of the fax machine, I truly believe we would have barely communicated that year with Dad and Mom. To be able to scribble out a quick note and hit a Send button was communication heaven. From then on there was rarely more than a week that went by that we were not waking up to each other's faxes.

Two years had passed since taking the position on *Sportsman*, and Dad was beginning to get restless. In almost every letter or fax we received there was mention of new job opportunities. There were many seemingly wonderful opportunities, which made it very difficult to decide. After chartering *Sportsman* a few times, their favorite guest, Sir Peter Ogden, had once again scheduled another charter. However that time, when the weekend was over he asked my parents to join him for dinner.

He had recently purchased a private island located in the English Channel between England and France. Peter had acquired the Island of Jethou (jet-TOO) on a ninety-nine-year lease, called a "Queen's lease." Peter invited my parents to visit Jethou and to consider becoming the island administrators. He explained that the island's other employees would come to work by boat during the week, and if necessary on the weekends, but Dad and Mom would be the sole inhabitants of the island.

Needless to say, that unique opportunity intrigued my parents, and true to his nature of always trying to top the thing he'd done last, Dad accepted the position. They fell in love with the Island of Jethou, and within a short period of time had settled in.

I knew once Mom had time to sit down and write her Island of Jethou journal, it was going to be great. They were so very busy in their new adventure that her journal was a long time in coming, but well worth the wait.

❧

Welcome to Jethou! I'm sorry it's taken me awhile to get this journal off, but when we arrived on the island, we hit the ground running and haven't stopped yet. The manor house was already totally gutted, and everywhere you looked was destruction and construction! Reconstructing the island was definitely a new experience, but taking on a new challenge he's never done before and being successful at it is what my Billy lives for.

My projects and responsibilities are coming along beautifully as well. My huge vegetable garden is a chef's dream but was a major undertaking. I planted hundreds of bulbs in our greenhouse, and I hear when spring arrives, Jethou will be one mass of color.

The Manor House will be done soon, and every once in a while, Bill catches me drifting off to la-la land as I fantasize about my new galley—oops, I keep forgetting, it's a kitchen. Peter is giving me my gourmet chef heart's desire. I've never seen a kitchen big enough to require roller blades to get around. I can't wait until Billy announces, "Kathy, it's time to put away your gardening gloves and put on your apron!"

Our cottage is now finished, and we find our humble little abode very cozy indeed. The one thing we enjoy about our cottage the most is the fantastic views. There is a different one out every window. Looking out at the sea, the boats sailing by, and the wildlife is like having a nonstop panoramic movie going on all the time.

I guess you can gather that we are very happy and excited about our new adventure. Going from years at sea to living on land was a major change for us, but I'm pleased to report that we do not feel at all detached from the sea. Actually we seem much more a part of it now. Still in all, during the quiet moments Billy and I make time to have our favorite champagne occasions—Sundays and absolutely no-reason-at-all days.

While reading the journal I was swept away to the Island of Jethou and captivated by its alluring beauty. As soon as I finished reading, I set the journal on the coffee table and got down on my knees to pray and ask God to somehow make a way for Donnie and me to travel there in the near future.

Scan this code
for informa-
tion about
Jethou.

chapter Ten

Jethou, Here We Come!

*M*y prayers were answered, and God was about to give me the desire of my heart. Donnie was going to take me to Jethou for three glorious weeks! Since we would enjoy such a lengthy visit, Dad thought June would be the best month to come for a number of reasons.

Apparently the weather in June is perfect and also the month of the Rolex Swan Regatta, which they desperately wanted us to experience. Also we would get to see them in action as Sir Peter would be entertaining guests on Jethou for a week. Once they were gone, we would have the island all to ourselves for two weeks.

It was only February when it was decided, so I still had months of anticipation ahead of me. With Valentine's Day right around the corner, I wanted to mail something to Jethou right away. I viewed holidays as "God opportunities," so I asked, "God, what would You have me send Dad and Mom for Valentine's Day?"

I immediately got a picture in my head of a perpetual calendar, one that stood up with pages that flipped over each day. On every page was a scripture from the Bible, and in my vision, the calendar was sitting over a stainless steel sink on a kitchen windowsill overlooking the ocean.

My first thought was of Isaiah 55:11, a verse that says God's Word never returns to Him void. I thought that was perfect; now they could get scripture in them every day.

God, this is brilliant. Thank You!

I searched and found the perfect perpetual calendar and greeting card to accompany my God-inspired gift and sent them both off to Jethou. I simply signed the card, not telling of the vision I had of the calendar. Little did I know what God was about to do.

One Amazing Vacation

Our reunion on their side of the Pond was no less exciting than when they had crossed over to see us. It was a short drive from the airport to the bustling harbor of St. Peter Port, and I knew I was going to love the place. Chris, the captain of the *Barbalotte*, which is Jethou's transport boat, greeted us at the dock. I looked all around on our way out of the harbor, because there was so much to soak in. It was as if I were in a different world, as if I were looking at a postcard, and I was in it.

Someone pinch me. Am I really here?

The first thing on Jethou Mom wanted to show me was their cozy cottage, and staying true to her passion for cooking, the first room she took me to was the kitchen. As we walked in, she started pointing out all the upgraded features, but everything in the kitchen, including her voice, was drowned out when I looked across the room. There, sitting on a windowsill that overlooked the ocean, just above a stainless steel sink, was the perpetual calendar I had sent them for Valentine's Day. My vision stood right before my eyes, and the calendar was even turned to that day's date. I stood there in complete awe.

The first time Donnie and I were alone, I told him about the calendar in the windowsill. We both laughed and rejoiced in the wonder of an awesome and exciting God!

That night while lying in bed, Donnie said, "Tonight when I was help-ing your mom with the dishes, I took a close look at that calendar on the windowsill. You know, she didn't just set that out because we were coming; almost every page has food splattered on it. God's purpose in having you send that calendar is being fulfilled. They are reading and being filled with Scripture every day, or at least your mom is anyway."

Bright and early the next morning, there was a kick at our bedroom door. As it swung open, in walked Miss Merry Sunshine with two cups of French-pressed coffee for us in one hand and that perpetual calendar in the other. With a cheerful voice, she sang, "Scripture for the day-ay, Scripture for the day-ay." Then she proceeded to read us the verse for that day and share her thoughts on it. As soon as she finished, she fluttered out the door and across the hallway into their bedroom saying, "Billy, here's our scripture for the day!"

Donnie and I stared at each other in amazement, and I said, "Well, baby, it appears my dad is being filled with Scripture every day too."

That day was the start to a very busy week. It was Regatta Week and Peter, his daughter, Tiffany, and their guests would be arriving later that day, and Peter's yacht, *Challenger,* a gorgeous sixty-five-foot Swan, had sailed in for the race.

Meeting Sir Peter and Tiffany was the highlight of the first day of Regatta Week. Tiffany was shy and so very sweet. Though her words were few, her continuous smile spoke the kindness in her heart.

After all we had heard about Peter, we were excited to finally meet him. One might think being a multimillionaire would make a person seem unapproachable, but that was not the case with Peter Ogden. His genuine friendly personality, generous spirit, and contagious laugh made him one of the nicest men I had ever had the pleasure of meeting.

The Rolex Swan Regatta, which took place off the Island of Guernsey, was scheduled to start the next day. Donnie received an unexpected surprise when Peter invited him to come on board *Challenger* and work the race as one of the crewmembers. I honestly could have knocked Donnie over with a feather at that moment. My husband is a man who lives for adventure and loves experiencing things he's never done before. He was so onboard (pun intended)!

Regatta Week was a smashing success and a week that will go down in history as one of the most memorable experiences of my life. We were sad to see Tiff sail off as she headed back to England with the crew on *Challenger*. She was certainly in good, safe hands as over the week we became great mates with Captain Criddy and First Mate Tom Williams. Peter was scheduled to fly out that day as well. We had thoroughly enjoyed getting to know him and felt as though he was much more than just my dad's employer. When the time came for Peter to leave the island, we had gained a new friend.

For the first time in a week, we were all alone on the island. The four of us were giddy, the sun was bright and shining, and the Manor House pool was calling our names. Once lunch was prepared Mom and I quickly changed into our bathing suits and monogrammed Jethou terrycloth robes. As I helped take lunch down to the pool, I found the guys were already doing laps. It was an absolutely splendid day that ended with watching movies in the old potting shed that had been converted into a state-of-the-art cinema.

The next morning we woke up to a frantic message on the Manor House recorder from Donnie's mom. Her dad, Grandpa Roy, had suffered a sudden heart attack but was stable in the intensive care unit. Donnie immediately called the hospital, and much to his surprise, when the nurse heard he was calling from Europe, she brought a phone in to Grandpa. Relieved, Donnie was able to talk to his grandpa. A short time later Dad came in and said we needed to call home. We both feared we were in for devastating news, and our instincts were right. Just hours after Donnie talked with Grandpa, he died in his sleep.

Following that phone call something happened that I will never forget. Dad, Donnie, and I were somberly sitting out on the deck, none of us saying much at all. Suddenly Miss Merry Sunshine walked onto the deck wearing a party hat and blowing a horn between her teeth. She was carrying a tray that held a bottle of champagne, four champagne glasses, and three more party hats.

What on earth is she doing? Doesn't she realize we're in mourning here?

I had come to appreciate her inability to stand back and let anyone be sad, but this was crossing the line.

Dad was the first to say, "Kathy, may I ask what you are doing?"

"I'm throwing a Grandpa party! We are all going to sit here for as long as it takes for Donnie to tell us every single Grandpa story he can remember. We are going to celebrate Grandpa's life today!" she declared.

When Mom placed the party hat on Donnie's head, for the first time that day his downcast face turned into a big smile. Just when I thought I was going to be irritated at Mom for the first time in a long time, I wound up admiring and loving her even more. For the rest of the afternoon, we sat on the deck and celebrated the life of Grandpa Roy Wilson. It was a glorious day!

By the time we had been on Jethou for two weeks, I had not only fallen in love with the island, I had also grown quite fond of the people who worked there. We had the pleasure of meeting several wonderful people. One in particular was Annie, who became my Jethou sister. Mom had spoken so highly of her in previous letters, and she was just as wonderful as Mom had described. We called her Little Miss Everything because she really did it all. Whatever Mom needed, Annie was right there!

One night at dinner, Dad announced that he and Mom were taking us to France on a private, chartered plane as a belated wedding gift. I almost fell off my chair! It was such a shock to us both; we had to ask if he was joking.

Paris! I'm actually going to Paris, France!

I jumped up, gave them a both a huge hug and said, "Thank You, Jesus!"

With a smile Dad teased, "Bean, I'm the one throwing down the American Express card, not Jesus. So you ought to be thanking your dear old dad!

I quickly retorted, "Dad, if it weren't for Jesus, you wouldn't have the funds to finance this trip."

"I can't win with you, Bean; I just can't win!" he said with a wink.

While dinner was being prepared that night, and we were visiting as Mom buzzed about in the kitchen, the master storyteller, Dad, shared yet another terrific tale.

This time it was about a sailing couple named Joe and Pam, who had suffered a near-death experience at sea. Here's how Dad told it:

"Our friends on the boat, *Sea Bass*, were sailing from San Juan toward Bermuda."

"Bermuda?" I interrupted.

"Yes, Bean, Bermuda, as in the Bermuda Triangle. Maybe an omen for what was to come for them. I don't believe in the Bermuda Triangle myth, but you know it is said that 'Bermuda is heaven, but to get there you have to go through Hades.' Our friends Joe and Pam were hit by a fierce nighttime electrical storm. The wind was blowing at least twenty knots, and they were up against seven- to ten-foot seas.

"When two people are sailing long distances, they will take two-hour shifts. Pam was down below, strapped in her berth asleep, and the autopilot was steering the boat. Joe is a very experienced sailor, but even the most experienced captains can make mistakes. Joe saw a splotch of oil on the deck, which could be slippery and dangerous. So he got a rag and made his way along the deck, being very careful to stay low on his knees, with one hand firmly clutching the lifeline for security. The boat lurched heavily, and when he braced himself against the lifeline, it gave way. He hit the water with the lifeline still in his hand, and when he looked up, he saw his boat sailing away with his wife down below asleep."

"You mean he wasn't wearing his safety harness?"

"No, Bean, he wasn't, and that was the mistake an experienced captain should never make! After he hit the water and came up for breath, he shouted for help, but *Sea Bass* was clipping away at a very rapid pace. He watched her sail off and said to himself, 'O, God, I have just killed myself.' He fully accepted that this was how life was going to end for him. He said his eyes were glued to the cabin doorway of the boat, and he was sure he was imagining things when he saw a movement on deck. When he realized it actually was Pam, the boat was so far away from him that yelling was pointless. All he could do was tread water and wonder what had awakened her or if she had heard his yell for help."

"I'll tell you what woke her up! It was the Holy Spirit; that's what it was! Oh, sorry for interrupting, Dad. Keep going, please."

"So now at least he had a fighting chance. Pam was nothing less than amazing. Her man-overboard training kicked in, and she did everything right. Somehow she spotted him and was able to keep sight of his head, which popped up only occasionally on top of the waves in the distance."

"Somehow? Dad, are you kidding me? That was totally God at work right there, empowering her and guiding her through."

"Well, yes, I'm sure you see it that way."

"She got him! Right, Dad? She found him because the Lord was right there directing her eyes!"

"Are you going to let me finish this story, Bean?"

"Oh, yeah, sorry, Dad; love you!"

Smiling at me he proceeded to finish his story: "This entire rescue went just as we had all trained ourselves for. Being prepared, knowing exactly what to do beforehand, and most importantly, keeping a cool head was what saved Joe's life."

When Dad came to the end of the story, Donnie and I were in awe of God, recognizing how He had orchestrated the events throughout this whole ordeal in order to save Joe's life. Even though Mom knew the story well, you could see the awe on her face as well; however, she was not giving God the credit as we were.

That became very apparent when she turned from the stove, put her hands on her hips, and asked in a kind but very sober way, "Why is it that you two always have to give God the credit for everything? Why couldn't it have been Pam's navigational skills that enabled her to find him?"

My mind was reeling; I had no idea what to say, but I knew for certain God would.

I quickly prayed a silent prayer, *Lord, that is a really good question, and if You could help me out here, I'd really appreciate it!*

God was so faithful to me in the intensity of that moment and gave me the words to speak, "Mom, we are all created beings, and anything we are good at or anything we excel in is because God first created that ability within us. If Pam was excellent in her navigational skills, it was because God gave her that ability when He created her!"

Mom just stood there looking at me, and like a wave washing away a mark in the sand, my answer washed over her somber and questioning face, and it changed to peace and satisfaction. She turned back to the stove without speaking a word.

I looked over at Dad as he told the story and became suddenly overwhelmed with a heavy burden for the fate of his and Mom's souls. This happened to me every time I thought about the fact that they had yet to ask Jesus into their hearts as Lord and Savior, and the thought of being eternally separated from them was more than I could bear.

The story about Joe and Pam offered me an opportunity with my dad I had never had before. I decided to seize it and said, "Dad, just promise me one thing—if you ever get into a position where you fear for your life, you will call on the name of Jesus."

Surprisingly, without any hesitation, he looked me right in the eye and said, "Bean, I promise you, if I ever get into a position where I fear for my life, I will call on the name of Jesus, but I have never been, nor will I ever be in a position where I am not in total control."

I knew my dad so well, and while to some people that statement would have sounded arrogant, I knew there was a lot of truth in his assertion. What Dad didn't acknowledge, which many people don't, is the fact that a day is coming in every person's life that he cannot control. On that day he will need a Savior. And Romans 10:13 is comforting because it says, "Everyone who calls on the name of the Lord will be saved" (NIV).

A BEAUTIFUL ENDING

Leaving Jethou was every bit as hard as I thought it would be. The two weeks we spent on their little island in paradise was more amazing than I could have ever imagined, but they went by so fast. As we boarded the *Barbalotte* and motored away, the only thing that made looking back at Jethou bearable was praying and believing in my heart I would return one day.

Our time on Jethou had come to an end, but our trip was far from over. We were off to Paris!

The two weeks on Jethou and our week in Paris with Dad and Mom were heavenly in every way. I had just experienced a once-in-a-lifetime vacation with three of my most favorite people in the entire world. We created many memories that I will cherish in my heart forever. If we had to do it all over again, none of us would have changed a thing. It was truly perfect!

After settling back home in Fresno, my normal morning routine was to be awakened at 6:30 a.m. by My Donnie with a perfectly brewed cup of coffee in one hand and a fax from Mom in the other. I loved my mornings. Donnie fluffed the pillows behind me, and I would lean back, sip my coffee, and read her fax out loud to him. They always produced our first chuckle for the day; her witty and playful way of writing always assured that. I loved being so familiar with Jethou that I could picture Dad and Mom's surroundings and everyday life on the island. Faxes no longer had to be descriptive for us to understand where they were or what they were doing; we could picture it all, because we had seen and experienced it all.

  On the morning of our sixth wedding anniversary, Donnie walked in with a fax from Mom and my coffee in hand. It had August 22, 1993, splashed across the top, and it was more of a handmade anniversary card than a fax, with well wishes signed by Dad, Mom, and the Jethou crew.

> *Still together! Is that due to Donnie's forgiving nature or Bonnie's irresistible charm?*
>
> > *Love,*
> > *Dad*

> *Words of Wisdom from Mom ♡*
> *"Guard well your spare moments—they are like uncut diamonds! Discard them and their value will never be known. Improve them and they will become the brightest gems in a useful life." –Ralph Waldo Emerson*
>
> *According to my calculations, you have been married 1,866,240,000 seconds. Hope all your treasured moments are too numerous to count. Can you count your uncut diamonds?*
>
> > *Love,*
> > *Mom*

> *Hope the two of you have lots of champagne on your anniversary. We certainly are!*
>
> > *Lots of Love,*
> > *Annie*

Donnie and I got a chuckle out of Annie's comment because we had no doubt that Mom had declared our anniversary an official champagne holiday on Jethou!

And so it went in the months to come, daily faxes to one another, and occasionally Mom and I would send love gifts in the mail.

I will never forget the day Donnie brought a small package that had arrived in the mail from Jethou. Inside was a framed piece of handmade artwork. At the top and bottom of the artwork were beautifully arranged dried and pressed flowers, and in the center were these words: *God made hugs, smiles, and little girls.*

Not being one to cry, I admittedly teared up! It was the "little girl" part that got me. She first knew me as the sweet little pistol running around the restaurant as if I owned the place. She then lived with an awful teenage troublemaker, who viewed her as nothing but an intruder. Now all grown up, we had come full circle. I not only thought of her as my friend, but as someone who I greatly loved and admired; someone I affectionately called Mom.

Those words said to me, "Bonnie, I knew you as a sweet little girl, I knew you as a hurting and confused teenager, and now I know you as a woman, and I have loved you through it all."

When I turned the frame over, she had written on the back:

Dear Bonnie,

Some lovely Jethou flowers I picked and dried for you with love from our beautiful Island of Jethou; your home away from home.

I love you, Bean,
Mom ♡

HAPPY HOLIDAYS

Dad and Mom could not come home for Christmas that year, so they made a quick trip to California in November to see us all. Even though they would not be with us, Christmas was still special because we celebrated in our new home we had recently built. Another thing that made that particular Christmas special for us was Mom's December journal. The special part was how she ended it. In all their journals over the years there was never an acknowledgement of God. Any mentions of God in past journals were made in vain or in jest. This one, however, was neither of those. It was an acknowledgement of His goodness to them. Here's how it ended:

It's been over fifteen years since I have actually lived in a house. Just imagine all those years of pent-up creativity. I have really enjoyed being Little Miss Homemaker this month. The Manor House looks so festive with all my decorations. I really believe that we have the most beautiful Christmas tree in the Channel Islands. My only Christmas wish is that we could share it all with you.

January should prove to be a very busy month. At this time we have forty people booked for two business conferences. One day after our last guest departure, our boss has invited us to fly to the Virgin Islands for a week aboard his yacht, Challenger, *a sixty-five-foot Swan. Oh, to be sailing again! So as you must know . . . God has been very good to us! Thank you, thank you, and happy birthday!*

Hope all you dear friends have equally as much to celebrate this holiday season. Merry Christmas and do have an exceptionally Happy New Year!

Merry Christmas,
Bill & Kathy

Right after New Year's on January 5 I received a fax from Mom. Financially, we really needed one of our spec houses to sell, and she had been praying for us.

Howdy, still sitting here next to the phone because I know you are going to call soon and let us know you sold the house. Yesterday when I was in town, I was thinking of you, and a little voice told me to buy a "this house sold" gift for you. Sooo, should I mail it or save it? Call, fax, or do something—we're dying to know!

We love you,
Mom and Dad

It was wonderful to be so close and connected to them. We knew everything that was going on in their lives, and they knew ours. The years of being disconnected, for whatever the reason, were in the distant past, and God had granted me the desire of my heart.

Apparently this feeling of complete family fulfillment was exactly how they were feeling as well, and they said so in a fax I received on January 11, 1994:

I'm feeling exceptionally happy this morning . . .

I enjoyed our talk on the phone, and after I hung up, your dad and I sat together with our morning tea and coffee and jawed on and on about how blessed we are to have such a wonderful family.

We just can't believe what super neat people you all are. We started with the youngest, Aaron, and went through the whole lot! Can't tell you how much it means to me to hear your dad go on and on about how proud he is of all of you. Gosh darn, we love you!

Love,
Mom

chapterEleven

Living the Nightmare

*S*urreal is a word often used to describe a tragic situation, but until you actually live through a tragedy, you can never truly grasp the meaning of the word. I was about to grasp it . . . The definition of *surreal*, according to Bonnie, is, "Beyond what the human mind can fathom as truth."

February 1, 1994: It was six o'clock in the morning on an anything but a normal day . . .

The US Embassy? Who is this Paul Howard? How does he know my dad? How did he get my phone number, and why on earth is he calling me Bonnie Clever-Floyd?

"Mrs. Floyd, Mrs. Floyd, are you still there?"

I knew I had to answer Mr. Howard. I could not hang up and pretend the phone had never rung; it was far too late for that now.

"Yes, Mr. Howard, I am still here."

With relief in his voice, he asked for the last time, "Mrs. Clever-Floyd, are you the daughter of William Norman Clever?"

After a long silence, I answered solemnly, "Yes, Mr. Howard, I am."

So now the inevitable was about to be spoken. My life was about to change in ways no one in their wildest imaginations could ever dream. But it was not a dream; it was a nightmare, and I was wide awake!

"Mrs. Floyd, I regret to inform you that your father has been killed aboard . . . "

"Is this some kind of a sick joke?" I interrupted.

"No, ma'am; I'm sorry, it's not. Your father is dead."

"You are a *liar!*" I screamed.

"No, ma'am, I assure you, this is not a lie."

I stood there numb in total disbelief with my mind racing a million different directions.

This just can't be true! Oh God, NO! Please, Jesus, don't let this be true!

I heard the shower go off in the bathroom and Donnie call my name, but I didn't answer him. I stood there looking at the phone that was no longer up to my ear. I was desperate to wake up from the nightmare. The phone in my hand became hot, and I viewed it as my worst enemy as my bedroom became the room where he died. *If I can get away from this room and this phone, he will still be alive. I have to get out of here!*

I threw the phone as hard as I could and ran out the door, down the hall as fast as my legs could carry me, but before I reached the living room, I came to a screeching halt.

What about my mom?

With the phone thrown on the floor in my bedroom, I now stood unable to breathe at the end of the hallway.

Not my dad, God! Please . . . NO! Not my dad! This just can't be true! How could it be? How could this happen? What about my mom? Please God not her too!

I suddenly realized I had to go back and pick up that phone if I wanted the answers to those reeling questions. I ran back to the bedroom where I found Donnie, soaking wet in a towel, picking up the phone. He had concern and confusion written all over his face. I ripped the phone out of his hand and screamed, "What about my mom?"

"I'm sorry, Mrs. Floyd, she too has been killed. Both your parents have been murdered aboard the yacht *Challenger*."

The room was spinning; I had experienced a lot of pain in my life, in fact it had become something with which I was very familiar. But this kind of pain . . . *never!* It ravaged through my entire body, and there was absolutely nothing I could do to make it stop. I wanted more information, yet I wanted to slam down the phone.

This just can't be true! Dad would never let himself be overtaken—all his training, all his experience, he was prepared for something like this!

I braced myself against the footboard of our bed and asked, "How, Mr. Howard—how did they die?"

"They didn't suffer, Mrs. Floyd; they were shot in their sleep."

O, God, please wake me up. This just can't be real!

I'm sure Mr. Howard was under the illusion that telling me they had been shot in their sleep would bring me some kind of comfort or peace. What he didn't realize was that his statement hurt worse than his telling me they were dead. A piercing and gut-wrenching panic shot through my mind and went straight to my heart. I fell to my knees and cried out, "No, God, *no!* They didn't have time! You didn't give them time to keep their promise to me . . ."

Donnie couldn't take it anymore, so he pried the phone out of my clenching fist and finished the conversation with Mr. Howard as I sat on the floor in shock and disbelief. I kept hearing an awful voice in my head, saying, *They're dead. They're gone, and they didn't have time to call on Jesus. It is too late, you are eternally separated from them . . . they are in hell!*

I had done all I knew to do to share Jesus with them. They had come a long way in their views of who Jesus was. They acknowledged His hand at work in their lives and in ours, and they were never against a suggestion to pray, but I knew it took more than that. They knew they had to call upon His name for salvation, but as far as I knew, they had never done that.

I knew I had to start making calls, but the thought of having to call my family and do to them what Paul Howard had just done to me was unbearable. As I made the calls, God gave me the strength and the words, because I had none of my own.

My phone call to Kimberly, my best friend, went much differently. I lost it! The only word I could form was *Daddy*, and then I wailed uncontrollably. All Kim could decipher through my hysteria was that something terrible had happened, and someone was dead. Because she could barely understand me, she first thought I was saying "Donnie." It took her some time to figure out that I was saying "Daddy," because I was crying so hard. She managed to get enough information out of me to know that my dad and mom had been killed. Within the hour, she was at my front door.

Mom and Dad Floyd, and other dear friends of ours began to arrive in record time and immediately stepped in, doing the best they could to try to control an uncontrollable situation. When my sister Susan arrived, I can only describe her as hollow. She was there in body, but when you looked into her eyes, it was as if she was not there. I knew immediately that on top of her agonizing grief over their deaths, she was also dealing with regret. On their last trip home in November she had not made time to see them. My already broken heart crumbled when I saw the pain of regret on her face.

My poor Donnie was devastated. I knew he wanted to just break down and cry, but he held it inside in front of me. He felt helpless, as did everyone else. There was simply nothing anyone could do or say that would make my pain go away. Donnie took some time alone in our room to pray and probably cry. When he came out of the bedroom, he walked over to me and said, "Baby, I have been praying and crying out to the Lord, asking Him why they hadn't had time to call on Him. He spoke to me, babe, and He said that He has them with Him in heaven."

I stared blankly at him, desperately wanting to believe what he had just told me, but I didn't. I knew he would never make something like that up, but what I did think was that he was hurting so badly, that out of desperation he willed it in his head.

Later that morning Sandy came to the door. For a long while we both just stood there and cried. Then she stepped back, looked me dead in the eye, and told me the Lord had spoken to her. Over the years "mean sister Sandy" and I had become closer than I would have ever thought possible. Her relationship with the Lord was one I often envied. If Sandy told you she had heard from the Lord, you had better listen up! I trusted the Lord in Sandy, and He knew it; He knew I would hear His voice clearly through her.

"On my way over here I was praying and asking God for answers and for Him to give me words to comfort you. And Bonnie," she paused as if to make sure she had my utmost attention, "God said to me, He has them with Him in heaven."

She had my attention all right! She just said word for word the exact same thing Donnie had just told me, that I couldn't bring myself to believe. *Okay, Lord, I know You are speaking to me! But how can this be true, if they didn't have time?* I knew deep inside that this was not something for me to doubt or question, but to just trust and believe.

I cried off and on throughout the morning. Looking back now, I believe I was mostly just in a state of shock. At times I felt disconnected and out of it; I would see my house full of people and hear their many voices around me, but I wasn't part of any of it—it was all just blurred noises.

The phone was being answered by others and only handed to me when it was necessary. One of those necessary calls was my pastor, G. L Johnson. Peoples Church is the largest church in the Central Valley of California, and with a church that size, it's difficult for a pastor to personally know every member of his congregation. I had visited with Pastor Johnson on a few occasions, but we really did not know one another. Nonetheless, he was my pastor—the one who ministered the Word of the Lord to me every Sunday at church. He taught me more about the Bible and how to understand it than all the godly people combined I had intersected with in my life. I may not have known him on a personal level, but I loved and respected him deeply. When I answered the phone and heard his familiar voice, I wanted to cry.

"How are ya doing, honey?

"Not good, Pastor." It was so hard to find the words to describe how I was feeling. "I know the Bible says not a sparrow falls to the ground apart from God knowing about it, but I'm having a really hard time with this one."

I will never in my life forget what Pastor Johnson said to me next. It immediately set my trembling, unstable feet on solid ground: "Bonnie, God could have prevented this, but He did not . . . and the one thing I know for certain is that God makes no mistakes!"

He might as well have said to me, "Bonnie, choose this day whom you will serve." I knew I had come to a fork in the road of my walk as a Christian. I could choose the path of peace, or I could choose the path of torment. God created me with the free will to choose. The day I willingly chose to accept His Son, Jesus, as my Savior, was the same day I started making wise choices based on what I knew to be truth from the Word of God, not on my emotions.

I knew I would have to take this one day at time, at first maybe even one hour at a time. The truth being spoken to me that day was what Donnie and Sandy had both said to me, which offered me peace and hope—God had them with Him in heaven. The other truth Pastor Johnson spoke to me was that God could have prevented it, but He didn't, and He doesn't make mistakes. Not only did this give me peace and hope but also an assuredness that God was in control of a seemingly out-of-control tragedy.

Missing Pieces to the Puzzle

Peter Ogden called from England after he knew the American Embassy had officially notified me. He was distraught and had been dealing as well with the tragic event since he was notified two days prior. Peter was actually able to fill in a lot of missing pieces for me.

Dad and Mom had flown to the island of Antigua (an-TEE-gah) earlier the previous week. They were met by the captain, Ian Cridland, also known as Criddy, and crewmember Tom Williams off Peter's yacht *Challenger*, both of whom we had met and come to know during Regatta Week on Jethou during our vacation. Criddy, Tom, and the galley chef, Allison, had been on *Challenger* in Antigua's English Harbor awaiting Dad and Mom's arrival. When Mom found out there was a chef onboard, she had quickly given her the week off.

When Peter told me that, I smiled for the first time, thinking about how, even while on vacation, Mom had to cook!

They sailed from English Harbor over to Green Island and moored there overnight before sailing the next day to the Island of Barbuda (bar-BEW-dah). Peter made contact with *Challenger* over ham radio on their first day moored off of Barbuda. Criddy told Peter they were having a grand time and that he wasn't sure out of the four of them who was actually on vacation, because Bill was always at the helm, and Kathy was always in the galley. In fact, at the time of their conversation, the two of them were out spear fishing for dinner.

Once again I could not help but smile at what Peter told me; it was so "them!"

The four of them had been overtaken and murdered that very night. It wasn't until Sunday, three days later, that a French yachtsman, after noticing no activity, boarded *Challenger*. He was the first to discover the horrific murders that had taken place. Peter was able to fill in a lot of blanks for

Scan this code for information about Antigua and Barbuda

me, but as for who did this and why, he knew nothing more than what I had been told. Peter assured me that he would stay in contact and keep me apprised of any new discoveries in the case.

For the next few days, people came and went, and just when I thought I had control over the tears, someone else who I had yet to grieve with would ring the doorbell. As the days went by, I felt so much frustration because of the lack information about what had actually happened to my parents on that boat. A very present fear began to overtake all of us about who had done it and the horrifying possibility that my parents had been targeted. That fear was certainly not unjustified, and I was being asked many questions by the authorities. They wanted to know if I knew any of my dad's current business dealings or if he had ever mentioned still having any connections to the National Security Agency (NSA).

I knew back when Dad was in the Service, that he was a cryptographic liaison and once held top-secret clearance for the Far East, but he had not mentioned that for many years. I received calls suggesting I not go anywhere alone, to stay aware of my surroundings, and remain alert for any abnormal activity until their murderers were found. Basically, all those people accomplished was to scare the living daylights out of me!

Within a couple of days, the media frenzy began, and I was inundated with calls from television and newspaper reporters wanting to get quotes from me for stories they were writing. My friends had been monitoring all the calls coming in, and until the media began contacting me, none of us had any real comprehension of how big this news really was all over the world. Everyone tried to shield me from what was being reported to keep me from hearing the horrifying details over and over. It was all over CNN and the BBC, and whenever I walked into the room, they would shut off the TV. Interestingly enough, there were also no newspapers lying around the house. I was being sheltered and cared for around the clock.

All kinds of food, made lovingly by friends and family, began pouring into our home, but no matter what sat on my kitchen counter, I could not eat. I couldn't eat or sleep. No matter how insistent everyone was that I needed to eat, there was just no way I could get any food past the constant knot in my throat, and sleep simply evaded me.

Pastor Johnson either came by the house or called me every day. He even gave me his cell and home numbers and told me that I could call him night or day. I looked forward to his visits; they always brought me comfort and peace. Each time he arrived he was cordial to everyone at the house, then after a short time, he would take me outside. Dressed in his business suit, he would sit right down on the concrete steps leading up to my house and have a long chat with me. He had an amazing way of helping me to open up and tell him how I was really doing and then guide me through ways to know how to deal with those feelings.

One of the most important things I learned from my dear Pastor Johnson was that it was okay and perfectly normal to ask God why. Like many, I thought questioning God was a form of disrespect. What Pastor taught me was that whenever we have a question that needs answering, we go to the one we think has the answer. When I ask God why, I'm acknowledging that He knows and has the answer. Pastor was quick to caution me that even though God has all the answers, there will be times—for His good purpose—that He will hold back from giving me the answer. It is in those times that I will learn to trust God more abundantly and in turn find that my faith is magnified.

For someone who had always claimed to be a noncrier, I surely did my fair share of it those first few days. The thing I hated most was not being able to control it.

The phone rang so often that it had become like constant background music. I was surprised when Kimberly said, "Bonnie, you need to take this; it's Mr. Howard from the US Embassy." I didn't even know the phone had rung.

"Hello, Mr. Howard."

"Mrs. Floyd, please, call me Paul."

"Okay, Paul, but you must call me Bonnie then. Okay?

"You have a deal. How are you doing, Bonnie?"

"I'm taking one day at a time, and my faith, family, and friends are see-ing me through."

"Bonnie, I'm sorry to have to tell you, I am calling you this morning to give you some very difficult and upsetting news. I know you are already deeply grieving the death of your parents, but I have information in regard to their case that I need to share with you before it hits the press."

Seriously? Difficult and upsetting news? You have got to be kidding me! They're dead! What other news could be more upsetting or difficult to hear than that?

I responded in a tone that tried not to reveal my irritation.

"Okay, Mr. Howard . . . Paul. I can't imagine any news that you could share with me that would be any more upsetting than the last time we talked, but go ahead; I'm listening."

"Bonnie, is there someone right there with you that can be of some sup-port?" he asked.

"No, Paul, there isn't. I'm in my room alone. I don't need anyone with me. Please, go ahead and tell me why you've called."

He proceeded to inform me that Antigua and Barbuda used to be part of the British Isles, until they gained their independence from England in 1981. In harrowing times such as this, the Antiguan government will, as they say, fall back on the Queen. Scotland Yard just so happened to be on Antigua investigating the murder of their customs chief. When they heard of the quadruple murders on Barbuda and that two of the victims were Brit-ish citizens, they immediately took over the investigation.

"So, Bonnie, at the request of Scotland Yard for investigative purposes, we were told to inform the family that the victims had been shot in their sleep. The truth is, your parents were actually bound and gagged for hours before they were killed."

The next few seconds were silent and played out to me as a slow-motion movie reel.

This was the upsetting news?

Unconsciously I fell to my knees—not in pain or torment but in relief. I immediately was very aware of where I was kneeling. I was bowing at the foot of my God in praise and thanksgiving that they had been given time— time to keep their promise to me!

Thank you, Lord, for giving them time!

I knew Paul was prepared for another cry of anguish. However, what he got from me was not at all what he expected. While staying on my knees in a position of worship, I said, "I know for most people, the fact that they were bound and gagged would be a torturous thought, but for me, it isn't. It is the answer I have been crying out to God for. Paul, I'm a Christian, and just six months ago, my dad promised me that if he and Mom were ever to get into a position where they feared for their lives, they would call on the name of Jesus. What you first told me left them no time to keep that promise; what you're telling me now does."

It took some time for Paul to respond, but when he did, he said, "Bonnie, your faith is amazing. To be able to take such horrific news and see it as an answer to prayer is a testament to how strong your faith really is."

"Thank you, Paul, my faith is strong, because He is a faithful God!"

After hanging up, I sat on the floor for a long while thinking about the complexity of all that had taken place. I thought more deeply about that conversation I'd had with my parents and their promise to me. How many times had I prayed for their salvation? I sat there with my Lord, thanking Him for answering my prayer. What Donnie and Sandy had said now not only made sense but was possible, because Dad and Mom had been given time!

Immediately, though, there was a tormenting voice in my head, trying to rob the precious gift God had just given me. *He didn't call on Jesus; that thought didn't even cross his mind. All your dad was thinking about was how to break loose and get free. He's dead; he's in hell, and you will never see him again.*

I shook my head to get rid of that awful voice and remembered the fork in the road. I could choose the path of peace or choose the path of torment. I learned from reading my Bible that the voice of God speaks words of peace, comfort, hope, and encouragement and that the devil, being the father of lies, speaks torment, despair, and doubt. Through all of that, I was learning how to recognize the voice of God over the voice of my enemy, the devil. That day I chose the path of peace that said, "I have them with Me in heaven."

As the days went by, I wasn't learning any new information about who had committed this horrific crime, and I was becoming very concerned that I might never find out. I remember praying and asking God not to let it be like "Who shot JFK?" I needed answers. I prayed that whoever had done it would slip up, and that God would lead those investigating the case right to the "scum of the earth" who killed my parents.

I did a little research of my own on the men from Scotland Yard who had taken over the investigation. I found an article about the case and the amazing men, who are often referred to as the World's Police.

By a stroke of luck, a team of Scotland Yard's elite international crimes branch, SO1, was already on the island of Antigua helping local police unravel the murder of the island's customs chief, who was hacked to death last year. So, the local government formally requested assistance from the Foreign Office in London, and Detective Superintendent Michael Lawrence, head of the Yard team and one of its most respected investigators, was assigned to the case that had just unfolded on the neighboring island of Barbuda.

This was not the first time Superintendent Mick Lawrence had been asked to investigate such a high-profile crime. Three years ago he was sent at the government's request to northern Iraq to solve the murders of the three members of the BBC film crew killed while covering the Kurdish rebellion against President Saddam Hussein. After months of painstaking work, Lawrence tracked the killers down. Superintendent Lawrence is one of a small group of senior detectives attached to the Yard's elite international and organized crime branch. These men are on eight-hour notice to be sent anywhere in the world to solve serious crimes.

Mick Lawrence's fellow officers are rightly proud of a colleague who they say combines the meticulous qualities of a Sherlock Holmes with the flamboyance and charisma of James Bond. "He is probably one of the finest detectives in the world," said a Yard colleague. If there's a difficult case abroad which the Yard needs solving they always send Mickey." And the crime he was just assigned to was no doubt a high-profile, difficult case.[1]

After reading the article, I gathered everyone around so I could share with them about Scotland Yard. When I finished reading, everyone just sat there with their jaws dropped in awe, not only because of the extraordinary team from Scotland Yard, but that a team like that would "just so happen" to be nearby and able to take over our case. There was no denying that it was divine intervention at work, because with God, there are no coincidences!

THE WILLS

Several years earlier, Dad had given me a tightly sealed and taped manila envelope with instructions to open it only in the case of both of their deaths. I had completely forgotten about that envelope until I was asked about a will. As I walked into my office to retrieve it, I was racking my brain trying to remember what Dad had told me all those years ago, but nothing was coming to me. I just had to trust that whatever their wishes were, they would be spelled out for me.

I was not to worry; all of their instructions were laid out, and the first thing Dad wrote on the outside of the will was this: "Hey, Bean, don't get excited. All I left you was my pet rock. Love, Dad." Those simple words showed me that, even in his death, my daddy was there for me, comforting me through something he knew would be difficult or at least make me chuckle.

I was named executrix of the wills, which meant I would be making a trip back to Jethou to go through Dad's office and the rest of their belongings with a detective from Scotland Yard. They wanted to look for any clues that might reveal if my parents were targeted or if this was a case of being in the wrong place at the wrong time.

Graciously, Peter took care of all of our travel arrangements, and the following week Donnie and I were off to London and then back to our beloved Jethou. It was painful to imagine stepping onto Dad and Mom's island paradise without them. There wouldn't be a spot on the island where I could escape a memory of them. They had left their mark on everything. Learning to live without them was going to be my life's greatest challenge.

chapterTwelve

A Certain God in an Uncertain World

*N*ever in a million years did I think I would be feeling so apprehensive about a trip to Jethou, but then I never thought my parents would be murdered either. Life is so uncertain, and that is why what Kimberly's mom, Shirley, said to me the day I got "the call" keeps me from fearing what tomorrow may bring. She said, "Bonnie, I know this has shocked you and shaken you to the core, but honey, this did not take God by surprise."

Couple that with Pastor Johnson saying, "God could have prevented this, but He didn't, and He doesn't make mistakes," and you've got a certain God in an uncertain world.

It is not God who makes our lives uncertain, it is those who choose to sin. God knew my phone would ring that fateful morning, and in His sovereignty He orchestrated His angels to watch over me, and He sent my brothers and sisters in Christ to come alongside me. Therefore, I rest in my faith, knowing that God can and will see me through anything.

Peter's assistant had made all of our travel arrangements. We would be staying with the Ogdens in London and flying over to Jethou for a day. Our ten-hour redeye flight to London was booked in business class. We were not expecting such a treat, but it was a wonderful blessing, to say the least.

Donnie was praying the trip would somehow bring me peace so that I could start sleeping and eating again. As exhausted as I was, sleep would still not come, and I had no appetite at all. That was all starting to take a toll on my body. As we settled into our comfy leather business-class seats, Donnie and I just turned and looked at each other, neither of us said a word; it was all still so surreal.

It's odd how differently people handle grief. I couldn't eat or sleep to save my life, and Donnie ate enough for the both of us, and if he could, he would have just lain down and slept the days away. A couple of hours into the flight, Donnie was sound asleep, and I actually felt myself relaxing and wanting to lay my seat back and close my eyes. I dozed off for a while until turbulence invaded my slumber. I tried to go back to sleep, but it wasn't happening, so I got up and moved to another seat so I wouldn't bother Sleeping Beauty.

There was a newspaper lying in the seat next to me, and without a thought I picked it up. The headline, in large, bold, black letters read, "SLAUGHTER IN PARADISE." There before my eyes were two pictures—one of Dad and one of Mom and a computerized sketch of the yacht's floor plan with four dead bodies lying in pools of blood. I gasped and threw the paper down, with heart-wrenching pain once again ravaging through my entire body. I was desperate to run away from that newspaper, now strewn on the floor, just as I had run from the phone the morning I first heard the news, but there was nowhere to run.

I laid my head back and closed my eyes.

Lord Jesus, I know you're with me. You knew that newspaper was beside the seat I chose to move to, yet You didn't direct me elsewhere. Why Lord? Why didn't You spare me this pain?

With my head leaned back and my eyes closed, I waited for an answer. I opened my eyes to the sound of a ruffling newspaper just as the flight attendant was placing it back on my lap. "Here you go, ma'am; this must have fallen off your lap when you dosed off. Oh, that headline! Such a horrible tragedy. It's been all over the news; those poor people!"

Unable to keep the tears from running down my face, I looked up at her and said, "Those poor people were my parents."

My own grief turned immediately to compassion when I saw the look of horror and regret on her face. "I'm so very sorry! Please forgive me, I had no idea . . ."

I interrupted her by reaching up and taking her hand, "It's okay; there's no way you could have possibly known. I'm actually on my way to meet a detective from Scotland Yard on the island where my parents lived. I'm going to help them look for clues as to how or why this could have happened."

For at least an hour, while My Donnie and the few people up in business class slept, she and I talked about what had happened to Dad and Mom. She asked me how I was handling it all, and I explained that without the Lord in my life I'd be a total basket case. I shared with her the story and the promise my parents had made to me just six months prior to their death. The pain on my new friend's face turned peaceful when I told her I had received a second call telling me they had actually been bound and gagged before they were killed. I then quoted what Pastor Johnson ministered to me about God making no mistakes.

I was telling my story to a total stranger, and all the while she just sat there intently listening. Before she got up she said to me, "I am in awe of your faith in God and have never heard it described in such a real and personal way."

As she walked away, I laid my head back once again and began to ponder many things. The first thing that came to my mind was realizing that the heart-wrenching pain had subsided and had been replaced with peace. It was at that moment, 38,000 feet in the air, in the midst of a conversation, I knew God was speaking to me.

Bonnie, do you trust me?

Yes, Lord, I do!

Then choose this day whom you will serve. Follow after me, and I will give you my peace that surpasses all understanding and my joy that will strengthen you through this.

I knew those feelings of peace that came over me had come from the Lord, because the newspaper that had earlier just thrown me into a tailspin was now sitting on my lap face up. When I looked down at it, the peace and joy God said He would give to me had replaced the anxiety and sorrow I had been feeling.

When Donnie woke up, I was back in the seat next to him, and he never even knew I had moved away. He saw the newspaper in my lap and reached for it, but I stopped him and said, "Let me prepare you first . . ." I had read the entire article by then and knew the gruesome details, but even so, God's peace sustained me, and His joy had strengthened me.

A fellow yachtsman sailed into Low Bay on Saturday afternoon and saw the yacht *Challenger* with its hatches open and its dinghy moored across the bay and thought nothing of it. But on Sunday he found it odd when *Challenger's* lights remained on long after daybreak, and the yacht seemed disturbingly unattended. At 11 a.m. Alan Whitehead paddled his dinghy across from his yacht, *Ulu*, and knocked on *Challenger's* hull. After getting no reply, he climbed cautiously aboard. A former Rhodesian military man, Whitehead was not easily shocked. But as he peered through the hatch, he saw something he will never forget.

The blood-spattered, partly clothed remains of three men and a woman lay slumped across the cabin floor. The *Challenger's* occupants had been brutally trussed up, their hands tied behind their backs, and their mouths gagged with thick masking tape. The bodies appeared to have dozens of deep stab wounds, many to the head, face, and neck.

The grisly scene bore all the hallmarks of a prolonged torture session, culminating in execution.[1]

Donnie took it hard, and my husband, who rarely utters a curse word, leaned his head back on the seat and said, "Those dirty b****s!"

chapter**Thirteen**

Love Can Build a Bridge

$\mathcal{E}$ven under the circumstances that took us on that trip, I was very excited to see Peter and Tiffany again. I was also looking forward to meeting the rest of the Ogden family I had heard so much about. It felt good to have a positive emotion inside my tattered heart. At the airport Peter's driver greeted us. He had been given instructions to take us directly to the Ogden home where we would meet with Mrs. Ogden. I was both disappointed and concerned when he told us that Mr. Ogden had to suddenly leave town for a family emergency and that we would most likely not be seeing Peter on this trip to London.

Peter's wife, Cathy, warmly greeted us at the front door of a stately five-story townhome, or "flat" as the British say, on Upper Phillimore Gardens. She was beautiful, just as I imagined she would be from having met Tiffany. She was small-framed with shoulder-length blonde hair, caring eyes, and a beautiful smile. Tiffany was definitely one of those children who is a perfect cross between her father and mother. Cathy welcomed us as though we had been friends for years, and she immediately offered us her sincere condolences. I could see by the pain in her eyes that she, too, was suffering from our great loss. What I didn't know was that the pain in her eyes was not only from the tragic loss of Dad, Mom, Criddy, and Tom.

As we followed Cathy into a beautiful sitting room for a cup of tea, I couldn't help but take in the uniqueness of their gorgeous home. When Cathy returned with our tea, she started our conversation by offering an apology for Peter's absence.

With concern I said, "Yes, we were told that there was a family emergency. May I ask what has happened?"

"Certainly you may, Bonnie. Much to our devastation, we received a call from Peter's mother just hours ago that Peter's father had suddenly passed away."

Both Donnie and I just sat there in shock and total disbelief. In tears, it was our turn to offer our sincere condolences. Poor Peter. How much more could this man take? My heart was breaking all over again for this family. I knew the entire Ogden family was grieving over my parents' death, and from our time on Jethou with Peter and Tiffany, I saw how they felt about Criddy and Tom. Now on top of it all, they had to suffer the very personal family loss of a father and grandfather.

Lord Jesus, please comfort them as only You can!

Later in the afternoon, when school let out, we had the great pleasure of meeting Peter and Cathy's sons. What fine young men they were! My parents had grown quite fond of all three of the Ogdens' children and it was such a pleasure to spend time with them.

We were scheduled on an early morning flight over to the island, so after a lovely dinner together, we were shown to our guest room. Once settled in, Donnie and I couldn't help but think about the flight that awaited us the next morning.

We chuckled at the memory of the first time we took the small turbo-prop plane from London over to Guernsey. What a memory it was!

I remember the day was dreary, gray, and raining when we took off, but the weather was no barometer of my excitement at the thought of spending three weeks with my dad.

To say the flight was bumpy was an understatement; to say it was downright turbulent would be accurate. I was "white knuckling" the armrests as the rapid jolts tossed the plane around and the sudden drops and bangs made it feel as if we were falling from the sky and hitting a concrete slab below. About that time the pilot announced that because of the severe weather they were considering turning back.

I remember it taking everything I had not to yell out, "Oh no, we're not!" Soon the pilot again made an announcement that they would make one attempt to land on Guernsey, but if it didn't work, they would indeed be turning back. At that point all we could do was pray.

As we were descending, all I could see were dark, gray, thick clouds. I was about to give up when suddenly I saw an opening of blue sky and land. The plane literally took a dive down through that opening and within fifteen minutes, the wheels of the plane were on the Island of Guernsey.

All I wanted to do was get off that plane, but the flight attendant made an announcement for all passengers to remain in their seats for a few more minutes. Simultaneously, a woman and two others stood up, collected their things and walked off the plane. I remember thinking, *What? Are you kidding me? Why do they get to get off the plane and I have to wait?*

When we finally disembarked it was still raining a torrential downpour. I paused on the tarmac to look up. As far as I could see in all directions was a solid mass of dark storm clouds. God had certainly parted those clouds and made a way for our plane to sliver through the seemingly impenetrable sky.

Donnie and I continued to reminisce as we thought about all the squeals, hugs and happy tears that had taken place inside that airport just six months prior. I remember wasting no time telling Dad and Mom what God had just done. At one point Mom interrupted and said, "Oh, we know, Bonnie! We saw it happen. We watched the clouds part, the plane dive through and then the clouds just closed right up. It was an amazing thing to watch."

The whole time I was telling Dad the story, he kept glancing over at Mom, and once in a while she'd throw him a wink. Finally I remember asking, "Okay you two, what gives?"

"Bean, do you know who was on that plane with you?"

"No, I have no idea. Who was it?"

"Oh, no one special . . . it was just British royalty!"

"What?"

"Yes, my dear daughter, you were flying with royalty. I'm sure having them on that plane had a little something to do with the pilot's determination to land and not turn back."

This was yet another time I was able to point out God's hand at work to my dad. With absolute resolve I remember saying, "Well, my dear father, then not only did God part the sky that we all witnessed, but He made sure that royalty was on *my* plane to ensure that the pilot didn't chicken out and turn back. Whatever the case may be, God did it, and there is no explaining it away."

"Okay, Bean, you got me on this one," he said with a smile.

"No, Dad, *God* got you on this one!" And I kissed him on the cheek.

At that memory I turned to My Donnie and said, "What I wouldn't do to be able to kiss his cheek again . . ."

After a short bit of time, there was a knock on our door. When I opened it, the Ogdens' youngest son was there with a big smile, holding a wooden tray with bottled water, two glasses, and some English cookies. It was so thoughtful and unexpected, I thought my heart would burst right then and there. He handed me the tray, and as he walked away, he said, "I hope you sleep well tonight."

For the first night since Dad and Mom died, I slept well.

On to Jethou

Detective Inspector Michael Barley of the Metropolitan Police, International & Organized Crime Branch, was our escort from Scotland Yard over to Jethou. With a title like that, you'd expect a guy in a stiff suit with the personality of Sergeant Joe Friday from *Dragnet*, but that wasn't the case at all with Detective Barley. He was very professional but also a caring, compassionate, and all-around great guy. He honestly turned a very difficult day into one I will always fondly remember.

Meeting Chris, my dad's right-hand man, at the airport was emotional, to say the least. I ran right up to him, and he gave me a hug. He offered his sympathy and expressed his own personal sorrow, but he could hardly look at me without tearing up. So, as most men do—especially European men—he would hardly make eye contact with me. He drove us in the Jethou van over to the harbor in St. Peter Port, and we boarded the *Barbalotte*. Everything was so familiar, such as the sights, the sounds, and the smell. Oh, the smell!

It had been only seven short months ago that I sat on that same boat with Dad and Mom, looking back at Jethou, praying and believing that I would one day return. I was returning sooner than I even thought to pray for but under circumstances no mind could fathom. As we motored over to Jethou, my mind was torn to shreds with so many thoughts that brought too many emotions. As I began to scarcely see the island on the horizon, my mind was taken back to so many memories. I was immersed with wonderful thoughts that filled my heart with joy one minute, and then the realization that my parents were dead would invade my mind the next. My mind was being shaken back and forth, back and forth, back and forth until I couldn't take it anymore.

I am not going to make it; I can't do this! If I can't even look at Jethou, how on earth am I going to step onto it? Lord Jesus, help me! Please, God, I am desperate for You!

At that very moment, Donnie called me away from the rail and over to him because Detective Barley had a few questions for me. Not realizing it until later, Donnie calling me away at that moment was actually God answering my cry for help and rescuing me.

Stepping onto Jethou was difficult, to say the least. The place I had returned to was my own Treasure Island. It held so many memories of special moments with my parents that I would treasure for a lifetime. I didn't allow myself to think about anything other than the business at hand. We started in Dad and Mom's cottage where Dad's office was located. We packed up the computer, went through all the files and looked through every drawer in the desks, dressers, and nightstands. I had no idea what I was looking for, but I was looking, and Detective Barley was right beside me.

As I came across things and looked all around the cottage, everything I touched and saw was so dear to me, and I knew it would be to Susan, Linda, Steven, and Aaron as well. As the executrix of the will, I knew getting their things back to the States was my responsibility, but that was not the trip to accomplish it. I was going to have to figure that out as soon as I got back to the States.

I heard Donnie calling me from the other room, and when I walked into where he was, he was standing there with tears in his eyes. In his hands was a beautiful, little yellow-and-green house made of wood.

"What is it, babe?" I asked.

"I believe this is for us . . ." his voice cracking.

"Why would you say that, because it's a house?"

"Well no, I mean yes! Just come over here a minute. Didn't your mom send you a fax last month saying that when she was in town she had bought us a present because a little voice told her to buy a this-house-sold gift for us?"

"Yeah . . . but just because it's a house doesn't mean that's the gift!"

"Okay, well why don't you tip the lid back on this little music box house and take a look inside," he said with an I-know-I'm-right smirk on his face.

"That's a music box?"

"Yep, it sure is!"

When I lifted the lid, the sweet music started to play, and tucked down inside was a Floyd Construction, Exclusively Designed Homes business card. On the back was written, "This House Sold."

I looked up at My Donnie with tears in my eyes and said, "I loved that woman!"

"And she loved you, too, honey," he said with a smile.

After searching through the cottage from top to bottom, we went up to the Manor House. Thankfully, the intent was to search only Mom's office right off the kitchen. There was no need to search the Manor House as Dad and Mom kept their personal things and even Jethou's bookkeeping confined to their cottage and Mom's office.

When we walked into the glorious gourmet dream kitchen that Peter created with Mom, I was overwhelmed. She was simply everywhere I looked. I saw her grinning from ear to ear as she popped up the food processor on her handy dandy, spring-loaded appliance lift. I imagined Mom standing at her stove, splattering food everywhere as she made her usual mess while creating a feast fit for a king! As I stood there lost in so many wonderful memories of Mom, God reminded me of something she told me one day when she and I were alone together in her kitchen. "Here on Jethou and in my kitchen, I feel as if I'm experiencing a little taste of what I imagine heaven will be like for me." In remembering her sharing that with me, I stood still, this time all alone in Mom's kitchen, and said out loud with a grateful heart, "Thank You, Lord, for all the memories!"

Mom's office was actually part of her huge kitchen. I walked over to her chair, turned it toward me, and eased myself down into it. I sat there for a long time, wondering why they had been ripped from life, why it had to happen that way, and how on earth I was ever going to live without them.

I looked down, and there on the counter was a Kodak envelope full of pictures. As soon as I flipped it open, I knew they were the pictures Mom had developed from their trip home in November. It was difficult looking at pictures of them smiling and so full of life. I loved the ones of them surrounded by all their kids and grandkids, who were definitely their pride and joy! As I continued to flip through the pictures, I came to some that were of the most beautiful tropical place I'd ever seen, and that's saying a lot, because through all their travels I'd seen many pictures of some breathtaking places. I remembered they went to Costa Rica for some R&R after leaving California. There was one exceptionally beautiful shot, and as I held it in my hand staring at it, I inadvertently turned it over to look on the back. There in Mom's own handwriting, were these words: "Beautiful place to visit, wouldn't want to live there . . . Been there, done that!"

As I read her words, I was amazed at how someone could say that about such a lush, gorgeous tropical place. I began to think about how Dad and Mom had many adventures and how they had literally traveled the world over, and yet with each new journey, Dad always managed to top the thing they had done last. It was at that very moment God revealed something very special to me. The only place they hadn't been, the only place that could top where they had ever traveled before, was heaven!

I had so dreaded going back to Jethou. As it turned out, it was a day filled with blessings and memories. It was there God had once gifted me with some of the most amazing moments I had ever had with my parents. It was there that I believe my parents' hearts began to be softened toward God. But most importantly, it was there that my dad made his promise to me.

The only thing I physically took away from Jethou that day was our This-House-Sold music box and that picture of Costa Rica. What I left on Jethou was another piece of my heart.

The Memorial Service

The memorial service for my parents was planned, and we were ready to face the inevitable—the day we would have to admit publically they were gone. I have found that there are days in life when you wish more than anything you could escape, but reality sets in, and you must push through and face it.

Peter flew in from London for the service, which we all thought was so kind and thoughtful, and it blessed our family immensely. My parents were deeply loved by so many people they had met while they were sailing around the world. We were blessed beyond measure that some of them made the trip to attend their service.

Pastor Johnson oversaw the service, but it was Aaron and I who spoke and shared the representation of who Dad and Mom were, what they meant to their children and to countless others around the globe.

I knew that anyone at the service who knew me would also know my parents through me, because I had always talked about them. In preparing and choosing what to say, I decided it would be best to share what other people had to say about them. I had received countless cards, letters, and faxes, so choosing just a few was a challenge, but two were especially dear to me:

Larry Carney, my dad's closer-than-a-brother lifetime friend wrote this:

> They lived the best, saw the best, and were the best. We were lucky to be with them at the apex of their life. What we shared was something few people ever have been fortunate to see or be a part of. If there were ever two people who enriched more lives than they did, I should have known them. There are so few people in this world who have ever reaped the harvest of living and love that these people, Bill and Kathy, have left us to remember.

Paul Preston, longtime friend and fellow yachtsman, said this:

> I feel a tremendous sense of loss. For me the world has suddenly become a lonelier place. They were very special people, and I feel

fortunate to have known them. It was obvious that they were very much in love, and I couldn't imagine one without the other. I held them as an ideal. I never once heard either of them complain or say anything untoward about anyone. They were truly lovely people!

Aaron walked up to the podium without any notes and spoke from his heart. He closed by sharing one of the last conversations he'd had with Mom while she was visiting him in San Diego. He said,

Mom always made sure to have some time alone with me. So, we went for a cup of coffee and some cheesecake one day. We began talking about family, marriage, and the bonds people have and how everyone is so different in that regard. I brought up the fact that Bill was older than she and that men tend to die before women. I told her there was a high probability that she would be alone for the last part of her life without Bill. She told me something that I didn't agree with then, and I was mad at her for even saying it. She said she would never want to be here without him and that she would rather die and be gone with Bill than live life alone.

As Aaron stepped away from the podium, we all heard him say, "And that's the way it happened . . ."

The memorial service was touching, it was moving, and there wasn't a heart that day that wasn't stirred. Steven, Aaron, Susan, Linda, our family and friends, and I felt a bond that cannot be explained. In short, we walked away feeling we had honored our parents in the best possible way and that Dad would have been smiling and giving me one of his many looks—one of utmost approval. It was now time to deal with life—life without Dad and Mom.

chapterFourteen

Purpose in Your Heart Not to Hate

*E*arly one morning, I answered the phone and quickly recognized the voice. It was no longer unfamiliar to me; I knew immediately it was Paul Howard calling from the embassy. I liked Paul; he had put up with a lot from me at first, but we had talked several times since that fateful morning, and I grew to know his personality and his character. I could tell he was a man of integrity. He always remained very professional, but there was a caring, soft side to him that would show itself when I talked personally about Dad or My Donnie.

"Do you have news for me this morning, Paul?

"Yes, Bonnie, I do, and it's good news."

"Good news? I could use some good news, Paul. What is it?"

"They got 'em, Bonnie! In just a matter of weeks, the detectives from Scotland Yard have captured and charged three men from the Island of Barbuda with the murders."

Purpose in your heart not to hate . . .

"Bonnie?"

"Yes, Paul, I'm sorry, my mind drifted. That is very good news—as news goes in these types of situations. That is exactly what we've been praying for—answers to who did it and why. So, you've given me the 'who.' Do you have a 'why' for me?"

"It's all just so senseless, Bonnie. After robbing the boat, they proceeded to shoot all of the victims. 'No witnesses' was the only reason given."

After hanging up with Paul, I sat for a long time pondering the thought, *Purpose in your heart not to hate.* Those words rang in my mind the instant Paul told me the three men had been captured.

I knew it was God speaking to me. I also knew hate was a form of unforgiveness, and if it were allowed to grow, it would become a root of bitterness. In that moment, God gently reminded me that the same forgiveness He had made available to me through His Son, Jesus, was also available to these men who had murdered my parents. The reality was, if any one of them came to a place of repentance and surrendered his heart to Jesus as Lord, I would be spending eternity with him.

Well, that certainly wasn't a place in my mind I was expecting to go, and when I tried the thought out on Donnie, it did not fit! My Donnie is a man of God, but the key word in that phrase is *man*. Donnie wasn't pursuing vengeance, but he was most certainly seeking justice. The thought of spending eternity with even one of those men was not a place Donnie was going in his mind.

The Burial

What Paul also discussed with me certainly wasn't a place where I wanted to go in my mind either. The investigation had progressed far enough along, and the final autopsies were complete. So it was time for me to make decisions about a burial.

My four siblings and I decided to bury their ashes at sea. It really was the best way for many different reasons, and we gave Dad and Mom one grand send-off at sea!

On a beautiful spring day in San Francisco, California, our family and some very close friends boarded a yacht and headed out beyond the Golden

Gate Bridge. The service included absolutely everything Dad and Mom would have wanted—their family, their friends, a yacht, the sea, a sunshiny day, and of course, champagne!

Traveling to Jethou with Donnie the week after they died provided me with the much-needed closure people seek after losing a loved one. Intuitively, Peter knew that and called me one day to offer an all-expense-paid trip to Jethou for the entire family. I was literally speechless and could not find the words to express my gratitude. In talking with Peter he wanted to make one thing very clear. He told me, "Bonnie, this trip I'm offering is as much for Bill's father as it is for you and the rest of Bill and Kathy's children."

Once again I struggled to find the words of gratitude.

Jethou had become so much a part of Dad and Mom that there wasn't a family member who hadn't wanted to make a trip over to Jethou to see them and "their" island paradise.

When the day finally came that Donnie, Susan, Teddy, Linda, Mike, Steven, Cyndi, Aaron, Grandpop, and I boarded the plane for our family trip to Jethou, we were all so happy we could hardly contain our excitement.

Our trip was amazing! Everyone got to see and experience Jethou and all of our parents' hard work. Donnie and I loved being able to tell them the stories we had learned from Dad and Mom on our visit. I watched my family walk alone in their own thoughts. I watched them gather all together in the dining room and, of course, the kitchen, while in my own mind I was imagining how much our presence there would have meant to Dad and Mom. Making that wonderful trip together as a family bonded us together and brought us the closure our hearts needed.

GETTING BACK TO NORMAL

Upon our return it was time to try and resume normal life again. Floyd Construction was crying out my name for attention. The last few months I had done just enough to get by, and it was time to get back to work. I managed to work a few weeks in the office, but as much as Floyd Construction demanded my attention, so did executing Dad and Mom's wills.

I had all their belongings from Jethou shipped to my house by a "slow boat to China." Any other way was ridiculously expensive. There was also the matter of their financial accounts. Not long before Dad died, he told me he needed to update their wills and mentioned that there were accounts they had added that were not listed in their current wills.

Scan this code for information on the Island of Guernsey

That proved to be a big problem, because the accounts I was aware of did not seem to hold the amount of money we all believed they had. That dilemma was working itself into another trip to Jethou. Well, not exactly Jethou, but Guernsey.

Guernsey is on the list of tax havens of the world, and I did notice when I was there that Guernsey had more banks than I had ever seen in one place. It seemed realistic that Dad would have put his nest egg in a bank near his home.

I enlisted my eldest sibling, Susan, to make the trip with me.

Prior to leaving on our trip, my phone rang early one morning at six o'clock. I could only remember one time when Paul Howard from the American Embassy didn't call me at 6:00 a.m., therefore with a voice of confidence I picked up the phone and said, "Good morning, Paul. How are you this morning?"

"You knew it was me?"

"Why yes! There's no one else who calls me at six o'clock in the morning. Do you have information for me today?"

"Yes, I do, Bonnie."

News from Paul had proven over time to be unpredictable, to say the least. So I asked, "Is it good or bad news?"

"Actually it's both. One of the three men in custody for murdering your parents escaped from prison."

My blood began to boil, and I could feel my face getting hot, but I said nothing.

"There was a shootout involved in recapturing him, and he was shot in the head, the chest, and the leg."

My immediate thought was, *Good! One down, two to go!*

But Paul would soon deflate that pleasing thought.

"However, Bonnie, he survived the shooting."

With as much sarcasm as I could muster I said, "So, which part of any of that would you call good news, Paul?"

"The fact that he didn't get away and was recaptured," he answered confidently.

"Oh, well, yeah, I guess someone might see that as good news. I would have preferred him to die."

Bonnie, I could have allowed him to die, but I did not, and I do not make mistakes! There was the Voice I knew all too well, guiding me, leading my heart and me down the right path.

In the midst of processing the thought that just filled my head, I heard Paul say, "Bonnie?"

"Yes, Paul, I'm sorry. That was not a nice thing to say at all."

"It's okay, Bonnie, I understand."

I sat for a long time by myself going over the things I knew God had spoken to me.

Purpose in your heart not to hate. That thought had come when Paul told me three men had been arrested for the murders. Then Pastor Johnson's first words of comfort came back to me: "God doesn't make mistakes."

God could have allowed that murderer to die, but He didn't, and He does not make mistakes. Once again I was reminded that God is in control. So why would God allow that man to survive after being shot three times? Why spare someone like that? There must be a reason.

Back to Jethou

Susan and I packed, repacked, and packed again. For the life of us, we just couldn't decide exactly what we needed to take. So, to our own demise, we packed it all. Our itinerary was to fly to Guernsey and take a few days to visit all the financial institutions, spend a night on Jethou because we were so close, and then fly to London. In London the plan was to meet with the detectives from Scotland Yard, who had completed their investigation on Antigua and Barbuda and had returned to London.

Exhausting and *futile* are the words that come to mind when I think about the days on Guernsey, going from one bank to another, over and over. We found nothing more than the one account we already knew they held at Barclays Bank.

Refreshing and comforting was our time on Jethou. Susan was so excited to be reunited with her buddy Pappy, the island rooster she had befriended when we traveled there with the family. As for me, I was just happy to be back, period! Any chance to be back in paradise and feel a connection with Dad and Mom again was like salve to my wounded heart.

Due to our excessive packing, coupled with our shopping spree on Guernsey, we got into a bit of a bind on our trip to London. One of my pieces of luggage had literally fallen apart on the flight over to Guernsey, so I came up with the not-so-brilliant idea of buying a new set of luggage, instead of just replacing the one damaged piece. With all that extra space and no husbands to reel us in, the two bumbling sisters wound up with four pieces of luggage, two carry-ons, and two purses.

Getting to and from Jethou and to the Guernsey airport was not as much of a problem because we had Chris and Annie helping us. It was landing back at London Heathrow Airport when we began to comprehend the trouble we faced. After mapping out the city, we realized we were going to have to take multiple trains on the Tube to get to our hotel.

What have we gotten ourselves into anyway?

If it was humanly impossible for the two of us to maneuver six pieces of luggage and two purses around in the airport, how in the world were we going to transfer from train to train to train?

We somehow managed to make it to the Metro station, and we just stood there and watched the trains come and go at lightning speed. The doors of the train only stayed open for a few seconds, and obviously the people getting on and off were much more experienced in doing so than we. Neither of us spoke a word; we just stood there in total fear, looking down at all the luggage and back at the train doors.

I finally told Susan we were just going to have to go for it. Her face was white, and panic was written all over it. When the train came, we began throwing the lighter pieces in before the now-angry passengers even started to disembark. The heavier pieces had to be dragged in, and when the "door closing" alarm went off, and the recording of the woman's voice kindly said, "Mind the gap," Susan panicked and fell down with only half of her body on the train. Without thinking, I reached down, grabbed the back of her coat with one hand and her last piece of luggage with the other, and with brute strength, driven by pure fear and adrenaline, I screamed and pulled them both in just as the door closed.

Once we were inside the train, the Londoners just glared down at the two idiot Americans, offering no support whatsoever. With no time to cry, panic, or assess our injuries, we were up on our feet planning our next escape. I'd like to say the second time went better than the first, but it did not. Not one time in all five of our embarking and disembarking experiences did we not fall into or out of the trains. I began to laugh uncontrollably every time I looked at Susan; she was completely disheveled and beat up. Susan's hysterical laughing was a defense mechanism to prevent her from having a meltdown. Not once did the train doors close without one of us letting out a scream of panic. We survived only by the grace of God and our pure fear of separation anxiety in a foreign country.

We had bruises on every limb of our bodies, and Susan had scratches on her forehead from falling face first in and out of the trains. That night in honor of Mom, instead of sitting in our hotel room licking our travel wounds, we decided to find a reason to celebrate. We popped a bottle of champagne and toasted Mom, brute strength, being together, and not getting lost or separated. Finally we toasted the extra-large taxi we would be hiring to take us back to the airport when it was time leave.

We had a late-morning meeting scheduled the next day. We were both very excited to meet the extraordinary detectives and experience the privilege of going into New Scotland Yard—the epicenter for world justice.

Once through security, we were escorted up to the office of Detective Superintendent Michael Lawrence, where two fine-looking gentlemen greeted us.

Detective Lawrence, known by most as Mick, was a tall, handsome man with a dark complexion, brown discerning eyes, and a great smile. Detective Constable Jim Johnstone was a very distinguished looking man. He had thick, straight, black hair with graying highlights and a close and carefully trimmed beard and mustache. He was tall and had eyes that got big with expression.

Mick started out by asking us, "Okay, what do you want to know and what don't you want to know?"

My cautious response was, "I want to know everything, and I want to see everything, all except pictures of them . . . well, you know, gone."

My wish was their command, and they proceeded to tell us everything from the very beginning, holding nothing back. It was so hard to listen to, but both of us wanted and even needed to hear what they had to say. At one point they told us that one of the men who had murdered our parents was having nightmares. They said he was awakened in the night with dreams of Mom crying and pleading for her life. I knew Susan was struggling with what they were telling us and that her heart was breaking all over again. I might be her little sister, but she'd be the first to admit, I was the tougher one. She could have easily excused herself from the room, but Susan knew I needed to hear every detail, so for me she sat right there and endured it all.

As I sat processing what they were telling us, a question came to my mind that started to burn inside me for an answer.

"Can I ask if the one having the nightmares is the same one who escaped from prison?"

Both of them just looked at me and then at each other, realizing they didn't know the answer to my burning question. So Jim began to ruffle through all their paperwork and didn't look up until he found the answer.

"Why, yes, Bonnie, it is one in the same person. It is Donaldson Samuel. How could you have possibly known that?"

I had no idea! *How could I have known that, God? Why would it be that the guy who escaped and was spared is the same guy having the nightmares? There must be a reason.*

Instinctively, I knew that was an opportunity to share my faith in God and howl He had been ministering to me over the last few months.

I always try to keep from sounding preachy. I never liked it when people got preachy with me before I accepted Christ, so I just simply told them my story—the condensed version of course! The silence that filled Mick's office after I finished my brief story was broken by Jim, who said, "You know, Bonnie Floyd, I don't believe the way you do, but my wife does!"

Susan and I looked at each other and started to laugh. What do you say to a response like that? I certainly had no idea, and by the look on Susan's face, she didn't have a comeback either. However, God always knows what to say. He is never without an answer. So I opened my mouth and said, "Jim, I cannot imagine living out a job like yours every day without the Lord in my life. What you have told me today, about just this one case, is enough to make a sane man crazy. It's enough to desensitize a person to the point where they have no feelings at all. I'm glad your wife believes, and I'll be praying for you, because in this line of work, you certainly need Jesus!"

Our meeting ended with an invitation to go to lunch with some of our new Scotland Yard friends, an invitation Susan and I eagerly accepted. During lunch, all at once all of their pagers started going off. Mick got up to make the call. When he came back he nonchalantly said, "There's been a kidnapping, and there's a ransom request. The handover is scheduled to take place at Harrods at three o'clock."

And with that, they resumed eating their lunches.

"Are you kidding me?" I exclaimed. "Don't you have to leave right now? Don't you need to get ready or something?"

"Ready for what? Do you think we need to go put on our capture-the-kidnapper suits?" he asked as they all roared with laughter.

I told him, "I don't believe you, Mick Lawrence! You're just pulling my leg!"

"Well, you will just have to see, won't you, Mrs. Clever-Floyd?"

Susan and I were disappointed when our lunch with this unique group of men came to an end. They were fascinating, funny, and full of baloney. But of course, they couldn't spend the whole day with us because they had to tend to the kidnapping caper!

Ha! To think I believed they actually got a call about a kidnapping.

Early that evening when Susan and I were back in our hotel room getting ready for dinner, we turned on the television. I almost burned the blouse I was ironing as I stopped cold in awe and disbelief at what I was seeing. Right there before my eyes was news footage about the kidnapping ransom exchange at Harrods. During the ransom handover, my new friends and Scotland Yard's finest caught the kidnapper and saved the day. I was completely, as they say in England, gobsmacked!

I stood there feeling a sense of pride, as someone would if they were seeing a close friend or family member being recognized for some great accomplishment. These extraordinary men solved the mystery of my parents' murder and captured the men who did it. Now the good-for-nothing murderers would stand trial and pay for what they did. Because of this fine team of detectives, our family now had our desperately needed answers. Closure and justice were about to be served. Or so I thought.

chapterFifteen

Justice at Last!

$\mathcal{D}$evastating delays, which led to furious frustration, caused our faith to flounder and doubt to set in. We thought the day would never come, but finally it did. After two long years to the day of their killings, the quadruple murder trial of William Clever, Kathleen Clever, Ian Cridland, and Thomas Williams was about to begin.

I had decided from the very beginning that I would go to Antigua for the trial. I could not imagine not being there in that courtroom representing Dad and Mom. We were told the trial would take two weeks, so that is what we financially planned for and the length of time we told our clients we would be gone.

Donnie and I flew into Antigua on January 27, 1996. Looking out the airplane window as we flew in made it hard to imagine that something so tragic could take place on such a beautiful island. I was full of emotion—I didn't want to be there, but at the same time, I was so glad I was.

My first impression of Antigua came from a man we met as we were deplaning. He was an Antiguan native named Keith Roy. He was a smartly dressed black man with a bald head, like Telly Savalas, and a smile any dentist would admire. He was as friendly as they come, asking who we were, why we were there, and where we were staying. The only thing we answered truthfully was where we were staying—the Halcyon Cove Hotel & Resort. He assured us our accommodations were at a great location on the island and a very nice resort. He went on to say what a wonderful and beautiful place Antigua was: "And the people," he said, "you will love the people! Everyone is so loving and friendly."

I just numbly looked at him and smiled. *Yeah, well I know of three who aren't so lovely!*

It didn't take but a minute for me to realize that it is just like God to put someone like that man in our path right off the bat—a person who represents Antigua for what the island truly is, rather than my skewed opinion of it. God was clearly showing me that I was to wait before I judged.

As soon as our feet hit the ground, we were introduced to the Antiguan way. We stood in a very slow line to go through immigration. So slow that we were sure our luggage was out there all by itself waiting to be claimed, hoping someone else had not claimed it. When we finally made it through, we found there was no luggage to claim, because it had not even been taken off the plane yet. After another fifteen minutes of standing in the humid heat, which I just knew was causing my hair to freak out, we were happy to see the luggage from our flight drive by on an airport cart. Then we waited and waited and then waited some more. We actually began getting dizzy from watching the belt go around so many times. After seeing the same few unclaimed pieces go around for the tenth time, we became concerned. Donnie began to search, and through a pigeonhole concrete wall he spotted our bags still sitting on a cart out on the tarmac. We found someone and asked why our bags were not unloaded yet, and he gave us a what's-your-problem look and said, "No problem, they're coming," as he walked away.

When our luggage finally made it onto the belt, we quickly grabbed them and moved to the customs line, where we waited another forty-five minutes. And there you have the "Antiguan way"—never, ever get in a hurry!

Once freed from the excessive waiting and red tape it took to get through that airport, two handsome, friendly, tanned Englishmen in shorts greeted us. I was thrilled to see them again! Donnie missed them completely because he was looking for proper-looking men in expensive business suits from New Scotland Yard. As soon as he saw me hugging these strangers, he realized in short order exactly who they were.

"You must be the famous detectives my wife goes on and on about," Donnie said, as he stretched out his right hand.

"And you must be the famous 'My Donnie' your wife goes on and on about," Mick said as he shook Donnie's hand. Mick and Jim led us to our car, and after loading the *boot* ("trunk" in America) with our luggage, we all piled in.

Our next Antiguan introduction was the roads—pothole city! There is no taking your eyes off the road on that island. If the driver isn't dodging potholes, he's weaving to miss sheep, goats, cows, donkeys, cats, and dogs.

I should have known from my first meeting with them in London, when they felt the need to educate me on how to speak "proper" English, that Englishmen, or at least these Englishmen, saw Americans as "works in progress." However, it became clear in just a matter of days that it wasn't Americans who needed educating—no, it was just me, Bonnie! Donnie thought it was hilarious and said, "Baby, it is obvious they love to tease you, and why shouldn't they? Your reactions are so animated. I'm sorry, my love, but you've got a target on your back with these guys."

Oh dear, this is going to be a long two weeks . . .

When we arrived at the Halcyon, Mick and Jim suggested we get settled into our room, change our clothes, and meet them at the Carib Bar located right on the beach for happy hour. Our room was nice but was located at the back side of the resort, and it had no television. Oh well, we had heard the television antennas weren't up and working after the recent hurricane anyway—bummer!

We found the Carib Bar, and it wasn't at all what I had imagined. It was more of a social place than a bar—a really fun place where all guests, both young and old, gathered to relax and enjoy themselves throughout the day. On the patio area there were tables and chairs for congregating, and for the more competitive guests, there were Ping-Pong and shuffleboard. If you'd rather sit in a lounge chair out in the sun or under a grass hut, the beach was only one step off the patio. It was most picturesque!

We found Mick and Jim sitting at the bar, along with Dave, who I had yet to meet. Detective Sergeant David Marshall was a big bloke. He was very nice looking with dark-brown wavy hair, closely set brown eyes, and thick eyebrows. He had a great laugh that was contagious and caused his whole face to light up. He was "Mr. Information," knowing all the great restaurants, when they were open, and what their price ranges were. He was a very organized man, so long as he had his fanny pack! Dave suggested Julian's, one of their favorite restaurants on the island, where the owners were friendly and greeted us warmly. They were genuinely glad to see The Boys were back in town.

The next day Donnie and I spent walking and exploring the resort. We wanted to familiarize ourselves with our surroundings while The Boys were at the jail meeting with Donaldson Samuel. They didn't tell us why they were meeting with him, but only that it was very important to the case and that it needed to go well.

Donnie and I were sitting on the patio by the Carib Bar when Mick, Jim, and Dave came walking up after being at the jail all day. The looks on each of their faces were somber and serious, and without knowing what they were about to tell us, my heart started to race. Mick began, informing us why they had gone to see Donaldson. "We need his testimony for the case to move forward. Donaldson, at this point, like the other two, is facing the death penalty. Capital punishment here on Antigua is death by hanging. We went to meet with him today to offer a plea bargain if he would testify against the other two."

Mick looked over at Jim as if to pass the baton. Jim, in a low and solemn voice said, "We offered him life in prison instead of facing the gallows, if he would turn queen's evidence and become a Crown witness. Bonnie, he refused." And without Donaldson's testimony against the other two, we have no case," Mick finished.

"So let me get this straight. What you're telling me is, if this scumbag, Donaldson, doesn't agree to testify against the other two scumbags, there will be no trial?"

"That's about the size of it," Dave answered.

"You've *got* to be kidding me! There is no way, absolutely no way, God has made a way for Donnie and me to come all this way for this long-overdue trial to have us turn around and go home tomorrow!"

All riled up and with my blood boiling, I tried to control my tone of voice and speak with respect, "Here's the deal: this makes no godly sense to me at all. What you guys need to do is go back to that prison tomorrow and offer this deal to Donaldson again. In the meantime, Donnie and I will call home and get a bunch of people to start praying. God will turn this around, you just wait and see."

Without any hesitation, Jim replied, "First of all, Bonnie Floyd, we are already planning to go back to the prison tomorrow, and second, you can do . . ." as he made a praying gesture with his hands "whatever you feel you need to do, and we'll just see how it all plays out." I had been around The Boys long enough to start to catch on to some of the British slang words they would typically use. Although they didn't say it, I could hear them thinking, *She is bloomin' off her trolley!*

So that is exactly what we did. We marched—well I shouldn't say "we" marched, as Donnie just walked fast to keep up with me—back to our room and proceeded to make some calls home. God's timing is always perfect and sometimes even amusing at times, because it just so happened to be Super Bowl Sunday back in the States. That meant we only had to make a few calls to get a whole lot of people praying, because everywhere we called there were Super Bowl parties happening where large numbers of people were gathered.

The next day, while waiting for The Boys to return from the jail, Donnie and I were out on the beach relaxing in lounge chairs. We were thoroughly enjoying ourselves, soaking up the Caribbean sun as we sipped on fruity drinks with cute little umbrellas in them. While leaning back with my eyes closed, listening to the surf roll in and out, my sun became shaded. When I opened my eyes, I saw three large, familiar Englishmen in business suits hovering over me with a bit of a jealous glare on their faces. I snickered at them a bit and said, "Good afternoon, gentleman. I'm so sorry you had to get sand in your shoes to find me, but I just knew my daddy wouldn't want me to suffer while here in the Caribbean."

"We see that, Bonnie, and from what we have learned about your parents, we're certain you're right," Mick said with a smile.

"Bonnie Floyd, we have good news for you. Donaldson agreed. He is going to be a Crown witness and testify against the other two," Jim said with a bit of cocky confidence.

"Oh, praise the Lord!" I said, as I bolted up in my chair. "That is exactly what we prayed for. I told you God would change Donaldson's mind."

"You know, when we were at the jail today and Donaldson agreed to testify, I remembered you had said you were going to . . . " And again, instead of Jim saying the word *pray* he made that praying gesture with his hands.

What is up with that? Why doesn't he just say the word pray? *And why does he always call me "Bonnie Floyd?" I think Jim and I are developing an out-of-the-ordinary but special relationship.*

The trial was to start the very next day, and Steve and Cyndi, or should I say Mr. and Mrs. Beilman were scheduled to arrive that evening and stay for the first part of the trial. Just as Mom and I predicted, Steve had recently made Cyndi his bride.

Justice at Last!

In the Courtroom

Surreal is once again the word I would use to describe what it felt like to be sitting in a courtroom waiting for the murder trial of my parents to begin. Surreal or not, there I sat in a white plastic chair that belonged in someone's backyard, not in a courtroom.

We're certainly not in Kansas anymore, Toto!

I was in a hot and humid, dilapidated courtroom. The floors, the stairs, and the walls were all made of concrete. It looked as if at one time they had tried to create a color scheme, or maybe that was just the only paint they could find. What remained now were gray walls with patches of white and aqua peeling paint. The courtroom was upstairs, and the exterior walls on the second floor had the same open-air concrete pigeonhole design we had seen at the airport. The courtroom smelled of bleach, Antigua's cleanser of choice. I'm sure it was to cover up the wet, musty smell I had become familiar with all over the island.

Donnie looked over at me and said, "Are you ready, babe? The feeling in the room has drastically changed; I think this thing is about to get going."

"Ready as I'll ever be. But why do say that?"

With a look of seriousness and discernment, he said, "Just look at the boys; they have their game faces on."

Boy, he wasn't kidding. By now I thought I had seen the many faces of these amazing detectives, whom I now called my friends, but I had yet to see them look like this. Grave, intimidating, and downright scary might begin to describe any one of them, except when they looked over at me. When I looked in their eyes, I saw a confidence and understanding that said, "Don't worry about a thing, we've got this under control!" Quite honestly, it was very similar to Dad's "Look #5," the one he gave me every time I was afraid.

I needed them there with me; I needed their strength and their assuredness, especially at that moment, because for the first time I was about to lay my eyes on the three men who brutally murdered my dad and my mom.

They walked in single file into the courtroom with their attorneys. First were Marvin Joseph and his lawyer, Gerald Watt. Then Melanson Harris with his lawyer, Clement Bird; and last was Donaldson Samuel with his lawyer, Ralph Francis.

Marvin looked like a human rat. He had a head that was shaped like a rat, with skinny sharp teeth and a straggly, sparse-haired beard that barely covered his long pointed chin. His hair was tight and wiry with a small, braided ponytail in the back that looked like a rodent's tail. He looked dead straight at me and smiled. I thought Donnie was going kill him right there, but Dave had hold of Donnie before he could make a move. I quickly realized then, that unbeknownst to us, we had been strategically seated by The Boys. They wanted to be sure Donnie and Steve did not do anything stupid.

Melanson Harris had a big head, and his facial bones were abnormally large. His forehead was huge, and his nose lay out across his whole face. He very much resembled the heavyweight boxer Mike Tyson. He walked in looking all around and seemed as though he was completely oblivious about why he was even there.

Walking with his head down, Donaldson Samuel was by far the most normal looking of the three. He had very strong facial features, and where Marvin's brown skin tone was light, Donaldson's complexion was dark, almost black. He never looked up, and it was obvious that he made no attempt at making eye contact with Marvin or Melanson.

You could immediately hear the hushed whispers running through the courtroom, demanding justice, which in Antigua is to be hung by the neck until dead. The three of them, all in their early twenties, stood there sweating and wiping their brows. Melanson wiped the perspiration dripping off his forehead with a yellow piece of terrycloth towel he clenched in his right hand.

With everyone in their places, the trial was set to proceed, barring any unexpected delays like the day before. Mr. Bird, one of the attorneys for the defendants, at the very last minute asked for a twenty-four-hour adjournment "to sort out some last-minute details." I was sure the judge, Albert Redhead, would not allow such a thing, since Mr. Bird should have been prepared already. Apparently, I was wrong.

I was not the only one displeased with this allowance; the entire public gallery stirred and grumbled at this unexpected delay. The British newspaper, the *Independent*, reported that the Antiguan people wanted this trial "to get started and be done with." The *Independent's* reporter, Bob Graham, interviewed several people from both Antigua and Barbuda, who said the murders had left an indelible stain on the reputation of both paradise islands. He further reported that in the eyes of many people on the islands, the murders were more than just the deaths of four people; they were an attack on the livelihoods of the islanders themselves. A taxi driver, who depended on tourism for his income, told Mr. Graham in his interview,

> This is a trial, man, not just for murders, but also for the attack on all
> of us living here! They can plead not guilty, but the people here know
> the truth. What's more important is that when they are found guilty,
> they gotta be hanged to give a message to every other young person
> who thinks they can import murder to Antigua and Barbuda.[1]

When I read that article, I wondered what the taxi driver meant by "import murder." Was it just a figure of speech? Or did it derive from the fact that Melanson and Marvin had both spent time in New York and were exposed to the city's gun-toting gangs?

O Lord, did my own country expose these guys to their wicked and violent behaviors?

Bright and early the next morning, the proceedings did start without a delay, with Marvin's attorney addressing the judge right off the bat. I did not like what I was hearing. I kept looking at Mick's face, trying to read it, trying to see if by his countenance I could tell if I was correctly comprehending all of this. Nothing. His face was stoic.

All I could get out of their proper English dialect spoken with a Caribbean accent was that Marvin and Melanson's attorneys were not one bit happy about Donaldson testifying against their clients. They wanted the judge not to allow the jury to consider his testimony. When it became clear that Judge Redhead had full intention of allowing Donaldson's testimony to be considered by the jury in regard to making a verdict, Mr. Watt said, "We wish to address the Court in the absence of the jury."

The jury was dismissed and sent out of the courtroom. I had a million questions, and when I quietly tried to ask Jim just one of them, he slowly put his index finger up to his lips and softly said, "Shush."

Marvin's lawyer, Mr. Watt, addressed the judge:

The first point I wish to make to Your Lordship—and I have spoken with Mr. Bird, counsel for Accused No. 1, Melanson Harris—is that we, the defense, had no indication that there was going to be a change in plea of the Accused No. 3, Donaldson Samuel.

Oh no, here we go. They are going to try and throw out his testimony! Please, God, don't let this happen.

In order to prevent a miscarriage of justice, the trial judge must not allow Accused Donaldson Samuel to plea to a lesser offence. I, however, do not presume to tell you what to do.

Nothing like talking out of both sides of your mouth! Tell the judge what to do, but then be sure to kiss up to him and tell him that's not what you're doing.

This testimony by the Accused No. 3, Donaldson Samuel, and particularly his plea of guilty, might dictate a serious influence that the others (Marvin Joseph and Melanson Harris) may also be guilty.

Ya think? Of course they're guilty, you bonehead!

This plea of guilt prevents the flow of evidence to the jury, who will now not hear the evidence against the Accused (Donaldson Samuel).

Justice at Last!

Am I hearing this guy right? Why does the jury need to hear evidence against Donaldson when he's already pled guilty to the crime? I don't get any of this—this is going to be a very, very long two weeks!

Pleading to a lesser offence is an inducement for the Accused to give evidence against the other two to save his own skin.

No duh, oh brilliant one. That's exactly why it's called "turning" Queen's evidence. He's trying to "turn" from getting hung!

After hearing all of Watt's attempts to sway him, Judge Redhead ruled in our favor to allow Donaldson's testimony to be heard by the jury. Immediately Mr. Bird, Melanson's attorney, stepped up and asked that a concession be made by the prosecution. The concession was asking the prosecuting attorney, Mr. Rex McKay, to not start the case by opening with the written statement of Donaldson Samuel made on February 21, 1994.

Why not?

Mr. Bird then stated that the admissibility of the statement would be challenged on the ground that it was not free and voluntary.

Huh? Not free and voluntary?

He went on to say that rather than putting forth his challenges now, he preferred to deal with the matters at such times as they came up in the trial.

What is he talking about? What is he up to?

Then Mr. Watt, Marvin's attorney, piped up and stated that he would be making an application for parts of Donaldson's statement to be edited.

Somebody better explain all this to me . . .

THE INDICTMENT

At 10:55 a.m. the jury returned. The jury roll call was taken—all present. Next, the indictment was read to the Accused No. 3, Donaldson Samuel. And the accused pled guilty to manslaughter. The Crown accepted the plea of "guilty of manslaughter."

Thank You, Jesus! I knew You would ensure that justice would prevail . . .
Keep our game faces on, everybody; we are going to have a trial!

No more than an hour after the jury had been recalled, sworn in, and seated, we adjourned for lunch. As much as I wanted to get this thing moving, I was *more* thankful for the lunch break. I was hungry, but not for food—for answers. I wanted to know the meaning of what Bird and Watt were saying after Judge Redhead allowed Donaldson to change his plea. I got the answers I was looking for as we walked to our first of many court day lunches, but not without a round of harassing first.

Mick explained to us that Bird seemed to have something up his sleeve. He thought Bird needed time to prepare himself for something specific before Donaldson would take the stand and give his testimony.

"Like what?" I questioned.

"Well, you heard him, Bonnie. He made some type of reference to the fact that Donaldson's statement was not given 'freely and voluntarily.'"

"Well, that's garbage! What's really going on in there?" I pleaded.

"Is she always this demanding and bossy, Donnie? I feel for you big time!" Jim interjected.

"Ahhh! Stop it you guys, and Donnie don't answer that! Mick, please keep going. I need to understand this," I begged.

Donnie pled the Fifth on the grounds that answering Jim's question might incriminate him. That created a big roar of laughter, along with The Boys telling him he was whipped!

Eventually Mick decided to return to my questioning. "I am speculating about Donaldson's statement, but I am sure that Watt wants to 'edit' out anything implicating his client from Donaldson's statement."

Feeling nervous about, well, everything, I asked, "Do I need to be concerned about that, because I'm freaking out right now!"

Without hesitation or even a glimpse of concern, Mick confidently said, "Bonnie, I predict that what we're about to have here is a trial within a trial, and though Judge Redhead's ruling allowed Donaldson to change his plea, the matter of his February 1994 statement being allowed in as evidence is still an issue. I don't think we've seen the last of that. Regardless, these men will hang for what they did to your parents, Bonnie. Do not worry another minute about that. Understood?"

With complete confidence and total trust in my Scotland Yard heroes, I pushed all worry out of my mind and turned it toward one of my most favorite things—food!

It was good to be out of the courtroom, breathing fresh air and surrounded by such tropical beauty as we ate lunch. We all sat outside together in a shaded courtyard but ordered from different places, as several quaint village restaurants surrounded us. With Donnie and I still new to the extremely eclectic cuisine on Antigua, we decided to go with a safe choice, tuna sandwiches and chips.

As we all sat down to eat, Dave handed us a bottle of Susie's Hot Sauce to put on our sandwiches, as if it was as common as a bottle of ketchup. I had noticed a bottle of Susie's on every table where we had dined thus far, but I had yet to try it on anything. I took the little bottle of liquid bright orange spice and sprinkled it all over my tuna sandwich. It was then that I saw the looks on The Boys' faces, but not one of them said a measly word.

It was too late, I'd set my fiery fate, and there was no way I would chicken out now. I bit right into my tuna sandwich, and *kapow!* My mouth flamed into a scorching, fiery frenzy, and my eyes lit up as if I had just been ignited! No matter what, there was no way I was going to be able to play this one off. I had just set myself up to be the brunt of the next several days' jokes! It was a great laugh, and we certainly needed one considering what we were about to face in the courtroom.

Over lunch Mick told us that McKay planned to get Donaldson on the stand as soon as he could. He wanted to get his testimony before the jury, in case Donaldson changed his mind.

"Could he do that?" I asked Mick.

"Sure he could, and these Barbudans are always saying one thing and doing another. Barbuda is a small island, and everyone is related to one another and . . . "

I could tell he was going somewhere with that "everyone is related to one another" comment, and we were about to hear it when Dave announced it was time to return to court.

PRESENTING EVIDENCE

The first person to take the stand after lunch was Johnny DeSouza, for the prosecution. Johnny was the owner of the shotgun used in the murders. He testified that on January 17, 1994, he discovered that someone had removed four louver panes from his bedroom window, creating a space large enough for someone to crawl through. When he realized his shotgun had been stolen from his bedroom dressing table, he immediately filed a report with the police.

Johnny was cross-examined by Mr. Bird, and as he stepped down from the stand, the judge announced it was time to break for the day. I now had to wait another day before the first murderer—the Crown witness—would take the stand.

The day Governor Ronald Reagan came to town. My dad, Bill, to his right and my mom, Rita, behind him.

The *Sarsaparilla!* Our family voyage to Baja, Mexico.

Dad would always let me chart the course and say, "I don't know why I always check your course, Bean; you're always right on the mark!"

Not only did I chart the course, but I was often at the helm.

"Laughter always filled the sea life air." Mom, me, and my sister, Linda.

Like father . . .

Like daughter . . . I wanted to be just like him!

I was Dad's personal dinghy chauffeur.

A successful day of diving! Lobster is on the menu tonight . . . and yes, there will be butter!

Celebrating Dad's birthday with lifetime friends, Betty and Larry Carney.

Silver Heels, setting sail around the world, fulfilling my dad's lifelong dream.

"Halfway There" celebration on their crossing to Hawaii.

Mom celebrating the halfway point in her handmade toilet paper Wahine luau top.

(Left): "Billy, Billy, look what our anchor caught; this will feed us for weeks!" I'll be breaking out all my most favorite clam recipes!"

(Right): "Not a bad accidental catch to go along with the bugs [lobster] we dove for this morning. All in all, Kathy, I think we had a successful day!"

(Right): They only needed each other to make a party!

Mom always provided fun surprises to delight the native children.

Just one of their many land adventures while sailing around the world.

A surprise wedding gift! Island treasures and the most beautiful seashell my dad found on a dive. Before sending it he had it cleaned and hand-polished by a native islander.

I threatened My Donnie,
"Don't you dare!"

August 22, 1987, Dad and Mom having a champagne toast to celebrate our wedding day in the Solomon Islands.

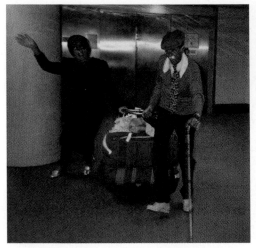

Dad and Mom donning disguises before they emerged from customs. They couldn't fool me, I knew the *old geezer* was Dad and I tackled him.

A toast—my daddy's home at last!

The Master Storyteller and his protégé back together again!

Having a blast on their first trip home, hanging out on (off) a cliff on the California coast.

Little did I know the "intruder" would become "my mom," who I deeply love and greatly admire.

It didn't take long for the four of us to become best friends!

The best in-laws ever! Dad and Mom Floyd and Sandy, a.k.a. "Donnie's dating dictator."

My Kimberly Noelle. She discerns when my first tear is coming; she successfully catches the second; and she faithfully stops the third. I have no one else like her.

Peter Ogden and his daughter, Tiffany, holding the trophy his yacht *Challenger* won in the Rolex Swan Regatta.

(Left): My sister, Susan, and I on our trip to England, where we had our first encounter with the greatest detectives in the world.

Two of the greatest men I've ever known—Detective Superintendent Michael (Mick) Lawrence and Detective Constable Jim Johnstone of New Scotland Yard.

After five weeks together in Antigua for the trial, I longed to meet the wives of the men who brought justice to my family. To my delight, we were all invited to Sir Peter Ogden's fiftieth birthday celebration.

The infamous John Fuller and his *real* treehouse!

Her Majesty's High Prison. "State your name and purpose."

The anxious ride from Antigua to Barbuda. So many unknowns to anticipate . . .

A long-overdue reunion . . .

"Family Picture"

Looking out over Low
Bay, reflecting on what
might *not* have been . . .

First Mate
Thomas Williams,
the yacht *Challenger*.

Captain of the
yacht *Challenger*,
Ian (Criddy)
Cridland.

"Oh, to be sailing again!"

Best friends forever!

chapterSixteen

The Crown Witness

The second day in court began as we had all hoped it would with the prosecution calling its Crown witness—Accused No. 3, Donaldson Samuel.

Until I felt myself getting lightheaded, I didn't realize I'd stopped breathing again. I had to keep reminding myself to breathe. Every time I took a deep breath, Jim would look over at me with a smile of confidence. I was growing very fond of Detective Constable Jim Johnstone; he was quickly becoming like an older brother to me.

Crown witness or not, when this twenty-three-year-old murderer took the stand, I glared at him with eyes that should have burned holes right through him. I was begging for him to look up at me, but he would only look at Mr. McKay when he spoke.

He was asked to give his name, his age, and where he was from. After that brief introduction, Mr. McKay dove headlong into this man's account of what happened on the fateful night of January 27, 1994.

Donaldson was frustratingly hard to understand, and within an hour my head was throbbing from straining to comprehend his accent. That frustration, coupled with the horror of listening to how they planned out and killed my parents, Criddy, and Tom was excruciating. "Planned out" is actually a stretch, as they really had no plan at all. He explained it this way:

> I was at Mel's house, and this was about 10:00 p.m. It was Marvin, Melanson, and myself. When I left house, I know where I was going. We were going to Low Bay. I know what we were going for. We were going on a yacht, not for a joy ride, to get some money at gunpoint. It was Marvin's idea. We left house, and Marvin got the gun that was buried in a sandpit. We used a boat that was parked by the jetty to cross over lagoon to get to Low Bay. Marvin held the gun, and me and Mel carried the *Sunfish* across the peninsula to the water. The *Sunfish* is a different boat to the one we get to Low Bay with.

How dare he say, "We used a boat." How about "We stole it"? And did he accidently leave out the details of how they calculatingly hid the Sunfish *in some bushes two nights before?*

The palms of my hands were sweating, and I kept rubbing them on my skirt. I tried not to fidget, but it was so hard to sit still. I knew what was about to happen, yet hearing it from someone who was there, from one of the men who actually killed them, was going to be more devastating than I thought. How was I going to react as I sat there listening to it all?

He continued, "We paddled the *Sunfish* with our hands to get to the yacht. All three of us went onboard the yacht. Marvin first then told Mel to pass him the gun. Melanson then went up. I last went up."

Dad, wake up! Why didn't you wake up? You always woke up at any little noise, any slight movement when we were on the boat! Why not this time, Dad? Why, God, why not this time?

"Marvin went down in the cabin of the boat with the gun. It was not locked, so he went down on a step . . ."

If only it had been locked, things would be so different now . . .

"Marvin stuck up the captain. All of us were down in the cabin. The captain shouted, 'We've got three men onboard!' The rest of the crew came out of their cabins. Melanson tied them up with rope, and we brought them upstairs. Marvin passed gun off because one of the guys got away."

Run, Dad! Jump! Go get help! Save Mom!

I knew in my gut it was Dad who got away, even before he said who it was. There was no way Dad was going down without a fight, and I knew beyond a shadow of a doubt he would lay his life down to save Mom and his friends.

The old married guy got away. So we tied their hands behind their backs and mouths with black tape. The tape was wrapped around their heads. Their mouths were tied up, just tape across. Marvin had the gun at that time, told me to go down and search. I went down in cabin alone. I searched. I found bird gun, about nine inches in length. I found camera. I found some EC, US, and English money.

That's it? The old married guy got away? What happened? How far did he get? How did he get caught? Who caught him? Did he put up a fight? Am I the only one who wants to know these things?

I searched the boat again with Marvin. Mel brought down the people from upstairs. I was down below at that time. I remained there until everything happened. The crew was sitting around a table. They were in good health. They were still alive. I was ready to go back at that time to *Codrington*, because we had finished what we went for. I was ready to go before everything happened, before the people died. They were shot. Mel and Marvin shot them. They shot them with the shotgun.

There it was; they were dead. As much as I had been anxious to finally be able to piece together every detail of what had taken place, before and after the murders, at that moment nothing else mattered. My parents were dead, and nothing was going to change that. For the remainder of the day, I sat numb; there was no more fidgeting. I tried to listen to how they got back over to the mainland of Barbuda and how they hid everything they stole in sandpits east and west of the airport, but all I could focus on was that my parents were gone. It was a very long day.

For the next two days I listened to Donaldson answer question after question. His story remained consistent, which said to me that he was telling the truth. The only thing he changed and revealed that he hadn't said the first day was that after the people were brought down below, he went up on deck to put the stolen items in the *Sunfish*. From up on deck he repeatedly said to the other two, "Let's go! We did what we came to do." But when they wouldn't answer him, he went back down below. It was then that the shootings took place.

Donaldson continued,

> I am positive Marvin shot the young guy. Then he handed me the gun and said shoot. I told him I don't know how to use it. I never touched it. Then he passed it to Mel. I realized at this time the promise that 'nobody get hurt' was finished. I fell back on the step, and my knees felt weak. I told them to leave the people alone. I did not know what was going to happen, but it did happen. Mel shot somebody. I was weak in my legs. I could not move. Mel helped me up when everything was over.

I sat there as Donaldson's words spun in my head over and over. He actually showed remorse, and apparently he had even tried to stop the shootings; that is, if he was telling the truth. Who really knew?

My mother-in-law often refers to me as "the stone that rarely weeps." It's a fitting statement, and it certainly rang true for me in the courtroom. We were a week into the trial, and I had yet to shed a tear. I was pretty confident after sitting through days of Donaldson's testimony that I was in the clear. However, something very strange started happening to me when Mr. Watt and Mr. Bird began to cross-examine Donaldson Samuel.

The first day of these cross-examinations appeared to consist of Donaldson repeating the same things he had already said, just in the form of an answer, rather than a statement. However, as the days progressed, these two defense attorneys turned brutal.

One morning as I listened to them badger him, things got heated. Bird accused Donaldson of changing his plea because he was afraid to die and just wanted to escape the death sentence. Donaldson adamantly denied the accusation, saying, "Everyone has to die someday, and I'm not afraid. I changed my plea because I never had any part to play in the actual killings. I never realized the plan was to be with violence."

I sat there listening to them badger him, and I thought, *They're being so mean to him* and then quickly came to my senses and corrected my erroneous thinking by saying to myself, *So what! Who cares if they're being mean to him! He deserves everything he gets, and more!*

But no matter how many times I caught myself sympathizing and correcting my wrong thinking, I kept feeling sorry for the guy. Feeling bad for him was really starting to irritate me and get on my nerves. I was relieved when it was time to adjourn for lunch.

We opted to have lunch at the courtyard where Dave took us the first day; it had become my favorite lunch spot. My palate had taken a real liking for the many flavors of Antigua.

During lunch I could not keep from thinking about how I was feeling in the courtroom that morning. I contemplated saying something but knew everyone at the table would have thought I'd gone bonkers. I elected to internalize it instead, making it my own little secret. Little did I know what was about to happen next in the courtroom would blow the lid off my little secret.

CROSS-EXAMINATION CONTINUED

Court resumed that afternoon, picking up right where we had left off with the cross-examination of Donaldson Samuel. What also resumed were my extremely mixed-up emotions. With Donnie on my left and Jim on my right, looking straight ahead was my only option. The problem with looking straight ahead was that directly in front of me was Donaldson in the witness box. I was losing the battle of the emotions going on inside of me, and it was beginning to manifest itself on the outside.

The badgering of Donaldson continued; they could not break him or cause him to contradict any of his testimony. It became obvious that they were just trying to confuse him with a battery of questions. Donnie took my hand, and we prayed against confusion, and soon it appeared that something washed over Donaldson. His countenance changed, and he said with boldness, "Stop trying to confuse me. I know days and times, but I don't know dates." At that the attorney began asking questions differently, and Donaldson was able to answer them correctly.

It was an amazing thing to sit there and discern confusion, pray against it, and literally watch God's hand move in that courtroom. Even so, I was still feeling so badly for Donaldson that I actually thought I might cry.

What's going on here? Who gives a rip about this guy? Certainly not me! Stop it, Bonnie, stop it now!

A lump developed in my throat, and I kept swallowing to try and get rid of it and the feeling that was causing it. The more they questioned him, the bigger the lump grew. I'm pretty sure whatever gland produces the lump we get in our throats is connected to the gland that produces tears. I started fidgeting in my chair to try and shake it off, as you would if you were trying to stay awake. Nothing worked, I was about to crumble, and my dried-up tear ducts had begun to flow.

I quickly turned my head to the left, away from Donaldson, to look outside. I could see the blue sky through the pigeonholes, and when I focused on the outside, the tears stopped. Once that stupid crying feeling went away, I turned my head straight forward again. Within a minute, the lump returned and so did the blasted tears. I turned my head to the left again and looked outside. This went on and on to the point where I literally would look forward, start to cry, and say to myself, "On," and then turn my head to look outside and say, "Off."

And so it went "on" and "off" and "on" and "off" until on one of my "off" moments, Donnie turned his head to the right and looked straight at me, sternly saying through gritted teeth, "Those tears are for him [Donaldson], aren't they?"

I froze at his words and the disconcerting look on his face. I didn't want to admit it, I didn't want to care, but I did, and I couldn't control it. I answered him through my uncontrollable tears, "Well, I really don't know what's happening, it's on and off and on and off . . ."

Again, speaking sternly through gritted teeth, he said, "I suggest you step outside and gather yourself."

Trying desperately to hold back the tears, I was able to utter, "I think that's a good idea."

As quietly and discretely as I could, I got up from my white plastic chair and headed for the side door that led onto a balcony. Once outside I took a few long deep breaths and viewed my surroundings. I was relieved to find I was out there by myself. The old concrete balcony was on the back side of the courthouse. It had concrete stairs that led down to a type of courtyard area that was enclosed by a chain-link fence topped with coiled razor wire. The view looking up at the sky was much better than the view looking down.

As I looked up I asked out loud, "Lord God, what is happening to me here?"

Instantly, and completely out of the blue, a story that my friend Marie's mom told me years before flooded my mind. She had been awakened in the middle of the night with a heavy burden for family members who had not yet come to believe in Jesus. She slipped out of bed and went into her living room to pray. As she prayed she began to cry for those unsaved loved ones. Her burden seemed to get heavier the more she prayed, and the more she prayed the harder she would cry. She told us she went from weeping to wailing and soon got to the point that her body physically hurt.

The next morning, still perplexed from her experience the night before, she called an older, godly woman she greatly admired and shared her experience. That wise woman of God said to Marie's mom, "Oh, how precious that God would allow you to experience just a sliver of His sorrow for those loved ones who do not yet know the Lord Jesus as Savior, because, my dear one, any more than a sliver would have physically killed you."

Just as quickly as that old memory came to my mind, so did these words: *Bonnie, what you are experiencing is just a sliver of my compassion for Donaldson . . .*

Peace like a river washed over me the moment I heard those words, and in an instant it became very clear what God was asking of me. So, on the balcony of that dilapidated courthouse, I looked up into the beautiful blue Caribbean sky, stretched out my arms, and prayed, *"Okay, God, here I am. Send me, and I will tell Donaldson about Jesus."*

The river of peace that had just washed over me started to dry up a bit when I thought about telling My Donnie and The Boys about my little episode on the balcony. So I offered up another prayer, saying, *"Lord, I'm willing, but there's a husband and three detectives in there that You are going to have deal with, who aren't going to like this idea one bit."*

I decided I would wait until after we got back to our hotel room to say anything to Donnie about my encounter with God out on the balcony. On the drive back to the Halcyon, he didn't say a word about my getting choked up or leaving the courtroom, and I knew why. He absolutely did not want The Boys to know I was getting weak for one of the murderers, because something like that would likely downright tick them off.

I was so apprehensive about telling Donnie. How on earth was I going to tell him that I wanted to meet with Donaldson so I could tell him about Jesus? I am not a controlling wife, and I can't stand it when I see a woman who manipulates her husband. However, I do know how to properly word things to My Donnie to keep the heat off me.

"Umm . . . baby?" I said sweetly. "Do you remember today when *you* suggested I go outside and gather myself?"

"Yeah, I remember."

"Well, when I was out on the balcony because you suggested I leave the courtroom for a while, something happened."

He looked at me, waiting for me to continue, and when I didn't say anything, he asked, "What happened?"

"So, when I was out on the balcony because *you* suggested I go outside and gather myself, God spoke to me . . ." I mumbled as I turned to look out the window.

"Oh no, baby, no!" he said in a whining tone and with a this-cannot-be-good look on his face. "What did He say now?"

With all the assuredness I could muster, I turned back around and told him everything that happened out on the balcony. When I was finished telling him the story, the look on his face was not promising. I knew I had to have his blessing or there would be no going to see Donaldson. It is never my job as a wife to convince Donnie of anything. It's only my place to share my heart and give him my thoughts and opinion. If I had heard from God, and I believed I had, then God would have to do the convincing and change Donnie's heart on the matter.

He looked at me with fury in his eyes and said, "I don't like this, babe, I don't like it one bit . . ."

He stopped himself as if to rethink what was about to come out of his mouth. I just stood there silently—not an easy thing for me—knowing if I opened my mouth, I would probably have done more damage than good.

The countenance on his face slowly changed, and with conviction in his eyes, he looked at me and said, "Far be it from me, babe, to stand in the way of what God is doing here. I just don't want you to say anything to Mick, Jim, or Dave about this yet. When the time's right, I'll speak to them."

chapter**Seventeen**

A Wink and a Promise

*T*he Scotland Yard forensics team arrived on the island in full force to give statements on all their findings. This elite group of scientists were fascinating in the courtroom, and before long, as I had their counterparts, I grew very fond of them.

The first to take the stand was Detective Sergeant James Gallagher, who was attached to the Science Forensic Laboratory of Scotland Yard. He testified that he was flown into Antigua to assist Jim in receiving and packaging exhibits in the case. The daunting task of collecting evidence from the boat, from the bodies, and from the investigative searches launched all over the Island of Barbuda took an entire month following the murders.

All exhibits were packaged and sealed in eleven boxes and one cool box by Jim in Detective Gallagher's presence. They took the twelve boxes to the airport and guarded them as they were loaded on a plane bound for London Heathrow Airport. Detective Gallagher boarded the same plane, and upon arrival supervised the unloading of the twelve boxes. He checked the seals and then drove them to the Metropolitan Forensic Science Laboratory in Lambeth, England.

From there he submitted the boxes to a team of six scientists whose duties were made most difficult due to the fact that the local Antigua police had made a terrible bungling mistake. Since the boat was moored off the Island of Barbuda, it needed to be brought back to the mainland for the investigation to ensue. For reasons best known only to them, and prematurely at that, the Antigua police decided to bring *Challenger* back to Antigua during a heavy squall. The seawater splashing aboard and rain pouring in damaged and destroyed much of the evidence. Worse yet, the rough seas rolled the boat back and forth, causing the bodies to be tossed about.

Even so, this brilliant Scotland Yard team was able to recover the necessary fingerprints, bloodstains, and other forensic science to put together a strong case for the prosecution.

The following days were filled with witness after witness taking the stand and giving their testimonies. Several friends, or should I say family, of the three accused men were brought over from the Island of Barbuda by the prosecution.

I say family because, as Mick alluded that day at lunch, everyone on Barbuda did seem to be related. Every time Barbudans took the stand, they were an uncle or cousin to somebody. Many of them had undeniably strong, and sometimes odd, facial features. So much about the Barbudans intrigued me, and I began asking around about their history.

I came to find out—though disputed by some—that back in the slave trading days, the sugar estate proprietor, Christopher Codrington, after whom Barbuda's only town is named, used Barbuda as a stud farm to provide slaves for sugar plantations on other islands.

In 1685, the Codrington family leased the Island of Barbuda from the English crown by King Charles II for the nominal price of "one fat pig per year, if asked." The Codringtons used Barbuda for slave breeding and as a source of supplies, such as timber, fish, and livestock. The Codrington family had rights not only to the land, but also to all wreckage from the many shipwrecks on the surrounding reefs. The income from such wrecks was significant.

They were an interesting people who suffered greatly at the hands of the Codringtons and today live a far better life, but still so different from anything to which I'd ever been witness.

A Hitch in the Proceedings

What was scheduled to be a two-week trial blew up the day Melanson Harris accused one of The Boys and the superintendent of police of offering him a bribe if he helped them in the investigation.

Our first indication that something had gone awry was when Norris Airall, superintendent of the Antigua police and officer in charge of the Criminal Investigative department, took the stand and was cross-examined by Mr. Bird. He seemed to focus his questions specifically on the day Melanson's house was searched. He suggested there were times when Melanson might have been alone with one of the Scotland Yard detectives, insinuating that Mr. Airall was not always within earshot of Melanson that day.

Mick was next to take the stand, and quite honestly, I'd been waiting for that moment. I knew what we were about to witness was going to be pure greatness, because Mick (a.k.a. Sherlock Holmes/James Bond) was literally the world's best! Not to disappoint, Mick was a force to be reckoned with on the stand, whether he was giving his statement or being questioned, he was the one in control. However, when it came to Judge Redhead, Mick displayed the utmost honor and respect when addressing His Lordship. Nothing ever rattled Mick, though he rattled plenty of other people's cages.

He started his statement literally from the beginning. He detailed the course of the investigation from the moment he was sworn in as the Special Constable of the Royal Antigua Police Force, to the day he conducted the investigation's first interview with the Accused Melanson Harris after a search warrant was executed to search his home.

All seemed to be going smoothly until Mr. Bird stood up and made an objection and things began to get bumpy, to say the least.

"In regard to Melanson Harris's statement, I object on the grounds that his statement given was involuntary, and I also object to his statement being given as evidence."

Immediately following this unexpected objection, Judge Redhead interrupted the proceedings and sent the jury out.

Once the jury was secured in the jury room, Mr. Bird addressed the judge, bringing light to his obscure objection:

> This is an objection that these statements were induced as a result of representations made. Superintendent Airall and Detective Constable Jim Johnstone made the representations to the Accused Melanson Harris prior to the oral statements and during the course of the investigations. I am instructed that Superintendent Airall informed Harris that he would help him with Scotland Yard, if he showed them the gun. I was further instructed that Detective Constable Johnstone, on a number of occasions during the investigations and in particular along the course of certain searches, offered Accused Harris that if he assisted in the inquiry he would ensure that the Accused will face only a term of imprisonment. Also, Mr. Johnstone told the Accused that the production of the gun would lead to the prosecution taking a likewise position and go easy at the trial. Furthermore, the Accused was informed by Mr. Johnstone of reward monies offered.

What? Neither Jim nor Mick nor Dave would ever do that! They don't need to bribe a lowlife to get information; they are far too gifted in their profession to do anything like that. This is ridiculous! This guy is really starting to tick me off!

Before we knew it, Judge Redhead was warning the press not to print anything they had just heard.

Things inside the courtroom were about to drastically change.

Without the jury being recalled, Mick was brought back to the stand. Not even slightly ruffled by this preposterous accusation made against his colleague, Mick confidently stated, "I did not force, threaten, or use pressure during the interview of Melanson Harris. I did not trick or use any inducement to get the Accused to make his statement or to answer any other questions. No one in my presence did."

Superintendent Airall was brought back to the stand to be questioned again by Mr. Bird, and he was quick to refute the allegations made against himself and Jim:

Neither have I, Superintendent Lawrence, Detective Constable Johnstone, nor anyone used any force, trickery, threats, or inducements to Harris before or after his statement. It is totally false that I made any promises that I would help him with Scotland Yard if he led us to the shotgun. It is totally false that Mr. Johnstone said to the Accused that if he assisted him he would get the reward money. That was never said.

What Mr. Bird suggested next caused Superintendent Airall's blood to boil: "May I suggest to you, Mr. Airall, that you told Mr. Harris you needed him to tell you where the gun was to be able to help him, and it was important to you because Scotland Yard had all the say . . ."

Before Bird could even finish, the superintendent retorted, "That is not so and totally untrue." And then he leaned back and laughed, as if to say the suggestion that he was jealous of Scotland Yard or was trying to get an upper hand on them was ridiculous.

After Superintendent Airall was excused from the stand, the jury was recalled and reminded of their oath. It appeared that Judge Redhead wanted to have full knowledge of what Mr. Bird was up to before he allowed the jury to hear these allegations against Superintendent Airall and Jim.

It was then time for my other Scotland Yard hero, Detective Sergeant David Marshall, to take the stand. Like Mick, with total resolve, he defended Jim to the hilt. One of Dave's duties as Detective Sergeant, and also having been sworn in as Special Constable of the Royal Antigua Police Force, was to act as scribe during the investigation's interviews. His testimony as scribe throughout the three interviews taken from Melanson Harris was crucial in defending Jim. Our prosecutor, Mr. McKay, was leading this testimony from Dave, but really he needed no leading at all. Dave knew exactly what to say, and he said it with utmost assurance.

> The three interviews were recorded, and the Accused, Melanson Harris, initialed each answer. The Accused also signed his name on each page of the statement and then subscribed his name on the last page of each statement. No complaint was made to me by the Accused Harris concerning promise or promises made to him. When he signed his name, no force, threats, or inducements were used to get him to sign his name.

When Dave stepped away from the box, the time had come for Jim to contest the accusations that were made against him, and I was a bit nervous about his taking the stand. I had grown very close to The Boys; my adoration was no longer just because they solved my parents' murders, but because I had become connected to them during the process. I knew their personalities, their characters, passions, and convictions. Out of the three, Jim had become like a big brother to me. He relentlessly teased me and was always watching out for me. He sat beside me every day in court and had the ability to discern my inward emotions, which I purposely tried *not* to show outwardly.

He was more than ready to stand up and defend himself. For days I watched the aggravation of these allegations mount up inside him and feared many times he might explode at even the smallest of provocations. Mick and Dave assured me Jim was completely under control and knew exactly how to handle himself and the situation. They knew far better than I, and of course I totally trusted them all. However, one thing was for sure, over the last few days, I was not the only one fidgeting in my white plastic chair anymore!

Jim took the stand, and his testimony began as all the rest:

I am attached to the International Organized Crime Group and sworn in as the Special Constable of the Royal Antigua Police Force. I was part of the investigating team in the murders on the Computa-center *Challenger*. I did not use any force, threat, or hold out any promise to the Accused Harris.

The rest of Jim's time on the stand was spent specifically addressing each allegation that was made against him. He would say to every accusation, "That is not true" or "It is completely untrue." Though not amusing to Jim, it became almost comical to Donnie and me, and even to Mick and Dave. I started mimicking him under my breath, even tried to guess his next, "It is completely untrue" or "That is not true" statement. His tone as he spoke was serious and unemotional, but his facial expressions screamed, *"Absurdity!"*

We thought we had heard it all until Melanson Harris took the stand and gave his account of how he had been enticed to give his testimony and was bribed to produce evidence.

He gave his name and where he lived and then began his tall tale. As soon as he opened his mouth, I could not help but think that the way he talked matched perfectly the way he looked: dumb as a stick.

He said it was the early afternoon when Superintendent Cosmos Marcelle and Superintendent Airall from the Antigua police and three Scotland Yard detectives came to his house and told him they had a search warrant. They gave it to him, and he read it . . . *I can't believe he knows how to read . . .* then told them to go ahead and search. *As if they even needed his permission!* He said it was Superintendent Airall who told him they were investigating the murders of four people. They searched the bedrooms, then the living room, and then began to search the bedrooms again.

I knew what was coming next because Dave had already told us about this day and what they found in Melanson's house. He said they were almost certain by that time that Melanson was involved in the murders, so when the first search came up empty, they knew they needed to search one more time. Dave told us that after the second search they came to a point when literally the only thing in the entire house that had not been searched was a shirt hanging on a nail in one of the bedrooms. It was Superintendent Airall who instinctively reached into the pocket of Melanson Harris' shirt. I would have loved to see the smile on his face when he pulled out seventy Guernsey notes (the currency of Guernsey) and realized the significance of what he had found.

It was the damning evidence they needed, because Guernsey notes are exclusive to the Island of Guernsey and can be used nowhere else in the world. When Melanson was asked where he got the money, he said he got it from his aunt in England.

Liar! Bingo, you buffoon, you're busted!

That part of his testimony was easy listening; from then on everything he said was like listening to acid rock. His fabricated story went like this:

During the search, Detective Johnstone approached me a minute after everyone walked out the room and told me that there is a reward of $100,000 out for the capture and convictions of the people responsible for the murders. I don't know why he was telling me that.

Then the detective tell me, if I assist him in the investigation, he would reward me. When another officer walked in the room, Detective Johnstone walked away.

Though we had already heard this from Mr. Bird, Jim was getting stirred up all over again. Poor Jim, he did not deserve that, and it was about to get worse.

Melanson went on with his fable:

Next day I was carried on a search in the afternoon. When we were in the jeep, Mr. Johnstone said, "You know who is responsible for those murders; help me, and I will help you." So I took them to Malleta Quarter; I was trying to cooperate with him. I led them to Rock's house to get shotgun. No shotgun there. I misled them. Then I take them to River Road at North End to look for gun. No gun. Detective Johnstone say if I won't help them, they cannot help me. I said okay.

The truth of the matter is that Melanson was not "carried on a search." He was the one who took the detectives on a wild goose chase. Later those turned out to be his very own words, admitting on the stand that he took the detectives on wild goose chases and had them aimlessly digging around in sandpits searching for the murder weapon. He would lie, admit he'd lied, and then lie some more. The guy was one with no internal moral compass or character—that was for certain.

Melanson continued his wild tale:

We were driving back to the village when Mr. Johnstone spoke to me. While we were driving, he look back from the front seat and told me, if I remember what he said. We arrived at the airport, and that is when I show them the bag.

That bag was my dad's, and finding it was a monumental moment in the case. First, it further implicated Melanson in the murders. Second, and what made it monumental was that, until that point, the people of Barbuda were not friendly or supportive of the detectives in any way. They followed them around and ridiculed them, accusing them of failing to understand Barbudans. They repeatedly claimed, "Barbudans would never commit such a crime." The detectives were heckled as they made their searches, telling them to go look elsewhere. But when Melanson Harris led them to a sandpit where two sticks were protruding from the sand, oddly marking a particular spot, the residents of Barbuda began to have a change in attitude.

Cosmos Marcelle, Superintendent of the Antigua Police attached to the Criminal Investigative department, began to remove sand from the area around the sticks, and in doing so, he began to uncover something—something that was blue in color. At that stage Marcelle stopped digging any further, and Jim put on a pair of rubber gloves, reached down into the sand, and pulled out the bag bearing the name "Captain William Clever, Island of Jethou." The crowd of Barbudans let out a collective gasp. From that point on, the islanders were behind Scotland Yard 100 percent, and three of their own were about to be disowned.

Finding Dad's bag was a great way to end a long, frustrating, and exhausting day for The Boys. The next search they went on would prove to be fruitful as well.

Eruption in the Courtroom

The following day started off with some real excitement in the courtroom. Unfortunately, my hotheaded husband caused it when he caught his first glimpse of Marvin ("the rat" as Donnie called him) and Melanson strutting into court. Marvin was wearing sunglasses and smoking a cigarette, and he and Melanson were laughing. The sight of Marvin with the freedom to sport sunglasses and smoke made Donnie's blood boil, and when you add their laughing and joking around, you have a recipe for a Don Floyd eruption.

Before anyone knew what was happening, Donnie rushed them. Just when he was about to go over the wooden handrail that separated them from us, The Boys had him. As they drug Donnie off, he blurted out what was bottled up inside him. "Stop laughing! Nothing in this courtroom is funny, and my mom and dad aren't able to laugh ever again!"

They sat Donnie back in his seat, and before Mick let loose of his arm, he told Donnie, "If you ever pull something like that again, I'll take you right out of this bloody courtroom—you got it?"

Donnie may have shrugged off Mick's hold on his arm, but he heard him loud and clear; everyone in the courtroom did.

Court began with Melanson being sworn in and reminded of his oath, which I found to be a total waste of time, because an oath means nothing to a liar. He continued with his cock-and-bull story from the stand:

After I showed them the bag, I was sitting alone in the Jeep. Mr. Johnstone approached me and told me he will help me in the court if I continued to cooperate with them, and I will not get imprisonment. I said okay. About midday the next day, they came for me and took me into a room at police headquarters. They began to question me, and Detective Constable Johnstone winked his eye on me, and that is when I gave the statement. Nothing else was said to me that day by any of the officers, just the wink from Detective Johnstone.

At that very moment, I thought Jim was going to blow a gasket! All at once he choked, shifted his position in his white plastic chair, and took a long, loud, deep breath. I wanted to stand up right there and call that creep out and tell him he was a boldfaced, lowlife liar! The trial had suddenly taken a sharp turn for me. I was hardly thinking about what this good-for-nothing sucker had done to Dad and Mom; I was now enraged that he was messing with Jim!

I was barely able to sit still, and now once again I was the one fidgeting the most in my white plastic chair.

Melanson Harris continued his lying testimony:

I was carried on another search. I took them to look for the gun. They didn't find it where I led them. I carried them up and down for the gun. I wanted to know if they would be true to their word to me as I would be true to mine.

Are you kidding me? True to your word? You wouldn't know the truth if it slapped you in the face, you ignoramus!

Then, when I was in the Jeep alone, Mr. Johnstone approach me again. He put his hand on my shoulder and said to me, I am lying to him again. Then he told me if I keep lying they would not help me in the court. What Mr. Johnstone promise me is why I show them the sandpit where the gun was.

Alas the murder weapon was finally revealed; we've got you now, sucker. You're going down!

A SURPRISING REVELATION

The trial continued on and on, day after day with Jim and Superintendent Airall returning to the stand to refute once again the allegations made against them. Mr. Bird called Melanson back to the stand as well. All of us in the courtroom would have rather had a root canal that day than have to listen to him all over again. Bringing him back to the stand with his broken, unruly grammar and communication skills was absolutely pointless. He offered no new information, just a lot more of the same garbage about a wink and a promise, until just before he stepped off the stand.

Mr. Bird's questioning was as monotonous as Melanson's lies. After yet another question asking the same thing, Melanson gave an answer that had absolutely nothing to do with the question posed him: "The Americans, they must have been Christian. The lady was shouting please, please not to be shot. She was pleading and crossing herself."

A piercing arrow shot into my head and straight through to my heart. I gasped as my mind tried to grasp all he spewed out of his mouth, and my heart could not handle the emotion of it all. It was devastating to think about Mom pleading for their lives and the dreadful torment they endured at the hand of these monsters.

To hear him say, "They must have been Christian" was what kept me from breaking down completely. What were they doing that would make

Melanson say that? I knew Mom crossing herself was from growing up Catholic. I'm sure she was saying, praying, and doing all she knew to do, but what did Dad do to make him say that? Did he keep his promise to me, to call on the name of Jesus if he ever feared for his life? I was emotionally torn in half by both the pain of their torture and the indescribable peace of believing their actions told me something I had been longing to know.

Sitting there, my mind foggy from all that had just played out before me. Suddenly, clarity came to me, and I realized that this portion of Melanson's testimony was a precious gift to me from God. They had indeed called on the name of the one true God.

The Trial Within a Trial

The talk inside the court, as well as what was being reported in the newspapers, was how there was no way this trial could wrap up in its projected two weeks. No one saw the "wink and a promise" coming, and that in itself added an entire week to the trial. Another unforeseen matter (though predicted by Mick) was the trial within a trial that was about to get underway.

So much of what I was hearing in the courtroom confused me, and I tend to be disturbed when I don't understand something. The trial within a trial was something I could not manage to wrap my mind around. What I could not figure out was why Bird and Watt were all in a dither over allowing Donaldson's written statement from 1994 in as evidence when he was literally on the stand saying the very same thing. What was the difference? Fortunately, Mick was always there to answer my many questions.

"Bonnie, do you remember the first day in court when Watt said that he would be making an application for parts of Donaldson's statement to be edited?"

"Yes, I remember, and I was confused then too."

"What Watt wants to do is suggest that I *led* Donaldson in my questioning of him. That I got him to say and not say certain things by asking and not asking specific questions while taking his statement. Judge Redhead sees what Watt's trying to do and, therefore, he's addressing the matter outside of the jurors' presence; hence, it's a trial within a trial."

The trial within a trial took place, and Judge Redhead's ruling was this:

Upon cross-examination, Counsel may put to the witness only inconsistencies. What is an inconsistency? If the witness said something different in his testimony on the stand than what he said in his written statement, this difference amounts to an inconsistency.

Fortunately, Donaldson's testimony was very consistent with his written statement. It is difficult for a liar to remain consistent, especially over a time span of two years. Regardless of what happened to me on that courthouse balcony, I was still looking for any reason to doubt this guy. I did not want to trust him, but he was consistently giving me no reason not to do so.

chapter**Eighteen**

Courtroom Drama

$\mathcal{I}$ had high hopes that the thirteenth day of the trial would prove to be more than just sitting there listening to Melanson continue to lie. In all my days, I have never known or even heard of such a liar—a self-professed liar at that. Literally every time he took the stand, he would say, "I was lying. That statement was lie. That part is true, the rest is lie. I lied."

One day, while being cross-examined by Mr. McKay, all at once this just poured out of his mouth: "What I said is not true. I lied to the court. I am a self-confessed liar to the police. I told a deliberate lie to the judge. I lied on myself." I sat there in total disbelief. It frustrated me to no end to think that someone that stupid and senseless could actually overtake my intelligent father, not to mention Criddy and Tom. I know there was a gun involved, but even so, it irritated me half to death.

I wasn't the only one sick and tired of Melanson's lies, and on that day McKay had had enough. He began his cross-examination by asking the following questions:

Q. Do you know what a fairytale is?
A. Yes.

Q. Do you know what an Aesop's fable is?
A. Yes.

Q. Do you know how to read?
A. Yes.

Q. Have you read an Aesop fable?
A. No.

Q. Have you read comic books?

Not waiting for an answer, McKay asked Melanson, "Is Marvin Joseph your friend?"

"No. Not close friends."

Out of the blue, McKay fired back, "I didn't ask you that! I asked you, is he your friend?"

From there a great argument broke out, as McKay's days of suppressed frustration seemed to erupt all at once. It appeared to me that he had been putting up with the lying for days, but today he was not going to be played. If he asked a direct question, he wanted a direct answer—*period!*

It was indeed turning out to be a great morning in court, and McKay just kept getting better as his anger turned to humor later on in the day. His cross-exam became quite comical, and McKay appeared to be at his best and having a little fun with the habitual liar. On several occasions he would turn to the jury, smiling as he pointed out lie after lie. It was pure greatness!

However, when McKay was through with him, the feeling in the courtroom quickly turned very serious. It was John Fuller's turn to cross-examine Melanson.

John was one of the lead prosecuting attorneys on the case and a very prominent man on Antigua.

John commanded the room; his demeanor demanded it. He was about to make a point on the effort it took to murder four people with one gun. He walked over to the evidence table and picked up the shotgun. It had an antique look about it; its original steel-blue color was faded and chipped. John was pacing in front of the jury box with the gun in his hands. As he made his way across the front of the jury box, he made visual contact with all nine pairs of eyes following his every move. He explained to them in detail how each of the four victims was shot at pointblank range, from no more than six to eight inches away. He went on by describing the exertion it took to shoot and cock that twelve-gauge, pump-action shotgun.

He stopped his pacing and cocked the gun; every eye in the courtroom was locked on him as he pumped the gun and pulled the trigger four times.

CHU-CHUNK . . . click! "Tom Williams."

CHU-CHUNK . . . click! "Kathleen Clever."

CHU-CHUNK . . . click! "William Clever."

CHU-CHUNK . . . click! "Ian Cridland."

The loud, eerie sound echoed throughout the courtroom—it was unnerving.

A YOUNG WITNESS

The seriousness of the morning session turned to intensity in the afternoon session. It was time for Kevin DeSouza, the fourteen-year-old cousin of Marvin Joseph, to take the stand. Kevin had only just turned twelve at the time of the murders, and his testimony was crucial to the prosecution's case against Marvin. Donaldson had confessed and given his testimony against Marvin, and Melanson had confessed on the stand as well. All the lying Melanson had been doing was about who was on the boat that night and whether he had actually pulled the trigger. He even lied several times about whether he shot one person or three. But Marvin never admitted to a thing. It was out of pure guilt and torment that Donaldson confessed. It was out of pure stupidity that Melanson lied himself right into a confession, but it was pure evil that kept Marvin hiding in the dark and concealing any action on his part.

All they had on him was Donaldson's consistent testimony. Eventually, even Melanson testified that Marvin was an accomplice and that he had shot the people. But with all the lying he'd done prior to implicating Marvin, his testimony didn't carry enough weight for a conviction. The prosecution needed something big on Marvin, and little Kevin DeSouza was it.

Poor Kevin, my heart was breaking for him as I watched him take the stand. Fear was written all over his face, and quite honestly fear was all over all of our faces. Kevin's fear was of Marvin and the courtroom. Our concern was that Kevin would become paralyzed with fear and not testify to what Marvin had told him the Monday after the murders.

On that particular Monday, the team from Scotland Yard was running their full-force investigation on Barbuda following the discovery of the murders. Jim met a young boy named Kevin, who told him about a conversation he'd had with his cousin Marvin Joseph. That conversation then led to Dave paying a visit to the young man's home and taking him to the police station to attain a formal statement. The statement taken proved to be damning evidence against Marvin Joseph.

When the preliminary hearing took place on Antigua a few weeks later, Kevin was brought before the magistrate to give his statement. He took an oath to tell the truth and then froze and could not speak. When he finally managed to speak, he did not tell the magistrate what he had told Dave in his statement. The magistrate showed Kevin his written statement and asked him if that was his signature on the bottom of the page. He nodded his head yes and said that if he could see what was written in the statement it would help refresh his memory. The magistrate read from his statement and asked him if he heard what she had read.

His response was, "Yes, and it is not true."

"Are you saying the police made up all I just read to you?"

"Yes, Mon."

Needless to say, every eye in the courtroom was fixed on the young, frightened boy. We desperately needed him to tell the truth this time. We were counting on the fact that he was two years older and that Marvin had been in prison and could not get to him. Unfortunately, Marvin was in the courtroom, and I was praying with all I had for Kevin not to look over and make eye contact with him.

With a quiet and trembling voice, Kevin began his testimony: "I know Marvin Joseph and Melanson Harris. Marvin is my first cousin; my mother and his father are brother and sister. I remember seeing Marvin on a Monday in the beginning of February 1994. I used to go visit him. We were at his house; it was just the two of us there."

That was all he got out, and then he froze.

No Kevin, no! Speak . . . get it out! It's okay; he can't hurt you.

He wasn't budging. The only thing that seemed to get him to speak was to ask him questions, but the questions could not be leading.

Q. How old are you Kevin?
A. I am fourteen years old.

Q. Do you have brothers and sisters?
A. Yes, I have seven sisters and three brothers, and we all live with my mother and father in one house.

Q. Do you go to school?
A. Yes.

Q. Did you go to school the Monday you went to Marvin's house?
A. Yes, I didn't have any homework that day. I went to Marvin's right away; he doesn't live far from me.

Q. Did you know about the yacht in Low Bay?
A. Everybody was talking about it, and I speak about it with my family. The police and Scotland Yard were there looking for those persons who committed those murders.

Q. Did you know anything about the murders, Kevin? (Silence.) Kevin, when you went to Marvin's house on the Monday, did you talk about the murders? (Silence.) Kevin, do you have friends?

A. I don't have a lot of friends in Barbuda. I don't have any buddies. Marsh sits beside me in school; we don't talk after school or at break. Benny sit on right of me; we don't talk. I don't talk to the one in front of me or the one behind me. Miss Daisy was my teacher, and Miss Henry was my head teacher. I go to church too; they don't baptize, and Mr. James is my preacher.

Q. Kevin, do you know what murder is?

A. I know murder is a crime, a very bad crime; I knew that when I was twelve.

Q. Kevin, did you talk to the police about the murders on the yacht?

A. I can't remember the name of the police officer I spoke to first. It was an English police. I don't recall how long we talk. This was after Marvin spoke to me in February. I don't see the second Scotland officer I talk to in court today.

Q. Can you tell the court what Marvin told you on the Monday after the murders?

He didn't answer. Once again he completely shut down.

No, Kevin, keep talking! Every time we get so close to the truth you clam up. Oh God, please help us here. Donnie and I need to pray now!

Just as I was about to take Donnie's hand to pray with him, Jim nudged me. I turned toward him, and he had this urgent "Well, aren't you going to do something?" look on his face.

"What?" I whispered.

"You know, Bonnie Floyd!" he hoarsely whispered back.

"I know what?"

"That thing you do (making that all too familiar praying gesture with his hands). Now would be a good time for that, don't you think?"

"Oh, good grief, Jim, just say the word! And just so you know, I was just about to *pray*, until you interrupted me."

I turned to Donnie, who already had his head down. I took his hand and joined him praying, begging God to perform a miracle. I prayed peace over Kevin, against the spirit of fear, and for him to have the strength to do the right thing. No sooner than we said amen, did it feel as if a wave of peace washed over the courtroom. Kevin lifted his head and very quietly spoke.

I spoke to the English inspector . . . that was the first person I was speaking to about the murder. I walked around with that knowledge from the time Marvin spoke it to me. I spoke to no one at all before that. I understand I have to tell the truth; if you don't, you go to hell. When I talk to the magistrate two years ago, I didn't tell that Marvin told me he killed people on the *Challenger*.

Oh, wow! He said it! Keep going, Kevin; you can do this. Jesus is right by your side. Oh, God, please . . .

"Kevin, why didn't you tell the magistrate about what Marvin told you?"

"I was frightened. When I'm frightened, I don't remember things well. I have a good memory when I'm not frightened."

"What are you frightened of Kevin?"

For the first time, Kevin raised his head, and looking straight at his cousin, he said, "I'm frightened of Marvin."

"Are you able to tell the court what Marvin told you?"

"Something happened that day. I can't remember what time it was. I saw a gun, and it was black. It was in Marvin's waist when I saw it. I asked where he got it from. Marvin tell me he got it off the yacht down by Low Bay. I cannot remember anything else he tell me . . ."

No, no, Kevin, keep going, don't stop. Tell them he shot the people, just as you told Jim and Dave. Tell them! Oh, God, please don't let this worthless scum get off. Empower Kevin, Lord; give him Your strength, please!

There wasn't a sound in that courtroom—no one fidgeting in the white plastic chairs; everyone was frozen still. Even the hustle and bustle you normally heard from out on the streets through the open-air pigeonhole walls was drowned out by the intensity of that moment.

McKay moved toward the evidence table and picked up the gun. He showed it to Kevin and asked, "Is this the gun you saw, Kevin?"

Looking at the gun and then down at the ground, Kevin said in an almost inaudible voice, "Marvin told me he killed three and somebody else kill one . . ."

Yes! Glory to God, he said it! Thank You, Lord. You are just and faithful in all Your ways. I know the eternal fate of every man lives in the hands of the Living God, but Lord, thank You for showing me justice today here on earth!

I wanted to run over to Kevin when he stepped down from the stand, but Jim saw it coming and stopped me flat.

"Let me go, Jim!"

"No, Bonnie Floyd. It's not appropriate; you must stay in your seat."

All I wanted to do was hug him, comfort him, and thank him for what he did. I knew he was scared, and I wanted to assure him he had done the right thing and tell him the Lord would protect him. But as much as I fidgeted in my white plastic chair, Jim was not letting me move. I could only sit and watch as that brave young man was escorted out of the courtroom and out of sight.

Donnie's Revelation

The topic of conversation at dinner that night was all about Jim having to put the reins on me to keep me from lunging on poor little Kevin. The harassing was relentless as I listened to their hysterical versions of how my attacking the young lad would have gone down. At one point Mick asked Donnie what it was like to be married to someone so impulsive and headstrong, at which I bristled. There was no defending myself with this lot, and Donnie only encouraged them by laughing at their every wisecrack.

Why Donnie thought sharing my balcony epiphany at dinner that night would be the right timing baffles me to this day, but that is just what he did, and it went over like a lead balloon.

"Absolutely not!" they all bolstered in unison. "There is no way she would ever be let into the prison to see that worthless piece of rubbish, and even if there were, we would prevent it."

Unlike the prisons in the United States, prisoners at Her Majesty's High Prison are shackled and chained and subject to hard labor. They have few rights and even fewer visitors. The prison on Antigua was built in 1735 and had not been improved much. The inmates were limited to only what is allowed by the superintendent, and from what we gathered, that was not much.

"Besides, Bonnie Floyd, you're not fooling me; I know why you want to get in there, and I'm telling you, he's not going to tell you where their missing stuff is," Jim added with a cocky tone, as if he were proving some great point.

"Stuff? What are you talking about, Jim? Donnie just told you why I wanted to get in to see Donaldson. I want to tell him about Jesus. And furthermore, I don't give a rip about their stuff; if I could have anything back, it would be *them*, Jim, not their stuff!" I responded with an even cockier tone.

With that, The Boys knew they'd hit a nerve, but I had clearly hit one with them too. Mick decided it was time to end this discussion and put a halt on my foolish notion of getting into the prison.

"Donnie, she'll never get in, and we have the power to stop her if she does. Her idea is ludicrous. That guy is a cold-blooded murderer, and her going to see him is a bad idea. There is no way a visit like that could end with a good result."

Donnie sat there for a while. I watched as he processed all that Mick just said to him, what I had said, and what God was saying. I knew more than anything that Donnie wanted to squelch that crazy idea of mine and agree with Mick, but I also knew Donnie trusted God in me and believed I had heard from Him. When he finally spoke up, I stopped breathing. Here's what he said:

> Here's the deal guys, I agree with you 100 percent and wish so badly that I could put the brakes on what my wife wants to do, but I can't. When she believes she's heard from the Lord, nine times out of ten she has, and I believe she has heard from Him this time. This trial is going much longer than any of us thought, and I have to leave on Sunday afternoon to get back to Floyd Construction. I know my wife, and regardless of what you think you can do to stop her, when God makes a way for her—and He's going to, trust me on that—I need at least one of you to promise me she won't go into that prison alone.

Without much hesitation at all, Jim, knowing full well that I'd never get access into the prison, piped up and said, "I promise, Donnie!"

"Great, Jim, thank you so much. I hate having to leave, but I have no choice. I just have too many houses under construction to be gone any longer than two weeks. Go a step further for me, would you, Jim? Just don't let her out of your sight until you've secured her in her room each night?"

Oh, good grief, I'm not a child!

"Yes, Donnie, I'll keep a close watch on her for you."

"Seriously, Jim, as if you haven't been already? You watch me like a hawk; I can't make a move without your questioning me."

"Well, somebody has to keep you in line, and clearly you have *your* Donnie whipped," he said with a wink.

"Whipped? Hardly! Man who hears from God? Yes! And I do believe if we're keeping score, Jim Johnstone, I just won. Bonnie Floyd, one; Jim Johnstone, the big *zero*!" I declared with a huge grin.

BACK TO COURT

The next day in court continued to not go well for Marvin, and I was thrilled to no end about it. I hated him. Okay, I know we are not supposed to hate, but I hated him. Every day before the court was seated, Marvin would strut in with an evil smirk on his face, smoking a cigarette. It still infuriated Donnie that he was allowed to smoke. Donnie had mentioned on several occasions how he wanted to crush that cigarette out on Marvin's face. His comments like that didn't concern me anymore, since The Boys told Donnie that the Antiguan police said if he had another outbreak in the courtroom, he would be escorted directly out of the country. I think The Boys still had their concerns about Donnie, because he was never out of arm's reach when court was in session.

The first person called to the witness stand that morning was a Barbudan named John Cephas. He testified that he saw Marvin coming out of the police station after all the commotion had happened. Marvin approached him and said he heard that John was going to Canada and that he wanted to go with him. John told Marvin he would have to talk with his brother (who was already in Canada) about it and let him know. A few days later, John needed to change his EC for US currency in preparation for his trip to Canada and heard Marvin had US dollars to sell. John said Marvin never told him where he got the US money, but he reminded John to talk with his brother about his going to Canada.

Marvin's little escape plan to leave the country was thwarted by his arrest just a few days later, and John's testimony had just put a few more nails in the sucker's coffin.

When a fifteen-minute recess was announced, I stepped out to the restroom. On the same floor of the courtroom was a long and very narrow hallway with only one door at the very end. The restroom was located behind that door. As My Donnie would say, that bathroom was a "one-holer." People normally waited their turn at the entrance, instead of forming a line in the narrow hallway that was barely wide enough for two people to pass each other.

When I opened the door and came out, there, lurking less than a foot away from me, was Marvin, standing alone and cornering me. His ratlike, beady eyes pierced right though me as he smirked. He was evil to the core. Without so much of a split-second thought, I screamed at the top of my lungs. The two idiot guards, who let him follow me, came running down the hall and grabbed him. They put him flat against the wall and turned to me, trying with all their might to get me to stop screaming. It wasn't long before Jim and Dave were standing at my side like human shields, letting the two guards know in no uncertain terms that they had just messed up *big time!*

It was another hour before I actually stopped shaking. My fear turned to anger in no time. How dare he torment me like that! I knew then, more than ever, that if Marvin Joseph were let off, he would murder again. There was not a remorseful bone in his body. He was pure evil, and he needed to hang.

GRACE BAPTIST CHURCH

When court adjourned that day, I couldn't help but think about how this was the last day I'd be in court with Donnie at my side. It was Friday, and he would be leaving on the Sunday evening flight. Our clients had been very understanding, but no matter how well things were running, they wanted the contractor present on their jobsites.

As we were leaving the courthouse, one of the police officers I'd seen regularly in the courtroom came up to us. "Excuse me, may I ask, are you Christian?"

Donnie and I quickly glanced at each other, knowing we were thinking the same exact thing . . . *Well, that's an odd question!*

"Um, yes, as a matter of fact, we are Christians," Donnie answered.

With discerning eyes, he looked at us both and said, "Ah, I thought so. My name is Superintendent Ephraim Gomes, and you are Mr. and Mrs. Clever Floyd, are you not?"

"Yes, yes, we are."

"Well then, may I invite you to join me this Sunday at my church, so that we might worship God together?"

Did he just say what I think he said? Oh my, how incredibly sweet and kind! Go to church? Worship God? Okay!

And before either of us consulted one another, we answered in unison, "Yes, that would be wonderful, thank you."

But then Donnie started thinking about the logistics and asked, "Where is your church located?"

Answering Donnie's question with a question, Superintendent Gomes asked, "I believe you are staying at the Halcyon, are you not?"

"Yes, we are."

"Then I will come there and pick you up and take you to my Baptist Church. Can you be ready at nine o'clock?

"Nine o'clock will be fine; see you then."

As we walked away in awe of what had just happened, I looked over at Jim to see him rolling his eyes.

"Do you just go around telling everyone you're a Christian, Bonnie Floyd?"

"No Jim, I don't need to. Can't you see the 'I'm a Christian, please invite me to your church this Sunday' written across my forehead?" I sarcastically responded as I rolled my eyes right back at him.

Sunday at nine o'clock sharp, Superintendent Gomes drove up to the Halcyon Cove Hotel lobby to pick us up for church.

Jim had asked me the night before at dinner where the church was, and when we told him we weren't sure, I asked him if he'd like to go with us as our bodyguard. He unequivocally said, "No!"

What we thought would be a leisurely Sunday drive to church was more like a cross-country adventure. Grace Baptist Church of Antigua was located on the opposite side of the island, and the already pothole-laden roads lined with farm animals and stray dogs became even worse the farther out you went. Not to mention that Superintendent Gomes's car needed new shocks, new tires, and new upholstery about 100,000 miles ago. We eventually made it to the church and quickly decided that it was well worth every bump, jump, pivot, and divot it took to get there.

Literally every member of the church was lined up waiting to greet us as we walked through the doors of the church, and there was no shaking of the hands—those people were huggers. After we had made it through to the end of the line and were about to be seated, a very large woman, whose heart was bigger than she was, came to greet Donnie. He politely reached out his hand to her, and she said in a loud, bolstering voice, "Honey, Mama don't wanna shake your hand; she wanna squeeze you tight!" And she wrapped her arms around Donnie and did just that. I didn't escape Big Mama's affection either, because I was next in line to receive her enveloping hug. Quite honestly, I didn't want to escape it. She was the most loving woman I'd met on the island, but it was what she said in my ear when she hugged me that was so endearing.

"Honey, I'm so sorry this happened to your mama and daddy on our watch. Please forgive us, honey, please."

Please forgive "us"? Did she just say that? How incredible that she would take responsibility for what happened to Dad and Mom as a whole rather than remove herself and place blame.

The sermon was out of the book of Colossians, which, of course, was perfect and just what we needed to hear. The pastor taught us, "Burdens shared are easily carried." And that's exactly what Big Mama said. She was carrying the burden of losing Dad and Mom with me, and she was carrying the burden of responsibility for the sin those three murderers had committed. I didn't realize it at first, but I felt so much peace, as if my burden had been lifted the moment Mama hugged me and spoke to me those precious words.

It was a great morning at Grace Baptist Church, and it certainly helped to keep my mind off the fact that Donnie was leaving later that day.

A Key to the Prison Door

I was given the privilege of sitting in the front seat on the way back to the Halcyon and thought for sure the ride had to be a little easier on my tushie than the backseat had been. I was wrong. No wonder Donnie had offered it up so quickly!

Not too far into the drive, Donnie said to me, "Hey, babe, why don't you tell Superintendent Gomes what God spoke to you out on the balcony?"

"Oh yas, please du!" Superintendent Gomes said excitedly in his very strong Caribbean accent.

"Okay . . . well . . . I believe I am supposed to go into the prison and meet with Donaldson Samuel and tell him about Jesus."

There was a very long and awkward silence while I watched Superintendent Gomes process what I had just said. When he finally spoke he said, "Oh yas, dat is nice to du, but you will nevah get in."

"But Superintendent Gomes, don't you believe if it's God's will for me to get in to see Donaldson and tell him about Jesus that God will make a way when there seems to be no way?" I asked in my best singsong voice.

"Oh yas, yas, yas, awbsolutley. God con du anyting!" he declared as he threw his hands in the air.

Whoa, whoa there, Superintendent. I'm excited over your enthusiasm, but would you please put your hands back on the wheel before we hit the next pothole or goat!

"But . . . you will nevah, nevah get in!" he said as he placed his hands back on the steering wheel.

Silence filled the car again, and I was very discouraged. If Superintendent Gomes didn't even think I could get into that prison, maybe I wouldn't.

Then all of sudden, he looked over at me and said, "But . . . if . . . you . . . du, it will be by way of Superintendent Abel Mac, M–a–c."

With my spirits lifted once again, I said, "Okay! Superintendent Mac, great! How do I meet him?"

"You don't!"

chapterNineteen

You'd Better Have Kept Your Promise!

*J*aying good-bye to My Donnie was so hard, but it was clearly harder for him than for me. If I were the one having to leave, I think I would have chained myself to the Carib Bar in protest.

Donnie did not leave until he had accomplished two things. First, he made arrangements to move my room closer to The Boys, which actually wound up being not only closer but sandwiched between them. The second thing was to remind Jim of his promise not to allow me to go the prison alone and not to let me out of his sight. Reluctantly, Jim renewed his vow.

After dining with The Boys for dinner, I retired to my new room and started scheming—I mean planning—all the ways I could get myself into that prison. Throughout the next week, I tried talking to The Boys about it several times. I was actually under the delusion that I could possibly make at least one of them change his mind. Not a chance; they would hardly even discuss it with me, and Jim always said the same thing every time I broached the subject: "I am telling you, Bonnie Floyd, they're not going to tell you where the stuff is."

Every day I walked around the courthouse introducing myself to people with the motive of trying to find someone or some way to get me into that prison. No matter where I wandered off to, Jim's watchful eye was on me. I even tried approaching John Fuller, one of the lead prosecuting attorneys on the case and also one of the most influential men on Antigua. His father, Nick Fuller Sr., went to Antigua in 1941 as US vice consul and decided to stay on the island and raise his family there. He sent his son John to the United Kingdom to study law. After passing the bar, John returned to Antigua and had since become the most prominent attorney on the island. So, if anyone had the power to get me in, it was John Fuller. What I did not know was that he could have easily been The Boys' fourth musketeer. Approaching John was a bad idea!

One day, while sitting in court, I saw Donaldson's attorney, Mr. Francis, outside the courtroom. I leaned over to Jim and nonchalantly said, "I have to go to the restroom." And I quietly got up and walked out into the hall. I approached Mr. Francis and got right to the point, "Would it be possible, sir, for me to at any time meet with Donaldson Samuel?"

"Why?" he questioned with a frown. "Who are you?"

I was quite surprised to find out he had no idea who I was. I mean I'm a white female with blonde hair and blue eyes, who has been sitting in the front row of the courtroom every single day. Who on earth did he think I was? After the awkward introduction was over, I said, "Sir, I would like just to speak with him for a while and thank him for testifying."

Without even seeming to consider my request, he said, "I don't think that would be possible." And he excused himself and walked away.

I stood there dumbfounded and disappointed. This was not going to be easy.

As soon as I returned to my seat in the courtroom, Jim harshly whispered in my ear, "Do you think I don't know what you just tried to do?"

Equally as harsh with a whole lot of sass in my tone, I replied, "Well, it doesn't matter anyway, Jim, because it didn't work. But I'm *not* going to stop trying!"

It's the little things in life that can often bring so much joy, and that afternoon a little incident occurred in the courtroom that brought some to me. During a long, hot, and tiring afternoon session, there was a loud snap sound that came from what seemed like Jim's chair. It startled me, and I think it woke Jim up from a little disguised nap.

"What was that?" I asked.

"I don't know. Where did it come from?"

"I think it came from your chair," I said snickering.

Clearly not believing me, he resumed listening to the witnesses on the stand and ignored my warning.

Another *snap!* And it was all over! Jim's white plastic chair crumbled beneath him, and he went crashing to the floor. I tried so hard not to laugh, but when I looked over at Mick and Dave, there was no holding back. I laughed so hard I couldn't breathe. Even Judge Redhead was laughing, along with a whole host of others. Keeping his game face on, Jim scrambled to his feet, picked up the pieces of his broken chair, grabbed a new chair, and was sitting down next to me in record time.

Dinner that night was delightful because, for once, I was not the center of harassment.

Welcome Friends

Tom Williams's parents, John and Beverly, came to Antigua to represent their son in court. Meeting them was one of the most precious times for me during the trial. When I heard they were flying in, I could not wait to meet them. In an inexpressible way, I needed them. It is difficult to describe all the emotions I was going through. To feel so close to these people, who had only been brought into my life through tragedy, was indescribable. The only commonality we shared was the pain ripping through our hearts.

The morning of the Williams's arrival, I was reminded of something Mom Floyd told me the day after I received the call that Dad and Mom had been killed. I remembered our conversation vividly. We were standing in the entry of my house with the morning sun shining brightly down on us through the transom window. She said, "Honey, I know you think that you have experienced the greatest loss someone could ever go through, and losing both your parents at the same time *is* a devastating loss. But Bonnie, there is a still a greater loss than yours, and that is when a parent loses a child."

I remember thinking, *This certainly isn't making me feel any better, Mom. Why on earth are you telling me this right now?*

But God's timing is always perfect, and though I found Mom's timing poor and her words pointless at that moment, I had never forgotten what she spoke to me that day. There I stood two years later, thankful that what she taught me enabled me to grasp the depth of pain that John and Beverly Williams were going through.

From the moment we were introduced, we looked into each other's eyes and saw the all-too-familiar pain. We hugged. No words were necessary.

As I watched them in court, my heart was torn to pieces as they listened to how their handsome son, only twenty-two years old with his whole life ahead of him, was the first of the four to be brutally murdered.

A Buoy Marked the Spot

One evening after dinner, I sat for hours with Beverly in the Ciboney Lounge at the Halcyon, sharing stories about Tom, Dad, and Mom and how hard it was trying to live without them. Beverly mentioned to me that John wanted to fly over to Barbuda before they had to leave to go home and asked me if I wanted to join them. Apparently there was a buoy anchored out in Low Bay marking the spot where *Challenger* had been moored that fateful night. I had thought about going over there, but after Donnie left, I did not think I could get my favorite detective/bodyguard to take me, and I knew better than to even think about going alone.

Two days later I found myself sitting on the tarmac at V. C. Bird International Airport in an old rickety twin-prop airplane, getting ready to take off for Barbuda with the Williamses. I guess Jim thought it would be safe, and I'm sure he was thrilled to hand over the reins on me to John for the day.

The flight over to Barbuda was . . . well . . . umm, let's just say I was glad it was only a fifteen-minute flight. It was rough!

John Fuller took care of all the arrangements for us. I knew John was one of the most prominent men on Antigua, but what I did not know was that his influence had spilled over to Barbuda as well. We were met at the airport and driven across the island to the lagoon where a man and his young daughter were waiting to take us to Low Bay. That sweet little girl was a needed distraction on the short trip across the lagoon as tensions mounted in the apprehension of actually seeing the spot that marked the place where Criddy, Tom, Dad, and Mom had breathed their last.

A peninsula about one hundred fifty yards wide separates the lagoon from Low Bay. I honestly do not know if the little cutie and her daddy left and came back for us or just stayed on the lagoon side of the peninsula and waited, because once my feet hit the sand, my mind was consumed with thoughts of life, death, beauty, and ashes.

Together the three of us crossed over to Low Bay. Breathtaking and beautiful sand beaches line both sides of the peninsula, but crossing over from the lagoon to Low Bay was a bit tricky. We had to walk through knee-high bushes with thorns the size of horns. There were mangrove trees over-head that provided plenty of driftwood stuck in the sand to trip us up along the way. When we finally made it through and looked up, it was a sight to behold. No wonder Barbuda is called "the pink jewel of the Caribbean." It was also very clear to me why Dad and Mom had chosen this island paradise to sail to for their vacation.

The coral reefs that surround the island have created a champagne color of sand that glows rose because of the crushed coral mixed in the sand. If I looked one way, the sand was silky white, and when I turned my head, it changed to a hue of pink. The remoteness was luxurious; there was no human-generated noise, only the sound of the ocean breeze and the waves breaking on the shore. The sea was the most beautiful clear turquoise color I had ever seen. I stood there in awestruck wonder of it all.

At that moment, I was the only soul on that beach, lost in my thoughts. I had forgotten I was with John and Beverly, and when I looked around for them, I saw that they, too, were lost in their own individual thoughts. Beverly was sitting in the sand close to the surf as it gently rolled in and out. She was positioned directly in line with the buoy marking *Challenger's* mooring. The buoy was much farther out than I expected it to be. There were no boats in the bay, and we were the only three people on the entire beach.

I was quite a ways down from Beverly, but I could not find John anywhere on the beach in either direction. I stood with my face to the sea and breathed in deeply, looking out to the buoy and imagining *Challenger* moored there. I saw the sails down, the dinghy tied off at the stern with three men relaxing up on deck. I could see my mom coming up from the galley with a bottle of champagne and four glasses and . . .

My wonderful imagining was interrupted when I caught a glimpse of something far out in the water. When I focused in, I realized it was John. He was swimming out to the buoy! And I thought, *Oh, John, the buoy is too far out there. You're too upset to swim that far; you'll never make it there and back!*

In urgency, I looked over at Beverly and found her mesmerized, watching John. I instantly knew in my heart that he was swimming for her too.

The Promise and a Handful of Wonder

At that moment I thought, *I want to go out there too*, and before I knew it, I found myself just walking out into the water, not even in the direction of the buoy. The farther I walked out into the ocean, the deeper my sorrow grew. The pain of losing my parents came rushing back as strong as the day I lost them, maybe even stronger. My head hurt, my heart ached, and my body began to tremble. I just kept walking farther and deeper out to sea.

The pain in my heart hurt so badly, I wanted to die. The water was up to my chest when I suddenly remembered the night I asked Dad to promise me that he would call upon the name of Jesus, if he ever feared for his life. I remembered his words; I remembered his promise.

I began to panic, worried that, if he had not kept his promise, I would never see him again, and worse yet, if he was not in heaven with Jesus, he was in . . . I began to shake violently; the water was up to my neck by now. I could not bear the thought of my dad spending eternity in hell. It was more than I could endure; I'd rather die.

I tasted saltwater pouring into my mouth, and I considered for a moment just continuing to walk, allowing the sea to consume me, but something welled up inside, and I began to weep uncontrollably. My weeping turned into wailing, and I began to shake my fist in the air, crying out to Dad, asking him if he'd kept his promise to me. My sorrow turned to anger, and with my fist still in the air, I yelled at Dad, no longer asking but telling him that he had better have kept his promise! With seawater choking me, I realized I was no longer yelling at Dad, but at God, because Dad's promise meant absolutely nothing if God does not keep His promise through Jesus to save all mankind.

I began to back up to get a foot on the sand below me, because the amount of water filling my mouth was keeping me from being able to shout at God. "If You don't keep Your promises, then what kind of God are You?" I cried out uncontrollably.

"You have to keep Your promise, God. You have to! You said Your promises are true. If I can't trust You, then my life means nothing to me, and I'd rather die right here."

At that hopeless thought, I gave up and began to sink down into the sea. Living without knowing for certain was no option for me. If God is not bound to His promises, then calling on Jesus meant nothing. But if God's promises are "yes" in Christ, then I was about to go to heaven and be with Him and Dad, and that was just fine with me.

Suddenly a tangible peace as real as the waves that were hitting my face washed over me, and I began to back up. I looked up into the purest blue sky I had ever seen and inherently and instinctively knew for certain that my God is faithful in all He does and trustworthy in all He promises. As I made my way back to the beach, a feeling of thankfulness swept over me. I was thankful for the absolute certainty that my dad had kept his promise, but even more significant, thankful for the assurance that my God had kept His.

When John reached the shore and came up out of the water, he and Beverly took hands and began to walk down the beach. I turned and decided to take a walk in the other direction. I discovered that though the sand might have looked silky, it wasn't silky soft at all. It was actually hurting my normally tough feet. I knelt down and scooped up a handful of sand only to find it contained millions of tiny pink clamshells mixed in with miniscule pieces of coral and pulverized skeletal remains of many other invertebrates. It was a handful of wonder, and I was not leaving the island without taking some with me, but I had brought absolutely nothing to put it in.

That beach had probably never even seen a piece of garbage. Who in their right mind would leave a piece of trash laying around in Paradise? That would be as bad as littering in heaven. I was determined though to find something to take some of that wonder home with me, so I could remember this day forever! I found myself back in the mangroves and thorn bushes, digging around for something, anything in which to put some sand.

Come on! There has to be some local who has littered at least once!

Just then I saw ahead of me something partially buried in the sand. It was reflecting the sun, so I knew it was not driftwood. As I approached, I saw it was a glass bottle upside down in the sand. When I pulled it out, it was an old Absolute Vodka bottle that still had the cap. Bingo, I had scored!

The trip back to Antigua was a quiet one, as all three of us had much on which to reflect. Waiting for us to return, in their usual spot at the Carib

Bar, were my three favorite detectives. This was the first day in almost three weeks I had not spent with them. I had actually missed them a lot!

DINNER IN A TREE HOUSE

One afternoon John Fuller asked The Boys and me if we would like to join him and his wife, Sarah, for dinner that night at their house. All of us, without any hesitation, accepted his generous offer. On the way back to the Halcyon that afternoon, Jim said to me with a smile, "You know, Bonnie Floyd, John lives in a tree house."

"Yeah right, I'm sure he does," I replied sarcastically.

"He does! Ask Mick and Dave, if you don't believe me."

Without even having to ask the question, they both piped up and said, "It's true, Bonnie; John really lives in a tree house."

"Ha! You expect me to believe you two? You say I'm gullible all the time; well, this time I'm not falling for it!"

No matter how hard I tried, I could not win with them. I only managed to further position myself as the center of attention and the brunt of all of their jokes.

To my dismay, John and Sarah Fuller lived in a tree house.

The moment we pulled up to the Fullers, the harassment began by their announcing to John and Sarah that I refused to believe they lived in a tree house.

Their house was uniquely wonderful; I'd simply never seen anything like it, except for Walt Disney's *Swiss Family Robinson* tree house. Trees grew up through and into the house, beautifully bringing the outside in. The dining room and living room are outside on a massive wraparound porch with no walls and always exposed to the elements. The rest of the main living area, the kitchen and a few bedrooms, are actually suspended above round like limbs on the tree. And Sarah was just as pretty as Dorothy McGuire, who played Mother Robinson in that movie. She was kindhearted and I enjoyed getting to spend the evening with such a lovely lady. Being with John was just like spending another evening with The Boys. He was a teaser as well, especially when it came to my being a Christian. Mick and Jim often gave me a hard time about it, but John was different; he knew the Bible and was always throwing scriptures at me.

The Christian teasing never bothered me; I knew my Bible very well and could hold my own when it came to their nonbelieving questions. I always just tried to use it as an opportunity; only God knew if I was really getting through.

When our fun evening in the tree house was over, John came over to me and said, "I have a little something for you, Bonnie." And he handed me a very old-looking piece of broken pottery.

"Why, thank you, John!" was the only thing I could think to say.

"You have no idea what that is, do you, Bonnie?"

"Well, uh, no I don't, John. But if it's from you, I'll treasure it always," I genuinely replied.

"That old piece of pottery dates back to the days of Christ, and I thought it might mean a little something to you," John abruptly said, trying not to make giving it to me a big deal or, God forbid, act as if that piece of pottery meant anything to him.

I reached out my arms and gave John a great big "Bonnie hug" and thanked him profusely.

"I love it, John, and I *will* treasure it always!"

chapter Twenty

God Will Make a Way

$\mathcal{W}$hen Marvin Joseph took the stand, I wondered if his testimony would be yet another series of lying and denying, or would something unexpected arise while he was in the witness box. The latter was not the case.

We were now four weeks into the trial, so sitting through that rat's lies made for another agonizing week. After one particularly long and exhausting day in court, I experienced a bright moment. When I walked into my room at the Halcyon, sitting on the corner of my neatly made bed was a white square envelope. Beautifully inscribed in calligraphy on the unidentifiable envelope was this:

Mrs. Bonnie Clever-Floyd
Rex Halcyon Cove Hotel
Dickenson Bay

In my excited curiosity I threw my purse on the floor, jumped up on the bed, and carefully opened the mystery envelope to find inside a very official looking invitation.

The Commanding Officer and Officers
H.M.S. Brave
Request the pleasure of the company of:
Mrs. Bonnie Clever-Floyd
For: V.I.P. Reception & Cocktails
On: Monday 26 February 6:30-8:00 p.m.
At: Deepwater Harbour, St. John's, Antigua
R.S.V.P
British High Commission

I about fell off the bed backward! I had actually received an invitation to a VIP Reception aboard the British battleship that I had just watched come into St. John's, Deepwater Harbour earlier that day.

What on earth will I wear? I didn't bring one thing with a sequin on it! *Oh, my goodness, this is so exciting! I wonder if Mick, Jim, and Dave received invitations.*

I scrambled off the bed and over to Dave's room to pound on his door. When he didn't answer, I knew exactly where to find him. I ran down the path, across the grass, and past the pool to our favorite beachfront hangout, waving the invitation in my hand.

"Guess what, guys, I got invited to a VIP reception aboard that battleship we saw come into the harbor today! Can you believe it? I get to go onboard a real British battleship. How stinkin' cool is that? Did you guys get invited too?"

I was not sure by their reaction if they were taken aback by my excitement or miffed about something. Surely it wasn't my excitement, since Jim mentioned quite often that I was "easily excitable."

"What's the matter, guys?" I questioned.

"Bonnie Floyd, do you honestly think we didn't get an invitation? We bloody well better have gotten an invitation, and the only reason you received one is because you are going with us! And the only reason you're going with us is because of that bloody promise I made "Your Donnie" that I wouldn't go anywhere without you," Jim curtly answered.

Well, miffed it was! Not really, though. Jim just liked giving me a bad time about my always having to tag along. I loved tagging with The Boys; everywhere we went was an exciting adventure and great fun. Our evening on the HMS *Brave* was no different.

I chose my best sundress, which certainly would not have been my first choice, if I'd had a choice, but it was all I had. So, to make up for not having the "perfect" dress, I decided to make big hair, which wasn't hard to do with my naturally curly hair in the tropic humidity. After living in Antigua for almost five weeks, the Caribbean sun had kissed my already blonde hair, which made for a nice contrast against my bronzed skin.

I did my best with what I had to work with, and when I met my escorts in the lobby, they were looking pretty sharp as well. On our drive over to St. John's, I took the opportunity to remind Jim of his promised responsibilities.

"Now, Jim, when we get there, it's going to be an awfully big ship, and I just want to remind you that you promised My Donnie you'd never let me out of your sight, not even for a minute."

Rolling his eyes, he said, "Now listen, Bonnie Floyd, I don't remember the promise I made Donnie going quite that way, but trust me, I do remember making the bloody promise, and I've regretted it ever since."

"Too bad," I quipped. "That's the way I remember it, so you're stuck with me. Just admit it, Jim Johnstone, you like it!"

When we arrived at Deepwater Harbour, I was overwhelmed by the size of this type 22 frigate (warship). It was 480 feet long and 48 feet wide. My heart was pounding inside my chest with excitement and anticipation; I absolutely *love* experiences like that.

As we approached the massive destroyer and waited to be invited aboard, I could not help but think about how much Dad would have loved this experience too. Being his daughter taught me to seize every opportunity put before me and to take a learned interest in everything. Doing that was more than just trying to be well rounded; it was about living life to its full capacity and always venturing out beyond the familiar.

It was Dad's adventurous life that had led me to mine, and his life began to flash before my eyes. Going from a broken home, abandoned by his father, to a private boys' naval academy, he graduated with honors and joined the army to become a cryptographic liaison for the National Security Agency (NSA), giving him top-secret clearance in the Far East. He left the army and got his underwater diver's license and started the first underwater rescue and recovery team for the New Jersey State Police. Then he dove for Jacques Cousteau. He left the East Coast for the West and became a successful entrepreneur. He left the West Coast for the sea to sail around the world, which led to the *Côte d'Azur,* where he met Peter Ogden and accepted his offer to become the administrator for the Island of Jethou. It was there he and Mom received their Christmas bonus, a chance to one last time sail the island tropics before going home . . .

So there I stood—Bill Clever's daughter—on a gangplank, flanked by Scotland Yard's elite, holding in my hand an exclusive VIP invitation from the Royal Navy and the British Embassy, granting me access to board a British battleship, the HMS *Brave.*

We were ushered on deck and to a greeting area. To use the phrase "we were treated like royalty" would not be an overstatement. We were formally greeted by a host of British sailors all smartly dressed in their perfectly crisp uniforms. Two handsome sailors eagerly took my arms and escorted me to the reception area. I turned back just in time to see Jim rolling his eyes.

This is going to be a great evening . . .

I could not get over how many people I actually knew, but then I had been on Antigua for almost five weeks with three Scotland Yard detectives, who literally knew everyone. I went from here to there visiting with different people from Antigua. Every person I had met on the island treated me with respect and great kindness. The statement, "I'm so sorry this happened to you on our watch," which I had first heard from Big Mama, was now something I heard on a regular basis.

As I spoke with some of the sailors, I learned that their seven-month deployment was to be a West Indies guard ship. Their duties could range from combating drug trafficking to various types of rescue missions.

At one point, when I was talking with two of them, I saw Jim walking over, so I asked the guys if they would go along with me on something. When Jim walked up, the first thing he asked was if they needed him to rescue them from me.

"Not funny, Jim! We are actually having a very interesting conversation."

"Who's doing most of the conversing—them or you?" Jim smiled.

"Ha, ha," I said rather sarcastically. "Not funny, Jim! As a matter of fact, they were just telling me they are spies."

"Spies?"

"Yes, spies! Ask them, if you don't believe me," I answered with confidence.

Not wanting to believe me at all, but fearing I just might be telling the truth, he looked at them and hesitantly asked, "What kind of spies?"

They waited just a bit to answer him and then said, "Well, Jim, we can't tell you, because then we'd have to kill you."

The look on Jim's face was priceless. I got him! I knew he had not actually believed they were spies, but I got him to wonder just long enough to get him to ask! We all got a very big laugh out of it.

DIVINE FINALE TO A GRAND EVENING

Toward the end of the evening, I saw Jim out of the corner of my eye, motioning for me to come over to him. When I walked up, he was talking with a man in some type of police uniform, so I knew he was from Antigua and not a sailor in the Royal Navy.

Jim introduced him with a bit of sarcasm in his tone: "Bonnie Floyd, I think there's one person left on the entire island of Antigua you have yet to meet. This is the superintendent of Her Majesty's High Prison."

What? Did he say superintendent of the prison? Oh, wow! It's him! What do I say? What do I do?

I'm sure the look on my face spoke volumes, and it did not help that when I finally mustered up the words to speak, I choked. Eagerly I reached out my right hand, and while vigorously shaking his, I blurted out, "Superintendent Mac, what a pleasure to meet you, sir!"

He was a great big man with very black skin. His massive arms were crossed in front of him as he looked down at me only with his eyes. Everything about him was intimidating. I suddenly realized how much this man resembled the actor, James Earl Jones, but right then did not seem like the best time to mention it.

He spoke with a deep, serious tone and asked, "How do you know my name?"

Quickly Jim exclaimed, "Yeah, how do you know his name?"

Searching inside myself for the nerve to do what I needed to do, especially in front of Jim, I looked up at the superintendent and said, "Well, sir, I've really wanted to meet you."

Without any movement he continued to question me, "Mrs. Floyd, what on earth could I possibly do for you?"

"Sir," I said, swallowing hard and wringing my hands. I took a deep breath and just let it all out, "I'm a Christian, and I believe that the same forgiveness that was available to me when I became a Christian is available to Donaldson Samuel, and I would like to get into the prison to meet him and tell him about Jesus."

There, I had said it. I got it out, and Jim couldn't stop me! It's all Yours now, Jesus.

I tensed up and wanted to put my hands in front of my face to shield the blasting I was about to get, but instead I just stood there squinting as I looked up at him.

There was a moment of silence while I watched Superintendent Mac consider my request. The countenance on his face appeared peaceful, and it caused my very tense body to relax a little. When he finally spoke, his words hit me like a tidal wave, and I almost fell over flat on the deck of that battleship.

"Mrs. Floyd, I am an ordained Pentecostal pastor. When would you like to get in to see Donaldson Samuel?"

I could *not* believe my ears; I stood there speechless in my disbelief.

Am I dreaming? Somebody pinch me! Oh, my Jesus, You did it!

Tears welled up in my eyes as I reached up with both my arms and hugged this wonderful Christian man, who just gave me access to the seemingly impossible.

"Thank you, Superintendent Mac, thank you so much! I've been trying so hard to find a way in to see him, but every door has been slammed in my face. I knew I'd heard from the Lord, I just knew it, and I knew if it was His will for me to meet with Donaldson, He would make a way when there seemed to be no way; and He did it!"

"We do serve an amazing God, Mrs. Floyd. I think it would be most excellent for you to speak with Donaldson about the Lord Jesus Christ. However, I think it best for you to wait to come and see him until after the verdicts come in. Can you arrange that?"

"Yes, absolutely. I have an open-ended ticket at this point, so I will make sure to allow for an extra day to come to the prison before I book my flight home."

"Excellent. Will you be coming by yourself?"

"Oh, definitely not. Jim has promised to take me, haven't you, Jim?" I said with all the I-told-you-so tone I could muster.

In all the excitement, I had completely forgotten about Jim standing there, and when I looked over at him, the look on his face said it all. God had gobsmacked him!

The drive back to the Halcyon was quite amusing as Jim referred to me as a social butterfly that fluttered all over the ship the entire night, and I razzed him about believing the sailors were spies. As I crawled into my bed that night, I lay there in awe of God's mighty hand at work. He was paving the way, and I was more than willing to follow the path He was laying before me. I was actually going to the prison to meet Donaldson!

chapterTwenty-One

The Three Summations

The day had finally come. All the witnesses had been called, all the evidence had been presented, and all the testimonies had been given. It was time for the prosecution and the defense to present their closing arguments.

Melanson's attorney, Clement Bird, went first:

> I would like to thank you for the patience you have exhibited and
> for listening attentively to the matter. Melanson Harris never denied
> having been on the boat. He admitted that he was on the boat with
> intent to rob. He admitted that he tied up persons on the boat. There
> is nothing to support Donaldson Samuel's evidence that Harris shot
> anyone. Samuel's evidence cannot stand alone. I am asking you to
> find that Melanson Harris went on board with the intention not to
> shoot anyone . . ."

Bird's closing summation went on for two-and-a-half hours.

Following Bird was Marvin's attorney, Gerald Watt. It took him almost four hours to say to the jury that Marvin Joseph did not confess to murder or that he was even aboard *Challenger*. To prove his innocence, Watt said, "Follow the trail of the BB gun." His point was that the only hard evidence against Marvin that had anything to do with the case was that he was seen with and admitted to having possession of the BB gun stolen off *Challenger*.

To follow the trail of the BB gun would be for the jury to believe Marvin's story, that he bought the BB gun from Melanson. The huge hole in that line of defense is that Marvin had the gun in his possession but admitted to never paying Melanson for the transaction. When he was questioned about why he had possession of the gun when he had never paid for it, he said it was because he was arrested before he got the chance to pay Melanson. Lies, lies, and more lies.

The Harbor Cruise

It was another long and agonizing day in court, listening to those lawyers go on and on, defending two cold-blooded murderers. On the way back to the Halcyon, The Boys assured me that the closing arguments were weak, and I had nothing to worry about. I couldn't help myself; I was worried. They also told me we had been invited to a sunset cruise in the harbor that night.

Oh great, another what-to-wear dilemma!

We were all looking forward to our outing that evening. The sky was as blue as ever, and some beautiful clouds had formed late in the afternoon.

We found our host for the evening was a sixty-foot, well-used sailboat. As we climbed aboard I did not recognize any of the crew and was beginning to wonder at that point who had actually extended us the invitation. We were introduced to the other invited guests, a few of whom we knew from the trial, but whose boat we were on still remained a mystery.

It was taking a long time to get going, and I asked The Boys what the holdup was. They did not seem to know any more than I did. While we were waiting to cast off from the dock, I noticed a van pull into the harbor parking lot near the dock where we were tied off. Out of the van poured about a dozen men all dressed in navy-blue pants and matching tropical print shirts. They were each carrying various sized drums, and I soon realized they were one of the steel bands that performed regularly on the island. It looked to me as if they were headed straight for our boat.

Kiddingly, I said to The Boys, "I wonder if they're headed down our way to serenade us as we take off."

We all laughed until we realized they were beginning to climb aboard our boat. Apparently they were not here to serenade us upon departure, but to serenade us on our cruise. What a delight!

It was a lovely evening for a harbor cruise; the sunset had begun to form beautifully, and there were a myriad of boats in the harbor to admire. The steel band was set up and going strong, and I took great delight in watching Mick interact with them, or better said, bedevil them.

I saw the harbor entrance ahead and knew we would soon be turning around as a harbor cruise was just that—a cruise around the harbor. When I realized we were not turning and that we were sailing straight for the open sea, I said to Jim, "We aren't leaving the harbor, are we Jim?"

He looked ahead, "It sure looks that way. Why?"

"Well, it's just that, oh never mind, it's nothing," I said trying to hide my concern.

"What's nothing? It's never 'nothing' with you, Bonnie Floyd. Why did you ask if we were leaving the harbor?" he pressed.

I firmly replied, "Well, Dad always told me never to go out of the harbor with a captain you don't know."

With a look of concern on his face, he said, "Your dad told you that?"

I knew exactly why Jim had a look of concern. He may have never met my father, but he most certainly knew him. Through their investigation and all the stories I had told them, The Boys were more familiar with Dad than most people who actually knew him. Jim knew if my dad said not to leave the harbor with a captain you don't know, you ought not to leave the harbor with a captain you don't know.

"Yes, Dad said that. So, do you know the captain, Jim?

"No, I don't know the captain. Do you?"

"Me? How would I know the captain? I can't even figure out who owns this boat. Besides, I'm with you! You're the one who is supposed to know the captain. Are you going to say something to someone?" I said, hopeful he might.

"I'm not saying anything. What would I say?" he asked to my disappointment.

We settled on not knowing, and out to sea we ventured.

I looked down at the handrail we were leaning against and noticed the white-knuckle grip Jim had on it. I asked Jim if he was scared, due to the condition of his hands against the rail.

"No, I'm not scared!"

"Why are you white-knuckling the handrail then?"

"I'm just not fond of water and would rather not go for a swim right now," he answered curtly.

Just then, a peculiar silence fell over the boat. We had motored quite far out beyond the harbor, and I noticed the steel band had stopped playing a while back. The only sound I heard then was the people onboard talking among themselves.

Jim noticed the silence as well and asked, "What's that?"

"What's what? I don't hear anything."

"Exactly!" he said.

"I don't know, Jim. Maybe they turned off the engine so we could bask in the calm silence of the open seas. It really is a lovely quiet, don't you think?"

"Yes, it is, but I think it would be 'lovely' if they'd start the bloody engine back up."

"I agree," I admitted.

Then bad news made its way up to us; there was engine trouble. Apparently there was water in the diesel fuel, and the engine was a goner. I immediately looked back toward the harbor. We had ventured out dangerously far, and though I wasn't about to admit it to Jim, I was very concerned.

"All right then, what now?" Jim asked.

"I'm sure they will just put up the mainsail and try to catch enough wind to get us back to the harbor," I answered confidently, my knowledge of sailing able to be heard. I had to admit, I liked being the one "in the know" for a change.

Next, more bad news arrived—the mainsail was in the shop for repair. Neither Jim nor I would admit to one another how worried we were with the situation. And the pending darkness was soon to be upon us.

"Now what?" Jim asked again.

"Well, hopefully, they have a jib sail or something and can figure out a way to hoist it up." I gave the answer, trying to sound as if there was still hope we would make it back before night hit us on the open sea. I was thankful when good news made its way up to the bow this time. There was another sail onboard, and they were about to raise it.

Praise the Lord and thank You, Jesus! I was really starting to get worried.

Although the sail was up, my spirits were not lifted with it, because it was impossible for me to put my hope in a sagging sail. Looking up at it brought a few words to mind—c*ollapsed, deflated, drooping, limp*, even *wet noodle* would describe it well. Clearly we were in trouble!

In desperation, Jim looked at me and said, "Don't you think now might be a jolly good time to, you know . . . " And he made that familiar praying gesture with his hands.

I hate to admit it, but in that moment I lifted my hands high in the air and prayed more to have fun with Jim than I did thinking the Lord would actually answer my prayer.

I prayed with hands lifted high, "Father God, in Jesus name, I pray You would breathe a breath of Your fresh wind, just enough to fill this sail and get us safely back within the harbor. In Jesus' name, amen!"

No sooner did I say amen than a slight gust of wind blew in, just enough to fill the sail.

Jim just about fell overboard! Admittedly, so did I.

Slowly as our broken vessel was limping its way back to the harbor, a small rescue boat came alongside us.

"Glory hallelujah! We've been rescued!" I exclaimed.

Even with the sudden breath of wind that filled our sail, it would take hours to make it back into the harbor. We were so relieved to see that rescue boat. We would soon be off this godforsaken sailboat and on our way back to land.

About the time we were ready to board the rescue boat, the steel band literally pushed their way right in front of us. By the time they had all boarded, the captain of the rescue boat announced that they had reached maximum capacity. There we stood, not believing our eyes as we watched the rescue boat motor away.

It was back to trusting in our God-filled sail to get us back to land, and though it took half the night, we made it back to the harbor, back to our car, and eventually back to the Halcyon. What was to have been the relaxing sunset harbor cruise The Boys and I had expected did not quite turn out that way. And as the British would say, we were all "right knackered," and morning would come far too soon.

THE PROSECUTION'S CLOSING

The next day in court started with our senior counsel, Rex McKay, delivering his closing summation for the prosecution. He blew holes through Marvin's defense. McKay "followed the trail of the BB gun" as Watt had suggested in his closing arguments. McKay painted the trail brilliantly, leading anyone with the sense God gave a goose to conclude that Marvin was indeed onboard *Challenger* that night. He also reminded the court of young Kevin DeSouza's testimony and of Kevin's marked fear of Marvin Joseph.

In regard to Melanson, it didn't take brilliance for anyone to believe he, too, was aboard *Challenger*. Melanson put the noose around his own neck when he told the court he was a self-confessed liar, admitted to stealing Johnny's shotgun used in the killings, and then led Scotland Yard and the police to the exact spot where that shotgun was buried in the sand.

When it came to Donaldson, it was obvious McKay was going for the maximum sentence of thirty-five years of hard labor in prison. He reminded the jury and me that it was Donaldson who savagely wrapped black tape around their heads and necks. It was with that same black tape that he covered their mouths and bound their hands behind their backs, making them helpless and defenseless. He clearly made the point that though Donaldson did not actually pull the trigger, he was in no way innocent of those horrific murders and deserved the maximum sentence allowed for manslaughter.

It was difficult to once again hear how brutal the murders were and to hear how Dad, Mom, Criddy, and Tom unbearably suffered at the hands of those men.

McKay brought back to mind the gruesome details that occurred on *Challenger* that dreadful night. That was the first time I had heard some of the details McKay was referring to, because when the original testimonies were given, John Fuller had insisted I leave the courtroom. Premeditation was a point he drove home by reminding the jury that Melanson testified they went looking for a boat to rob on Tuesday, but there were no boats in Low Bay. As a result, they went back again on Thursday and found the yacht, *Challenger*.

All of these details just reopened the wound in my already gaping heart, especially when I heard McKay say that Dad was the only one of the four who did not have his hands tied behind his back. Melanson said he kept getting loose, so they bound his wrists in front so they could keep watch on his hands.

It infuriated me to hear how Melanson tortured them by having forced conversations, asking them questions to the point that he could testify to their nationalities by their accents. He even described Mom as being "kind of crossed-eyed." It greatly disturbed me that he knew them all by name, except Dad; for some reason he called him Norman.

Why did Dad give them his middle name as his first? Odd, very odd! I know there was a purpose; Dad always had a purpose in everything he did.

The description of how they died was the most traumatic for me. Because the weapon used in the killings was a shotgun, there was not a single bullet wound to the bodies, but multiple wounds. A single shotgun shell is made up of hundreds of pellets that scatter as they leave the barrel of the gun.

Thomas Williams, the youngest of the four, and just starting out his life as an adult, was the first to be shot, a shot to the chest. Melanson said in his statement when asked why Tom had gunshot wounds in the back of his head as well as on the front of his chest, "Marvin did that; he thought he wasn't dead, so he shot him again."

The blow to his head killed him instantly. The coroner said, "The head was below the level of the shotgun," which is to say, the wound revealed the shotgun was pointing downward. "Distance of discharge: six to eight inches."

Oh God, how horrible! Please, Lord, bring justice here. So much wrong was done to these innocent lives. Please, Lord, make them pay for this!

I could not help but ponder the horror that would have instantly consumed my parents and Criddy the moment they heard the gunshot and witnessed Tom falling to the floor. Until that moment, I'm sure they hoped beyond hope that these thugs would abandon the crime scene as robbers, not murderers. That first shot changed everything.

My precious mom was next. Petrified and trying to hide behind Dad as she pleaded for her life, she was shot in the chest. According to the coroner, her wounds did not cause instant death.

Oh, Lord, I trust that she was knocked unconscious and did not suffer.

Dad, guarding Mom the best he could, was also shot in the chest, but unlike her, one of the scattered pellets tore through the ascending aorta of his heart, and he died instantly.

But not before he watched his beloved Kathy shot right before his eyes. *Oh, God, I can't even imagine their torment; this is unbearable!*

Ian Cridland was the last victim to be shot and killed. He, too, was shot in the chest area, and like Mom, death was not immediate.

McKay emphasized their disturbing lack of remorse or conscience by pointing out that Marvin heedlessly smoked cigars he had found on the boat during the harrowing hours they were on *Challenger*. He recalled that Melanson described how he and Marvin left the yacht laughing after the murders were complete. The most poignant moment in McKay's three-hour long summation was when he said, "The killings were a senseless, savage, and sadistic execution."

Before the jury could retire to consider their verdict, Justice Albert Redhead offered his closing summation. What I didn't expect, because I'd never seen this happen in a U.S. court of law, was how long Judge Redhead's charge to the jury would be. It started out seemingly normal, but what followed turned out to be our longest day in court. Here's some of what he said to them:

> Mr. Foreman, ladies, and gentleman of the jury, both the Accused Melanson Harris and Marvin Joseph are indicted on a charge of murder. They have both pleaded not guilty. The Accused are jointly charged, but you must consider the evidence against each Accused separately. And only if the prosecution proves the guilt of that Accused are you entitled to return a verdict of guilty. If the evidence presented in relation to any of the Accused leaves you in doubt as to the guilt of that Accused, you must return a verdict of not guilty.
>
> You will bear in mind that you are the sole judges of the facts, the supreme judges of the facts in this case. You have heard addresses by the learned counsel, Mr. Bird and Mr. Watt, on behalf of the defense

and senior counsel, Mr. Rex McKay, on behalf of the Crown. If anything any of them says to you appeals to your reason, you may adopt it as your own, and it becomes yours and not theirs. But you are at liberty to reject everything they said to you, because you are the sole judges of the facts.

During my summation, I may make observations on the facts, and you are at liberty to decide what evidence you accept or reject. If I omit to mention evidence, which you think is important, you must disregard the fact that I omitted it. However, you will take your directions on the law from me without question, because I am the sole judge of the law.

You must not allow yourselves to be influenced by any sympathy for either of the Accused . . .

Who on earth would have sympathy for any coldblooded killer, especially these two pigs?

. . . and you will not take into consideration any prejudice against the victims or their relatives. The fact that the victims are white should not influence your decisions one way or the other. You may very well say that four people were brutally murdered, but you should approach your task without any emotions.

At that statement, I leaned over to Jim and said, "It would be all right by me if they did!"

His response was quick wink and a smile.

You must analyze and assess the evidence dispassionately. Approach your task seriously and responsibly.

I know you have been a very attentive jury. In fact, a more attentive jury I have not found. I ask you to pay special attention to what

I am going to say from now on. If I say something you do not understand, please indicate and I shall repeat or explain.

Donaldson Samuel, as you know, was charged with the two Accused; he was indicted with them for the offense of murder. He pleaded guilty to manslaughter. The fact that he pleaded guilty to manslaughter does not mean that the two Accused are guilty of the offense of murder. In fact, Donaldson Samuel is now no longer in this case of murder, but will be judged separately for the charge of manslaughter, and you will have to dismiss Samuel from your minds, so far as this case against him is concerned. Of course, he has given evidence in this case before you, and you will have to consider his evidence very carefully. Donaldson Samuel is a person who is regarded in law as an accomplice. He was involved in the actual crime for which the other two Accused are charged. You will have to scrutinize his evidence very closely, because so far as the prosecution is concerned, he is an important witness.

It is dangerous and unsafe to convict the Accused, either of them, on Samuel's evidence alone. The reason being that Samuel may want to exculpate himself, take himself out, or minimize his part in the common crime. In fact, it was put to him repeatedly by both counsels for both the Accused that he was minimizing his role in the whole crime. The defense is saying that Samuel's evidence is suspect. The defense is saying that he had agreed to give evidence for the prosecution to save his own skin and, therefore, you should not rely on his testimony as evidence.

That's baloney! The defense is trying to muddy things. Donaldson is the only one who has consistently told the truth! He's guilty, no question on that, but not relying on his testimony as evidence is stupid!

Judge Redhead's closing summation went on for several more hours, detailing the five weeks of the trial. He went over all the evidence submitted and reread statements taken during the investigation and the testimonies given in the courtroom. The events of that dreadful night were once again comprehensively put before the jury. Judge Redhead wanted to ensure that the jurors had a full and complete understanding of the law and, in turn, all of us in the courtroom became well educated on the terms of law. He literally defined terms—according to book of law—such as, *murder, manslaughter, joint enterprise, common intention, Queen's Peace, corroboration,* and *circumstantial evidence,* just to name a few.

At half past three in the afternoon, after more than six grueling hours, Judge Redhead finally said the words that caused my heart to race, my stomach to knot up, and my hands to wring: "Mr. Foreman, Members of the Jury, you may now consider your verdict."

chapterTwenty-Two

The Verdicts

$\mathcal{A}$fter five weeks of roasting in that sweltering courtroom, I was well done. I had experienced a gamut of emotions during the trial and felt I had handled all of them well, but waiting for the jury to return the verdict was an emotion I had never experienced, and I had no idea what to do with it.

"How long will they take?" I asked.

"Not long, Bonnie," Dave said with confidence.

"Do you still think I don't have anything to worry about?"

"Absolutely nothing; they will hang," Mick answered.

I wanted to believe them, and I did, but really no one can be 100 percent certain until the verdict actually comes in. Dave asked me if I wanted to get out of the courtroom for a while, but I could not bring myself to leave that room. Mick came over to tell me the word was getting out that the jury was deliberating, and many locals were beginning to gather outside the courthouse.

I could not imagine their bringing in a verdict so late in the day, because I thought it would take hours for them to review and discuss all the evidence and testimonies. I settled in my mind that the very best I could hope for was for them to bring us a verdict the following morning. Hoping for that was a stretch, since in my country juries in high-profile cases often take weeks to deliberate. The wait was on.

An hour had passed, my palms were sweating, and I kept wiping them off on my skirt. I wanted to stand up, but then I would just sit back down in my white plastic chair, only to repeat the process a few minutes later. I didn't know what to do with myself! I thought maybe some fresh air would be good for me and possibly alleviate some of this nervous behavior. As I walked out onto the balcony, the crowd that was surrounding the courthouse blew me away. As I stood there looking down at the sea of people, one of them made eye contact with me and yelled out, "You just keep lookin' up, honey. Jesus is with you!"

I smiled down at her and noticed more and more people had now seen me. They began to call out to me, "An eye for an eye, honey, don't you worry!"

Another said, "They're gonna get what's comin' to them."

My eyes began to sting with tears as I looked down at the people. I looked up at the striking blue Caribbean sky and out over the city of St. John's. I had grown to truly love this island. It was such a beautiful place, and wherever I went, the people were always so kind and sympathetic. As I waited to hear the fate of the two men who had murdered my dad and mom, the islanders were shouting out words of encouragement to me.

Still lost in my thoughts, Jim came up from behind me and gently said, "Bonnie, the jury has a verdict."

I snapped out of my daydream and quickly walked back into the courtroom.

I turned to The Boys and looked at them with eyes begging for assurance. As always their demeanor was strong and confident, but after five weeks, I knew them well—well enough to know that their outward appearance never showed their inward thoughts.

We all took our places in our designated white plastic chairs and waited for the jury to come back into the courtroom. I kept getting lightheaded and had to remind myself to breathe. I had almost rubbed my hands raw from wringing them, and the fidgeting in my chair was excessive.

Finally the door to the jury room opened, and I saw the five men and four women that made up the jury file into the courtroom and take their seats. Melanson and Marvin were brought in by two police officers. My nerves were at a high they had never known.

Please, God, please let it be guilty!

It was 4:59 p.m. The jury had been out for only one hour and twenty-nine minutes.

The jury was roll called, and all were present.

Judge Redhead, poised and ready for the verdict, asked the foreman if they had reached a verdict. The foreman affirmed that they had.

"What say you?"

"Melanson Harris: guilty of murder."

"Marvin Joseph: guilty of murder."

I sat there with a burning stare into the two who had just been found guilty of murdering my parents. I didn't make a move. I heard it, I heard the verdicts, but for some unknown reason, I froze with fear that I had somehow heard it wrong. Of course, I didn't; they had been found guilty.

Thank You for justice, Lord; thank You!

I broke. The tension throughout my body suddenly released, and I crumpled in my chair and cried.

Tears of relief.

Tears of justice.

Tears for Dad and tears for Mom.

Tears for Tom and Criddy.

The courtroom became like the day I first received the call that they were gone. I felt disconnected and out of it. I saw a courtroom full of people, and I heard the many voices around me, but I was not part of any of it; it was all just blurred noises. What brought me to my senses was when the court was asked to rise for Judge Redhead to read the death sentence to Marvin Joseph and Melanson Harris.

I held back my tears as I listened to Judge Redhead say to both of them:

It is the unanimous verdict of this court that you should be taken to a lawful place of execution where you will suffer the penalty of death by hanging, and upon which your bodies shall be buried within the prison. God have mercy on your souls.

The only reaction from Melanson was a smile that spread across his face as he nodded his head. I couldn't believe my eyes! Was he really that stupid? Or did he really not care? Marvin Joseph on the other hand just kept staring at the judge.

Smile or stare, it doesn't matter what you say or do anymore; you are going to pay for what you did. Justice has been served; you will never be free to hurt another person.

I heard crying and turned to find two women weeping openly. They were Marvin's mother and sister. I looked around for someone who might be there on Melanson's behalf, but those two women were the only people who seemed shaken by the verdict.

Marvin and Melanson were led out of the courtroom. They had laughed as they left *Challenger* that night. They had laughed time and again during the trial. Melanson had smiled when the verdict was given. But now, neither of them was laughing or smiling. My eyes followed them out of the courtroom.

Good riddance!

THE THIRD SENTENCE

It would soon be time for Donaldson to be brought in for his sentencing. The night before, I tossed and turned in my bed unable to sleep. My thoughts consumed me. I was filled with worry that Melanson and Marvin would somehow get off, but I was also consumed with fear and doubt about going to see Donaldson.

Okay, God, here I am, send me, and I will tell Donaldson about Jesus.

It seemed so long ago that I had stood out on the courthouse balcony and said those words. It had been easy for me to say when it was a meeting that would take place in the future that might not even happen. That was no longer the case. Having met Superintendent Mac, I now had a sure way into the prison, and meeting with Donaldson was no longer a date in the future. Rather, it would be taking place within the next two days.

I began to doubt if I had actually heard from God. Was it really His will for me to go and talk with Donaldson? I had somehow forgotten all He had done to confirm that I had heard from Him correctly; I needed another sign.

As I tossed and turned that night, I lay there remembering the story of Gideon in the Bible and how he, too, heard from God but needed a sign to be sure. God gave Gideon the very sign for which he had asked, but still Gideon doubted and asked for another. Once again, God gave Gideon a sign. So just like "doubting Gideon," before I went to sleep that night, I asked God for another impossible sign.

My request was to see God's hand of mercy move on Donaldson's behalf. He was facing a sentence of thirty-five years to life. I needed to see him get less, way less. I needed to know that my feelings of mercy for Donaldson were a reflection of God's mercy on him.

As Donaldson was led in, all I could think of was my request to God. If He gave me this sign, I would move forward with my plan to go to the prison; if not, all plans were off! It was time.

Mr. Watt stood before Judge Redhead, pleading Donaldson's case: "I rise this afternoon to ask for leniency to the prisoner."

"Leniency, you ask?" Judge Redhead questioned.

"Yes, Your Lordship, Donaldson Samuel is only twenty-three years old."

At that Judge Redhead abruptly rose from his chair, leaned over his bench and bellowed, "Tom Williams was only twenty-two!"

His words echoed in the silent courtroom until Watt spoke again.

"Yes, Your Lordship, but Donaldson Samuel didn't shoot anyone."

"No, but he bound and gagged them with black tape!"

Oh dear, this is not going well at all. You're going down, Donaldson, and I know what that means . . . no going to the prison for me!

Mr. Watt proceeded without seeming to be phased at all by the judge's heated rebuttals. "I appeal to normal thinking persons in Antigua; remorse of the Accused."

Judge Redhead interrupted once again, "Remorse does not change the fact that he was a part of this crime."

"Yes, Your Lordship, but remorse that the prisoner exhibits has caused him to give important evidence in the case. He has been contrite throughout. Without his evidence, the course of events would have been different. The Accused gave evidence to the prosecution from the onset. I ask that for his assistance substantial credit to be given."

When Watt finished his seemingly pointless appeal to Judge Redhead, the court recessed.

"Well, that went well, don't you think?" I sarcastically said to The Boys.

"Bloody well!" they all replied with equal sarcasm. The Boys were certainly not standing with me in my desire for Donaldson to receive a lesser sentence; they were as pleased as they could be at the judge's responses.

In just fifteen minutes, the judge returned with his sentencing. I was actually feeling a bit relieved that Watt's plea for Donaldson didn't go well. As much as I was willing to go into that dreadful prison and meet with Donaldson, I think a part of me wanted just to hear the sentencing, walk away, and never look back.

Judge Redhead looked directly at Donaldson Samuel and said, "I sentence you to fifteen years hard labor."

I almost fell out of my white plastic chair! I started to choke, and Jim looked at me and said, "Are you all right?"

"Uh, yes, I'm good. I'm fine," I answered.

Will wonders never cease? Fifteen years! That is less than half of what he could have received! I am so going to the prison now. What happened? How did Redhead come up with that sentence after the righteous anger he had just displayed? Never mind, I already know how; it was You, God.

As Donaldson left the courtroom, I did not take my eyes off him. Jim told me he had gotten word that Donaldson had agreed to meet with me after the verdicts came in, so I expected he would look over at me. I waited for just a glance, but it never came. I think Jim read my thoughts, because he leaned over and said, "He only agreed to meet with you because he thought it might help with his sentencing. Now that he just received fifteen years hard labor, don't be disappointed when he refuses to see you."

"He'll see me, Jim," I responded.

"Don't be too confident about that, Bonnie Floyd."

"My confidence is not in him, Jim. He'll see me. I know he will."

When we left the courtroom, we were met by a frenzy of people—reporters, cameras, and a celebration of justice served. It took me aback a bit, but it made me feel good inside to know they, too, wanted justice for my parents, Criddy, and Tom.

A reporter made a beeline straight for Mick. He had become quite famous as the head detective, and the reporter wanted his initial response to the verdicts. He answered the impromptu question as though he had prepared for it:

Two years ago, these two men carried out four coldblooded murders aboard the yacht, *Challenger*. I am delighted for the sake of the relatives of those who died that we were able to trace, detain, and finally convict those responsible for the barbaric murders. Today the course of justice was completed with the rightful conviction for a killing, which was without reason.

I stood there beaming, looking at him in awe with great pride; he was simply remarkable.

Dad, you would have loved this guy; in so many ways he reminds me of you.

Just then I was approached as well, first by a camera crew and then by several newspaper reporters. They were all asking me the same questions. "How did you feel about the verdicts of Harris and Joseph? Are you upset about the leniency shown to Donaldson Samuel?" And I answered this way:

I feel that justice has been served in the verdicts and sentencing of Harris and Joseph. I am very glad I came to Antigua for the trial, and I can definitely see why my parents chose this place to vacation. During my five weeks on Antigua, I have come to realize that this is a beautiful place, full of kind and loving people where something very, very bad happened. In regard to Donaldson Samuel, I didn't want his sentence to be harsh, though it looked like it was going that way. I am satisfied with his sentence.

Jim took me by the arm and escorted me away to where Dave was waiting for us in the car. As we drove away, I heard people saying, "We got 'em, honey; an eye for an eye!"

chapterTwenty-Three

Behind Prison Walls

It was over. That was our last drive back to the Halcyon after those long days in that hot courtroom. I couldn't wait to get back and call home. There were so many family members and friends who had been praying me through the ordeal. I would only have time to make a couple of calls, and then they would have to spread the news. My first call was to our Floyd Construction office, where I knew My Donnie and sister Susan would be waiting to pounce on the phone.

They did not let me down. All I said was, "Melanson and Marvin were found guilty of murder; they're going to hang. Donaldson got fifteen years." And the tears of relief began to flow. I heard Donnie yelling a huge, *"Yes!"* And I visualized his fist pumping the air as an athlete does after a great play. I knew an enormous weight had just been lifted from his shoulders.

I told them as much as I could, but in my eagerness, I kept jumping around in the story, and the battery of questions they were both throwing at me did not help our chaotic conversation. It was hard to hang up, but I had to make my second call to Kimberly.

"Oh Bon, I know you're so relieved for so many reasons. I knew it would go that way; it just had to. I'm even more excited that you get to come home now! Well, I mean after you go see Donaldson. Are you ready for that?"

"Ready as I'll ever be, I guess," I answered apprehensively.

"Do you know what you're going to say to him?" she asked with concern.

"Are you kidding? I haven't a clue what I'm going to say. And you know what? I'm not going to concern myself with it either. This is God's deal, not mine. I'm just going to pray hard and then go in there. I know in my heart God is going to give me the words to speak."

"That sounds like a perfect plan, Bon."

After a quick change of clothes, I was back out the door for the victory dinner celebration with The Boys and several others.

It certainly was an evening of rejoicing; we were all in high spirits. What we had expected to take two weeks had turned into five, and that was the end of a very long and difficult time in all of our lives. The fact that we did not have to head back to court the next morning was a reason in itself to celebrate, but of course our elation was for so much more than that. We celebrated that justice was served, we celebrated the world's finest detectives, and we celebrated the lives of Dad and Mom, Criddy, and Tom.

It was festive, sentimental, and downright fun, which we all desperately needed. All went along well until I blew the wind out of their sails at the mention of going to the prison to see Donaldson the next day.

"You are not still serious about going to see him?" Jim asked with a you-have-to-be-kidding-me tone.

"Of course I'm going! Nothing's changed, including your promise to My Donnie that you would go with me."

"That bloody promise! I told you, Bonnie Floyd, he's not going to tell you where the stuff is, and he's not going to agree to see you tomorrow. His fate is set, fifteen years hard labor, so agreeing to meet with you now is of no benefit to him."

"And I told you, Jim Johnstone—in fact, I keep telling you over and over—I don't care a thing about where the stuff is. All I want to do is tell him about Jesus!"

"I will take you to the prison tomorrow, Bonnie," Dave said from across the table.

"You will?"

"Yes, what time would you like to leave?" he asked.

"Well, I really need to contact Superintendent Mac to be sure, so I'll call him in the morning. Okay?"

"That will be fine. Just ring me when you have a time," Dave said.

"So, you're going to back out, Jim Johnstone?" I inquired.

I got no response at all.

"Fine then, I have my ride and my escort with Dave. I'll be sure to let Donnie know you bailed."

At breakfast the next morning, Jim was dressed and ready to go to the prison with us. I actually never doubted for a minute that he would go. On the way, Jim felt he had to prepare me one last time for the disappointment he thought I was about to face.

"You know, Bonnie Floyd, he's probably not going to agree to see you now that he has been sentenced."

"Yes, Jim, you've mentioned that to me."

"And if he does by chance agree to meet with you, he's not going to tell you where the stuff is."

Seriously Jim, you're saying that again? I've told you, I don't care where the stuff is!

"Yes, Jim, you've mentioned that to me too."

"And I'll tell you another thing, I'm not going to sit there with you and listen to your conversation with him. I'll have no part in that!" he said with adamancy.

"That's fine, Jim; you don't have to go in with me. I'm really okay with that."

"As a matter of fact, while you're in meeting with him, I'm going to go and check out the gallows."

"You know, Jim Johnstone, I think that's a fine idea and very appropriate for your sick mind," I said with sarcasm and a smile.

I noticed Dave drove the car in silence, not saying a word.

Come to think of it, over the last five weeks, Dave always seemed to clam up whenever any of our conversations broached the subject of God or Christianity. Hmm, I don't think I've ever noticed that until now.

When we pulled up to the prison, it was similar to what I imagined it would be, except for the thick iron door painted bright red. That thing looked exactly like something a Hollywood director would do in a prison movie for the sake of emphasis.

When we walked up to the intimidating red iron door, there was a big brass knocker that was mounted to the upper left of the door. After Dave reached up and gave it a few bangs, we stood there and waited for something to happen. There was an eight-by-eight-inch horizontally barred cutout in the door that had its own little obscure door that slid side to side. After a few minutes, the little door slid open, and a guard gruffly said, "State your name and your purpose!"

Dave stated, "I am Detective Sergeant David Marshall, and we are here to see Superintendent Mac. He is expecting us."

The little door slammed shut, and there we stood.

"What do we do now?" I asked nervously.

"We wait," Jim answered.

My heart was racing, and I was wringing my hands again. I kept trying to imagine what it was like behind that big red door. It could not be good. From the outside it was daunting, but then I guess any prison anywhere would appear that way to me. It was the conditions inside that concerned me. Just knowing people were hung until they were dead and then buried inside that place was creepy enough.

Eventually the big red door opened, and we were told to step inside. Jim went first, and then me, and Dave followed. Basically they flanked me on either side, and I was fine by that! Once inside we were escorted up an open staircase and then down a covered balcony to Superintendent Mac's office. When we reached the doorway, Jim made his exit, and Dave went with him. As they walked away, I heard Jim asking directions to the gallows.

Superintendent Mac rose from his desk to greet me and then had me take a seat in one of the two chairs that were in front of his desk. To my surprise they were wooden chairs, not the white plastic chairs to which I had become accustomed. I chose the chair farthest from the door.

Superintendent Mac and I talked for a long time. It was great to freely discuss our faith without any naysayers in the room. He told me he was quite impressed by my faith and the mercy I was about to show Donaldson. I was quick to let him know that this was a sheer act of obedience, and I completely trusted the Lord to give me the strength and the words to get me through.

Superintendent Mac told me his desire to share Christ with the prisoners and how challenging and difficult that was for him. "That is why I made a way for you to come here and meet with young Donaldson. There is hope for these prisoners; the same hope offered to us. That hope is Jesus."

"Exactly!" I said excitedly. "I believe the same forgiveness that was available to me when I accepted Christ is available to Donaldson. I am painfully aware of Donaldson's sin. He is a sinner, but so am I . . ."

"Yes, yes, and Jesus is the sacrifice for all sinners who believe in Him!" Superintendent Mac said, finishing my sentence for me.

I was thoroughly enjoying our conversation, but I couldn't help noticing how much time had passed.

When on earth is Donaldson going to get in here? I'm ready to do this now before I lose my courage!

Finally I heard footsteps walking down the balcony, and soon in the doorway stood a guard and Donaldson Samuel. Superintendent Mac immediately got up from behind his desk and went to the door. He excused the guard and put Donaldson in the chair next to mine.

I immediately noticed two things: one, they had allowed him to change into street clothes, and two was how he smelled. Somewhere between his cell and Superintendent Mac's office, he had clearly found a bottle of Brut cologne and appeared to have emptied the entire bottle on himself. He smelled so strongly of that ancient obnoxious men's cologne, and within seconds the whole office reeked of Brut.

I remembered that potent smell well because Grandpop wore Brut, and whenever he came into a room and left again, the smell of him lingered on for hours. Not only that, but whenever anyone hugged Grandpop, they would smell like Brut for the rest of the day too. In the midst of being overcome by the potency of this cologne, a thought filled my mind.

Bonnie, this is the way he prepared himself to meet you. It was the only way he had to show you respect.

I was sobered by that thought just in time to see the superintendent take his seat behind his desk. He looked directly at Donaldson and said, "I presume you know who this is?"

"Yes, Mon, I du."

"Mrs. Clever-Floyd is the daughter of William and Kathleen, two of the four who were murdered on the boat that night."

"Yes, yes, Mon," he acknowledged, now looking down at the floor.

"Do you know why she is here today?"

Looking up at the superintendent, he said, "No, sir, I'm not too sure bout dat." And then turning to look me straight in the eye, he said, "I didn't shoot your mom and dad."

Looking straight back at him, I said, "No, Donaldson, you didn't, and I believe you, but you did go to the boat that night to steal, and stealing is a sin. There's a price to pay for sin, Donaldson, and yours is fifteen years."

"Yes, Mon."

"Do you know who Jesus is?" I asked him.

"Yes, the superintendent has been telling me bout Him. I don't know much."

"Donaldson, I am a Christian. I became a Christian when I was twenty-four. Someone told me all about Jesus, that He was the Son of God who came from heaven and died on a cross to shed His blood for the sacrifice of my sins. I'm here because I believe I'm supposed to tell you about Jesus, just as He was shared with me ten years ago."

"Yes, Mon."

"I had been telling my dad and mom about Jesus before they died. I believe that everything I shared with them they remembered that night on the boat, and that is why Melanson said he thought they were Christians."

I stopped and waited to see if he wanted to say anything, but he just looked at me and nodded.

"Donaldson, you almost died by being shot when you escaped from prison that night, didn't you?"

"Yes, Mon."

"My pastor told me something the day I found out my parents had been killed. He said, 'Bonnie, God could have prevented this, but He did not, and the one thing I know for certain is that God makes no mistakes!'

"That was very hard for me to understand at first because I couldn't understand why God didn't prevent it. As time has gone by, I've seen God's grace, and I see His hand moving in all this. Donaldson, God could have allowed you to die when you got shot while escaping the prison, but He didn't, and He doesn't make mistakes."

Superintendent Mac had been sitting behind his desk observing and not saying a word, and then without so much as an "excuse me," he had something to say; and it was powerful.

"Donaldson Samuel, do you understand what this young woman is saying to you?" And without giving Donaldson a chance to answer, he went on, "She is here to offer you Jesus and the forgiveness that believing in Him offers. Do not be misled in your thinking. Do not be confused in why she is here today. By rights she should want one thing and one thing only for you, and that is vengeance for her parents; death by hanging, the same sentence the other two received. She is not here out of love for you but out of the great love she has for the Lord Jesus Christ. She is not seeking vengeance, but offering you mercy—the only mercy that can save your soul—and that is Jesus Christ."

I sat there in awe of the words that came from his unexpected interruption.

Wow! That was certainly just putting it right out there! That was awesome, Lord. Thank You for giving him the words to speak; now don't forget about me!

He listened intently to every word Superintendent Mac said to him, and then Donaldson turned his eyes back on me, and I continued: "I believe your time here in prison needs to be spent getting to know Jesus, so when you get out and go back to Barbuda, you can tell people your story. How God saved your life, twice!

He would nod, acknowledging the things I was saying, and when I took a breath, he would say, "Yes, Mon."

"I also believe you can speak to kids on Barbuda about the importance of choosing the right friends and the consequences of making bad choices. That's what I've been doing and will continue to do. I will tell my story about how good God has been to me through all this. How He has healed my heart and given me peace. How I believe all my efforts of telling my dad and mom about Jesus were not in vain, and that when it really mattered, they acknowledged Him as Lord, and He saved them!"

"How He save them?" he questioned.

"There is only one way to be with God in heaven, and that is to believe in His Son Jesus. Donaldson, heaven is real, and so is hell. When God created us, He gave us the free will to choose. We can choose to confess we are sinners and ask Jesus to be our Lord and Savior or not. That one choice determines where we spend eternity. I have no doubt and believe with all my heart that my parents kept a very important promise they made to me before they died. The promise was that they would call on the name of Jesus if they ever feared for their lives. In keeping that promise, God saved them, and they are living in heaven right now. God may not have saved their lives here on earth, but He saved their souls for all eternity, and that is all that really matters."

Donaldson listened equally as intently to me as he had Superintendent Mac. I began to search my mind for what else there might be to say, but there wasn't anything. I had said what I went there to say; the seed was sown, and the choice was his. In my mind, it was time for me to go.

I looked over at Superintendent Mac to let him know I was finished, and he began to speak. I have no idea what he said, because my mind began to have some crazy thoughts. It didn't take me long to figure the crazy thoughts weren't mine, but God speaking to me.

Obediently, I turned to Donaldson and said, "Donaldson, would you like to pray with me?"

Without any hesitation, he said, "Yes, yes, I would like dat."

I turned my chair to face him more, and in turn, he did the same. As I bowed my head, another crazy thought came: *Bonnie, you rarely ever pray with anyone one on one without holding their hands.*

I looked down at his lap, and there before my eyes were the black hands that bound my parents. These were the hands that made them helpless. In an instant, any compassion, any mercy, any sympathy I had previously felt toward this murderer were gone. I froze in panic. Not only wasn't I going to touch those hands, I didn't even want to pray anymore! Fear had completely taken over my mind.

Go ahead, run. Nobody would blame you! You don't have to do this; you said what you came to say! Get up and go! Now!

Before I let another thought of panic and fear speak, I reached out and grabbed his hands.

No! I will not run. God has brought me too far, given me too many confirmations and too many signs to turn and run now. I will finish this.

Donaldson squeezed my hands tightly, and I began to pray for him. I prayed for his time in prison and for his future. Then without even knowing it, my prayer changed from praying for him, to praying with him, which led to Donaldson himself praying the words that would save his soul for all eternity.

Tears filled my dried-up eyes as I realized exactly what was happening.

Lord, he accepted You as his Lord and as his Savior. This is surreal; it is too deep for my mind to fathom. You actually used Dad and Mom and me to lead this man to You. How is any of this even possible? You are amazing—I am simply in awe of You.

As soon as we finished praying, Donaldson looked up and announced to me, "I know how to write! You write me?"

A little taken aback by his sudden announcement, I stammered, "Uh, you do? Well, umm. that's great."

I looked over at Superintendent Mac, who had a very pleased look on his face, but he offered me no assistance.

Looking back at Donaldson, I suggested, "How about we do this? I will give Superintendent Mac my address, and if you write to me, I promise, I will write you back. Does that sound like a good plan?"

"Yes, Bonnie," saying my name for the first time. "That is a good plan."

"Okay then, that's what we'll do. I think I need to go now, because the detectives are waiting for me."

"Are you married, Bonnie?" he asked.

Stopping me in my tracks, I answered, "Yes, Donaldson, I am, to a wonderful man. His name is Don. He was here with me in the beginning of the trial but had to fly home to run our construction company."

"Maybe I meet him?" he said.

"Oh? Well, I don't know, but maybe. He's really busy, so I don't think he'll be coming back here any time soon," I stuttered.

Oh, yeah, that'll be the day when Don Floyd comes to visit you, the day pigs fly!

I got up from my chair, and so did Donaldson. He turned toward the door, and more crazy thoughts entered my head: *Bonnie, you rarely ever pray with anyone without giving them a hug afterward.*

Are You kidding me? No way, Lord!

Yes, Bonnie, show him. Treat him as you would anyone else.

But he smells so badly of Brut!

"Donaldson, may I have a hug?" I blurted out, before I lost my nerve.

He turned and looked at me with forlorn questioning eyes, not seeming to believe that I would ever consider such a thing. I looked back at him with compassionate, confirming eyes, and without an ounce of forethought, I lifted my arms to him. He cautiously moved forward and gave me a most respectful gentleman's hug.

He walked toward the door, and as he stood in the doorway, he stopped and turned back. With the brightness of the noonday sun shining in behind him, all I could see was his silhouette, but I heard him say, "You come back?"

My heart wrenched, knowing I would most likely never return, but I said with all the confidence I could muster, "Donaldson, I never thought in a million years I would ever be here in the first place, but if you pray and I pray, one day maybe I'll return."

I saw him nod, and then he obediently put his hands behind his back and stood there as the guard shackled and chained him, then led him away. Although I was elated that he had accepted the Lord, I actually felt sadness in my heart as he vanished out of sight.

Why does that upset me? Why do I care? I did what You sent me here to do, Lord. You never said anything about caring.

Just as I suspected, Jim and Dave were more than ready to depart the prison premises. I had given Superintendent Mac my address and said my good-byes to him. Before I left, he said, "You know, Mrs. Floyd, he *will* write you."

"Yes, sir, I do believe he will, and I will keep my promise to always write him back."

On the drive back to the Halcyon, Jim just had to ask the question that was burning inside him, "So did he tell you where the stuff is?"

Looking straight ahead and not even turning to face him, I simply answered, "I didn't even ask him, Jim."

Neither Jim nor Dave said a word of response, but out of the corner of my eye, I thought I saw a smile of approval appear on Dave's face.

chapterTwenty-Four

Going Home

$\mathcal{S}$aying good-bye was definitely bittersweet for me. I was so excited to go home to My Donnie, my family, and my friends, but the thought of saying good-bye to Mick, Jim, and Dave only put a huge lump in my throat. A lump so big, no matter how many times I swallowed, it just would not go down. It was the same familiar lump that came up every time I had to say good-bye to Dad.

The Halcyon Cove Hotel had been home to me for five weeks. The East Caribbean cuisine, especially Susie's Hot *(kapow!)* Sauce (more sparingly, of course), had become one of my favorite foods, and I had grown very fond of my sun-kissed bronzed skin. As fond as I had become of those things, I could easily give them all up. But it was the crystal blue sea, the clean white sand beaches, and the soothing sound of the surf that was the most difficult for me to leave behind.

I loved the ocean; I had loved it since Dad had shared his love of the sea with me when I was a little girl. Everything I knew and loved about boats and the ocean, I learned from Dad. When I am by the sea is when I feel the closest to him, so in essence, leaving it behind was like having to say good-bye to Dad all over again.

When the time came to say good-bye to The Boys, I didn't cry. I wouldn't let myself cry, not in front of them anyway. I kept my tears at bay by getting all their contact information and making future plans for Donnie and me to fly to England for a visit. I couldn't wait to meet the wives of these three amazing men I now called my friends. I had heard so much about them, I felt that I already knew them.

After hugging them each a hundred times, I walked out of their sight and found the nearest restroom to lock myself in so I could let my emotions run freely. I had gained a splitting headache from holding back the tears; they came spilling out with the force of a fire hose. Once the waterworks started, I had a most difficult time turning them off. I had hoped that once I let them loose, the pressure headache would subside; alas, it didn't. I needed some Excedrin.

I had the most unexpected surprise waiting for me when I checked in at the airport. I had been upgraded to first class! I had no idea why, who, or how, but I was certainly thankful. I settled into my window seat and sat there gazing out the airplane window. I can't say my mind was reflecting; it was more like flooded with thoughts of the last five weeks, the last two years, and all that had occurred in that short time span. Would life ever be normal again?

My dad and mom were gone. I had just spent five weeks on an island in the West Indies with three of Scotland Yard's finest detectives. I had an encounter with the reality of God in the Caribbean Sea. And I held hands and hugged one of the men who aided in the murder my parents.

Where do I go from here?

As we took off and I looked down at Antigua, the tears came again. I had a glorious view of the whole island, and I knew most of the landmarks. I could see the three places we frequented the most—Antigua's biggest city, St. John's; English Harbour with nearby Shirley Heights; and, of course, Dickenson Bay and the Halcyon Cove Hotel. I looked out as far to the northwest as I could, but Barbuda was hard to see.

My plane landed in Fresno just before eleven o'clock in the evening, but the late hour did not keep my family and friends from gathering together to give me a big welcome home celebration at the airport. My Donnie was at the front of the pack with Susan, Kimberly, and Mom Floyd standing directly behind him. I was truly blessed by everyone who came to welcome me home.

Walking into our house and taking in the familiar sights, sounds, and smells was very comforting. When I walked out into the backyard, my precious Gordon Setter, Lochmoor, ran over to shower me with slobbery kisses only I could love; he had missed me too. It was so good to be home!

The plan for my first full day at home was to wake up to a lazy morning with My Donnie and then make our way to Mark and Kimberly's for the rest of the day. Mom and Dad Floyd and Kim's parents, Charles and Shirley, would be joining us as well. It was days like those when I wished my mother didn't live out of town, but I was thankful to be with these other two moms who loved me as their own.

We sat in the living room together as I told every detail of my five weeks on Antigua. Many questions were interjected along the way, which made for quite a lengthy story. However, the one part I left out was my encounter with the reality of God in Low Bay, Barbuda.

Miss Shirley, Kimberly's mother, was captivated by the events that took place in Antigua. Because she was Kim's mom, she had also lived out the last two years with me. Shirley Barber was the director of women's ministries at Peoples Church and was intent on asking me a question: "Honey, there have been so many people praying you through this who want to hear what happened while you were in Antigua for the trial. How would you like to gather them all together and tell them your story? We can reserve a room at the church, and you can update them on all the events as they unfolded in the last five weeks."

"Oh, I think that's a great idea, Miss Shirley. I would love to share all that God did while I was there, and let's face it, it's a long story! I can't imagine having to tell it over and over. I do have a job, and Donnie and Susan are more than ready for me to get back to the office."

A week had passed, and I was enjoying getting back into the swing of things. I was especially excited to be walking into Peoples Church again. My first Sunday back with my church family and seeing Pastor Johnson was just what my heart needed. My pastor was so personable; I loved how his face lit up whenever he saw me—his face lit up for all people, but I liked to think I was special with the familiar way he would say, "Well, hi ya, Bonnie; how are you today, Honey?" It always warmed my heart.

Being back at work felt good too; there was a lot to catch up on, which was keeping me very busy. One afternoon while sitting at my desk, the phone rang, and I answered to hear the sweet voice of Miss Shirley. I assumed she was calling to set the date for the little gathering at the church we had discussed. "Honey, do you have any plans for Saturday, April 20?"

"Well, that's Donnie's birthday, but we haven't made any plans yet. Why, Miss Shirley?"

"Bonnie, I've been thinking about everything the Lord did for you and for Donaldson when you were in Antigua. It truly is an amazing story that so glorifies the Lord and speaks about the importance of forgiveness. What would you think about telling your story at the Ladies Spring Luncheon?"

This is a joke. She cannot be serious! That will be five hundred women! What happened to the small group of friends we were talking about? There is no way I'm getting up in front of five hundred women!

"Excuse me, what did you say?"

"Honey, I'm asking you to share your story with the women at the Ladies Spring Luncheon."

"Miss Shirley, that would be a big no! I can't possibly speak in front of that many people. I'm sorry, there's no way; the answer is no."

"Honey, I need for you not to say no right away. I'm asking you to talk with Donnie and then the two of you pray about it, and if the answer is still no, then that's perfectly fine. Would you do that for me?" she asked in her very sweet voice, the one that I loved so dearly.

"Okay, Miss Shirley, but I don't think talking to Donnie is going to change anything."

That evening over dinner, I told Donnie about Shirley's ridiculous idea. I didn't expect his response, and I didn't think any more highly of it than Shirley's crazy idea for me to speak at the luncheon.

"Babe, I think this is what we should do. I think we should fast and pray for three days and then make our decision. Okay?"

"Okay, whatever you say, babe, but I think this is nuts to even consider. I couldn't even get up in front of my class in school and give a book report without breaking out in a nervous red rash. How on earth would I do something like this?"

At the end of three days, after starving myself and admittedly not doing a whole lot of praying about something I already knew the answer to; I approached Donnie.

"I didn't get anything different, did you?" I asked with a hunger-induced irritated tone.

"Yep, yes I did, and you're doing it!" he answered with full confidence.

"What? You can't be serious, Donnie. I can't do that!"

"Yes, you can, baby, I know you can. God did not bring us through all this for nothing. God reached out to Donaldson through this story, and I believe now, after praying, that God wants to use what happened and all He did in a bigger way than we can imagine."

"Fine then, you get up there and speak for the luncheon," I sarcastically replied.

"Babe, you are going to do this, and I think you know down deep inside you're supposed to; so please call Shirley and tell her you'll speak at the luncheon. Will you do that for me today?" he asked with a soft but firm tone.

I knew that tone all too well. It meant, "We've completed our discussion, I've considered what you've said, but I've made the decision for us."

223

Oh, how maddening it is when I know he's right!

Miss Shirley didn't seem a bit surprised when I called her with my decision. I've never known her to be wrong when it comes to discerning things from the Lord, but she will never tell you, "The Lord told me you're supposed to do this or that." She is adamant that a person should hear from the Lord personally. I love that about her!

There was much to do in preparation for that frightful event. How on earth was I going to tell this story in forty-five minutes? I had some serious work to do! The only part I thoroughly enjoyed was shopping for my outfit with Kimberly.

The week before the luncheon, I was sitting in church for the Sunday evening service. A woman about my age had been asked to give her testimony that night. When she got up to the podium, she was obviously very nervous; I could so feel her pain. About halfway through her testimony, I was an absolute wreck! She was stammering, losing her place, apologizing, and having to go back in her story to give forgotten details. I sat there frozen stiff, paralyzed with fear. That was it—I was not going to do it, and nobody was going to make me! It was still a week away; Shirley would have time to find someone else.

When the service was over, and before I had even stepped out of the pew, Miss Shirley appeared out of nowhere. She looked at Donnie and said, "I'd like to talk with Bonnie in my office right now. Will that be all right?"

"Oh yes, Shirley, that's fine. No problem at all," he answered with "She's gonna bail" written all over his face.

Before Shirley could say a word, I spoke up emphatically, "I know why you've brought me to your office, Miss Shirley, and there's nothing you can say to change my mind. Did you just see that? That was totally me up there! This is no longer about my fear of speaking in front of people; this is about letting down hundreds of women, who put out money for a ticket and wound up just wasting a Saturday afternoon."

"Bonnie," she said in the firmest way I've ever heard her sweet voice sound, "you need to listen to me. I know that this evening did not go well, but let me tell you why. When a person is asked to share their story in a public setting, having notes is good only to a point, and then they become a hindrance. You cannot become tied your notes, as though they are a script for you to follow. You know your story, you lived it, and nobody knows it better than you. You just need to pray and trust that the Lord will guide you as you speak. If you forget something you've written down, it may be that it wasn't necessary to the story. If it is significant, don't announce that you forgot a part, just simply add it in."

She made it sound so easy, and I knew why—she was right, and experience was talking now. Every word she went on to speak to me described what I had witnessed that night and addressed every fear I had about sharing my own story at the luncheon. I walked out of Miss Shirley's office with a newfound confidence; that is, until I woke up in a ball of nerves at five o'clock in the morning on April 20, 1996. I would much rather have awoken to a day of just celebrating My Donnie's birthday, but instead I awoke to the thought of standing in front of hundreds of women. I lay there, praying to God that when I opened my mouth, intelligible words would come out.

The Women's Ministries team had once again outdone themselves. The luncheon was decorated beautifully with all things spring. My admiring all the lovely surroundings lasted only a moment as I realized how many round tables of ten had been crammed into—I mean set up—in that room.

I honestly felt as doubtful and scared as I had just over a month earlier when I looked down at Donaldson's hands and wanted to run out of that dismal prison room. The stark contrast to that day and this one was poignant in my mind. There I was surrounded by darkness, a twisted and warped world. Here I was encircled with life and beauty, with new beginnings. Yet the same feeling was evident in my heart—I was scared and overcome with fear.

This time there was no voice telling me it would be okay to run as there had been in that Antiguan prison. There was most definitely a voice screaming in my head that I didn't have what it takes to do this, but as for running, I knew without a doubt that was not an option. The time was nearing for me to take the stage; I felt a squeeze on my leg. I looked over at Kimberly, who was giving me the "You can do this, Bon; I know you can" look. I nervously smiled back at her and then over at Susan, who had the exact same look on her face. Shirley introduced me, and as I stood up Susan gave me one of her beautiful smiles and a nod of absolute assurance.

I wish I could tell you how I did it, but I can't. When it was over, I had no idea what I even said, except for one thing. At the end of my testimony, I had become burdened, thinking about someone in the room who might have never prayed to accept the gift of Jesus. I summed up my testimony and said without any forethought, "Please don't be deceived in thinking that, like my dad and mom, you, too, may have the opportunity to be bound and gagged before you die. The Bible says, "Today is the day of your salvation." The words just flowed out of my mouth, and I knew instantly they were not mine.

As soon as I stepped down, Miss Shirley came up to close. She has such an eloquent way with words, bringing everything together perfectly. She said she would be remiss if she ended the luncheon without offering an invitation to pray with those in attendance who may have never asked for Jesus to forgive them of their sins and be their Lord and Savior.

I will never forget what I saw next. A young girl, who did not buy a ticket to attend the luncheon, but who worked for the catering company, weaved her way through the tables from the back to pray with Miss Shirley and ask Jesus into her heart.

I sat there in total awe of my Lord. A soul had just been saved from eternal damnation, her eternal life in heaven with God now secure. And it was all because of what God had done through the life and death of my parents. All because I faced my fears and told my story.

chapterTwenty-Five

*Anticipated Correspondence and
an Unexpected Cruise*

I went to the post office in the morning as I did any other Monday and put the key into the door of box 391. I reached in and pulled out our Floyd Construction mail, and I saw an odd letter in a manila envelope. When I flipped it over, I saw unfamiliar, feminine handwriting and was baffled about who it could be from until I noticed an unusual marking in the left-hand corner. It was an oval dark blue ink stamp that read "H. M. Prison Antigua." I had to take a step back to keep from falling over.

Was it him? Oh my, I can't believe Donaldson may have actually written to me!

It had been a few months since I left Antigua, and I had wondered if he would really ever write to me. I wanted to rip it open right then, but I thought I should wait until I was back in the car. As I scrambled to open the door and jumped into the seat, a feeling of anxiety washed over me. I carefully examined both sides of the envelope, stalling now to somehow avoid the inevitable. When I finally opened the letter, the handwriting inside changed to a masculine print. Of all the things I could have imagined the first line of his first letter would say, it certainly wasn't this: "Greetings in the name of our Lord Jesus Christ!"

While the grammar and wording were not perfect, his letter was full of genuine concern for me and how I was doing in dealing with the loss of my parents.

"Bonnie, be strong. I know you are strong. Hold in there, I'm praying for you."

He expressed what meeting me meant to him: "I don't know, but ever since we have met, it's just like a bond between us. I respect you a whole lot. Meeting you was very important, and I'll never forget that. I liked it when we sit and speak and pray."

He spoke of how he was holding up and how prison life was changing him: "I'm balancing myself out. Things I used to do, I blank them. I'm becoming a man in prison. I'm getting to understand life more."

He asked about Donnie and told me to tell him hello. I chuckled at the thought and the look on Donnie's face when I read that to him. Donnie supported my going to the prison and was sincerely glad Donaldson had accepted the Lord, but that's where it ended for Don Floyd. He had said more than once that he was just glad the whole thing was over, and we'd never have to go back to Antigua again.

DÉJÀ VU

One morning I answered the phone in my office to hear the cheery voice of my friend Carrie Millett. She and Peter had moved to Oregon a few years back, and even with the distance between us, we had remained close friends.

Carrie was calling with one of her bright ideas. "Bonnie!" she said excitedly, "Peter and I need two things. The first is a vacation and the second is a Floyd fix, so I think we should go on a vacation together, and I think it should be a Caribbean cruise."

I immediately started to laugh and said, "Carrie Millett, you can't be serious! Do you realize it's been less than a year since I spent five weeks on an island in the Caribbean?"

"Yes, I know, but that certainly was no vacation, and Donnie wasn't even with you for three weeks of it," she argued.

"Oh, Carrie, there is just no way. Floyd Construction is booming. We could never take a vacation with this many houses going," I argued back.

Carrie is never one to take no for an answer, especially when it comes to having fun. After two weeks of phone calls back and forth, with even Peter getting into the mix and calling Donnie, we relented.

"Okay, Carrie, we'll go, but it can't be until after the first of the year. We think we can manage some time off in February. But here's the deal: you have to be the travel agent. My plate is so full right now, I need a side plate. I have no time to research cruises or plan a vacation. Whatever you decide is good with us."

Carrie took on that challenge and planned the whole thing. All she had told us was that we were going on a seven-day Caribbean cruise that departed out of San Juan, Puerto Rico. Even though we fought going at first, we were actually very excited about our upcoming vacation.

Just days before we left for the cruise, Donnie and I realized we needed to get serious about preparing for our vacation. One night we grabbed the cruise packet to have a look, and what we read thrilled me to no end and threw My Donnie into a raging tailspin.

"We are not going to Antigua! Did you know about this?" he heatedly questioned me.

"No, babe, I swear I had no idea!" I said in my own defense.

"Well, call Carrie right now; we're not going!"

Calmly I replied, "Baby, yes we are going. We can't *not* go. The cruise is nonrefundable. Please don't get all upset, Donnie; it will be fine. Antigua is a beautiful island; we both know that."

"Bonnie, we both know it's not an ugly island. I'm not concerned about that!"

Oh boy, I knew exactly where he was headed, and I knew we were about to have a very heated discussion. There was no doubt in my mind that, if I was going to step my foot on the Island of Antigua, I would most definitely be going to see Donaldson.

The air in our home for the next few days was thick. Every time I would broach the subject, Donnie would erupt. We finally came to a decision that we could both live with, but Donnie still was not a happy man—not in the least! I couldn't really blame him, though; he definitely made the biggest concession, and I made no concession at all. It was decided that I could go to the prison to see Donaldson, but Donnie would have no part in it. All he needed to say now was that he'd agree to "go to the prison but only to check out the gallows," and I'd be having a bad case of déjà vu!

THE DAY'S AGENDA

Our cruise ship was the *Monarch of the Seas*, and it was a royal beauty. We had no trouble picking up our dear friendship with Peter and Carrie right where we had left off. Quality time away from building houses and being on our first real vacation in a long time was what Donnie and I needed, as long as the name Donaldson never came up.

Mentioning his name became inevitable when, after only two ports of call, Antigua was on the horizon. Before leaving Fresno I did some fast work behind the scenes—making calls to Superintendent Mac to request another visit with Donaldson. The plans were set in place for my return visit to Her Majesty's High Prison.

I should absolutely not be this eager to visit him again. It is so odd, and if My Donnie knew, he would be downright irritated.

Our ship came into St. John's during the night, so when I woke up and Antigua was before my eyes, I was thrilled to be back. I played down my excitement at breakfast, trying hard to contain myself and not spend that time rattling off my personal agenda for the day. Carrie broke the ice and asked in her cheery voice, "So Bonnie, what are our plans for the day? After all, this is *your* island!"

"Well, I was thinking I'd first like go to the police station to try and see

Superintend Gomes, then over to the prison. After that, I'd like to go to John Fuller's office and then we can head to English Harbour and end the day at Shirley Heights. That will make for a full day, and I'm pretty sure we can fit it all in by the time we have to be back on the ship," I said in a happy, matter-of-fact voice.

"Sounds like a plan to me!" Carrie answered.

That girl was game for anything. She had told me time and time again how much she wanted to go to the prison with me and that she had appointed herself as my personal prayer warrior. I was fine with that and thankful to have her support.

The police station was a small office, nothing at all like Peter and Carrie were expecting.

"Is this it?" Carrie questioned.

"Yep, this is it," is all I said.

When we walked in, the man behind the counter looked at us with a bit of suspicion and doubt. Not many tourists go to the police station or even know where it is. I walked right up to his desk, put out my hand, introducing myself and asked if Superintendent Gomes was on duty. He told us that he was scheduled to work that day, but his shift had not started yet. I asked, with as much emphasis as I could, to please let the superintendent know I had come in on the cruise ship for the day and that I would very much like to see him.

Walking out of the police station, I quickly proceeded to the next thing on my agenda—to hire a taxi for the day. It did not take long for the cabby to figure out who was riding around in his car as I told him all the places we wanted to be taken.

"Can you please take us first to the law office of John Fuller? Then we need to go to Her Majesty's Prison for about an hour. After that, I'd like to show our friends English Harbour and Shirley Heights."

I had told the Milletts that literally everyone in Antigua knew about the *Challenger* murders over on Barbuda and that the daughter of the American couple had been in court every day for the five-week trial. Our cabby seemed somewhat honored to be our driver and expressed that it meant a great deal to him that we would choose to return to Antigua for vacation.

"I don't think I'd use the word *choose*," I heard Donnie say under his breath.

My perfectly planned day seemed to be unraveling when John's secretary told us he would be out all day.

"I can't believe I keep striking out," I said disappointedly.

As we were walking back to the taxi, I heard Donnie say to Peter, "Hopefully she'll hit strike three at the prison, and then we're outta here." He and Peter chuckled, but I failed to see the humor.

The next stop was the prison. In accordance with the agreement Donnie and I had made, he would walk me up to the door, but he was not going in. The big red iron door was just as intimidating to me as the first time I approached it with Jim and Dave. But showing no fear, I marched right up, grabbed the brass knocker, and gave it three bangs. The little door slid open, and the unfriendly voice said, "State your name and purpose."

"I am Bonnie Clever-Floyd, and I am here to see Donaldson Samuel. Superintendent Mac is expecting me," I said with confidence.

"Donaldson Samuel is out on a work crew today and will not return until three o'clock!" the voice gruffly answered and abruptly slammed the small viewing window in the door shut.

As much as Donnie was elated to hear that Donaldson was not available for my visit, he held his tongue, knowing I would be crushed by the news. Before a word could be spoken, I turned from the iron door and looked at My Donnie dead in the eyes, firmly stating that we would return promptly at three o'clock!

Not at all pleased with my determination to do that, he gave me an affirming nod. As we climbed back into our taxi, I asked to be taken to the fourth location on my agenda that day, Shirley Heights. That breathtaking spot is by far the most beautiful lookout on the entire island of Antigua. The view from Shirley Heights Lookout is the number one tourist attraction and certainly warrants its fame. It is a picturesque panoramic view overlooking English and Falmouth Harbours. On a clear day you can see the neighboring islands of Guadeloupe to the south and Montserrat to the southwest, with its active volcano soaring from the island.

As soon as we got out of the taxi, our friendly driver felt the need to gather the locals around and announce to all of them, "This is Bonnie Clever-Floyd, the daughter of the American couple who were murdered on the yacht *Challenger* off Barbuda."

All of the islanders were full of sorrow as a community for the crime committed against Dad, Mom, Criddy, and Tom. They said to me, "Please forgive us, honey, for the heinous actions of the three who murdered your parents while on our watch."

Once again that phrase was used, *on our watch*. Though it had become familiar to me, I still found it deeply profound that the three men who committed the crimes were not even from this island but from the neighboring Island of Barbuda, yet these people still took responsibility and bore the shame for what the men had done. It became evident to our friends why I had fallen in love with the people of Antigua.

The next stop on my agenda was English Harbour, where we would have lunch. I was very excited to return and anxious for Peter and Carrie to experience its beauty. The mountainous island surrounds the harbor and provides a towering shelter for the many fascinating and charming sailboats. I never tired of the long drive it took to get to that peaceful and alluring part of the island because it was the last harbor from which Dad and Mom had sailed.

A SURPRISE MEETING

Just before we reached English Harbour, we were brought to a standstill in construction traffic. While sitting in the taxi contemplating our next move, which was either to wait it out in the taxi or to walk the rest of the way,

Donnie looked out the window and stammered, "Babe, is that . . . no, never mind, it couldn't be."

"Couldn't be what? Who? What do you see?" I diligently questioned while straining to see whatever it was Donnie was seeing.

"Oh, my!" I yelled as I scrambled for the door handle. "It's John Fuller!" I couldn't believe my eyes. "John! John Fuller!" I yelled as I made my way through the stalled traffic.

He spotted me just as the traffic in front of his car cleared. As he drove away, I heard him say, "Meet me at . . ."

"Where? Meet you where?" I called back, but to no avail. The traffic was moving at almost a full pace by now, and Donnie pulled me back to the taxi—the one that was about to drive off without us. As we jumped into the moving taxi and slammed the door, Carrie said to Peter, "Well, there is certainly never a boring moment when we're with the Floyds!"

My many concerns of where to look for John and how we would find him were quickly dashed when we pulled into the first parking lot at English Harbour. John calmly stood there leaning against his car smoking a cigarette. The look on his face said, "I knew you would find me."

After giving him one of my big hugs that he knew was unavoidable, we updated him on what had brought us back to Antigua. I slyly mentioned that I desired to make a trip to the prison during my visit. His less-than-thrilled reaction didn't surprise me in the least.

I patiently listened to him as he lectured me once again, saying, "I still don't like the idea of your going to the prison and offering forgiveness to Donaldson. He should not have been given a prison sentence; he should be waiting to hang right along with the other two."

"Yes, John, I know full well how you feel about my visiting Donaldson, but nothing stopped me last time, and nothing's going to stop me now."

John looked directly at Donnie, and before he could say a word, Donnie piped up, "I've tried, John, believe me, I've tried! But when I see that look in her eye, I know God is making a way for her, and I am to stay out of the way."

John's only response was an exaggerated roll of the eyes.

A Shocking Gift

Out of the blue, John eagerly informed us, for some mysterious reason, earlier that very morning while he was at the courthouse, he had been handed all of the transcripts from the trial. Apparently they only keep transcripts for a year, and they were scheduled to be destroyed if he didn't want them.

He then said something we never would have expected to hear. "When they asked me if I wanted them, I thought to myself, *What would I want with them? I have no use for them.* But for some unknown reason, I accepted the transcripts, and they're here in the boot of my car. Do you want them?"

Donnie gasped and, choking on his own spit, managed to get out, "Yes, we want them! I just can't believe this. We need those for the book Bonnie is going to write!"

With raised eyebrows John said, "Really? You're going to write a book, Bonnie?"

Now it was my turn for an exaggerated eye roll. "According to Donnie I am," I said unenthusiastically. "I'm still not quite sure about that, John."

"Well, I think it's a good idea, and Donnie seems very sure about it—about as sure as you are about getting into that prison again." The antagonism dripped from his words as he reached down into the boot of the car to fish out the transcripts.

"Oh, great, now you, too, John? Family, friends, and even the dog think I should write a book. I'm just not feeling it. And honestly, I'm not sure we have room in our luggage for these transcripts."

"Oh, yes we do! I'll buy an extra piece of luggage to get them home, if I have to!" Donnie chimed in with that don't-argue-with-me-babe look on his face.

Once that was settled, John encouraged us to come into the restaurant and have lunch. "I believe there is someone inside I'd like to introduce you to, Bonnie."

As we entered the restaurant, John was immediately taken to his own table. The unexpected run-in with us had apparently made him late for his lunch appointment. The four of us were shown to a table across the room from where John was seated.

A VERY SPECIAL INTRODUCTION

Halfway through lunch I noticed John was making his way over to our table. "Bonnie, can I steal you away for just a minute?"

"Of course! Where are we going?"

"Why do you always ask so many questions?"

"It's my nature," I answered with a wink.

I followed him across the dining room and noted that we were headed in the direction of a long table where many official-looking people were seated. I had no idea who any of them were.

John led me to the head of the table. A man who appeared to be in his late fifties—tall, broad-shouldered, and distinguished—was seated there. His face was familiar to me, but I didn't know why.

"Bonnie, I would like to introduce you to Antigua's prime minister, Mr. Lester Bird."

What? Are you kidding me? Could you have given me a little heads up here? The prime minister of Antigua! What do I look like? Am I properly dressed? Oh my, what do I say? How do I address him? Is it Your Lordship? No wait! It's My Lordness. No, no, it's My Lord. Aghhh!

"What an honor it is to meet you . . . sir," I said with a respectful smile.

"The honor is mine, Mrs. Clever-Floyd. It grieves me to think of the pain of your loss at the hands of those three men. I extend my deepest condolences."

"Thank you, sir. It was most certainly a tragic and devastating loss for my entire family and me. God has been very faithful, though, and He has seen me through to the other side of that pain."

"I want to personally assure you, Bonnie, that the men responsible for that horrific crime will pay for what they have done. I guarantee you, justice will be served, and they will hang in the very near future, in accordance with their sentencing," he said with absolute resolve.

"I do feel justice was served at the trial, and I am pleased with all three of the verdicts. Throughout my five weeks on Antigua last year during the trial, I was shown great kindness and compassion. The people of Antigua grieved for me and with me. I came to learn that what happened to my parents, Ian Cridland, and Tom Williams deeply affected them as well. As I said after the trial, this is a beautiful place, full of kind and loving people where something very, very bad happened."

"Bonnie, I thank you for those kind and affirming words. Everyone I have spoken with in regard to this trial has spoken highly of you. What brings you to Antigua, and what are your plans for your stay here?"

"I was brought on a cruise ship, very unexpectedly I might add, so I am only here for the day. There were a few special people I hoped to see again while I'm here, and one of them is John," I said with smile as I looked over at him. "I won't keep you any longer, sir. Thank you very much for taking time out of your lunch to meet me; it has certainly been a pleasure."

John walked me part of the way back to my table, and before he turned back to his, he quietly said, "Very nicely done."

As I took my seat, the looks on Donnie's, Peter's, and Carrie's faces told me everything I needed to know—somebody had told them who I had just encountered.

chapterTwenty-Six

A "Trip" into Prison

*I*t was three o'clock sharp when our taxi pulled up in front of Her Majesty's High Prison. The weather had taken a drastic turn, and we were now in a torrential downpour. A common afternoon thunderstorm had blown in during our drive from English Harbour. With no umbrella and nothing to cover us, we forged the storm and once again approached the intimidating red iron door. I thought my heart was going to beat right out of my chest.

Please, Lord, let Donaldson be here. There is no way I'll ever get Donnie to bring me back for a third attempt at this, and we are running out of time before the cruise ship sails away without us!

For the second time that day, I grabbed the brass knocker and banged on the door. That familiar sound resonated off the iron makings of the door: *Bang! Bang! Bang!* The small viewing window in the door slid open to the all-too-familiar and unfriendly voice, "State your name and purpose!"

"I am Bonnie Clever-Floyd, and I am here *again* to see Donaldson Samuel. Superintendent Mac is expecting me!" I yelled into the little mini viewer. I was angry now—angry at the unfriendly way they treated us, angry that a blasted storm had blown in, and angry at Donnie for reminding me just before we got out of the taxi that he was only walking me to the door.

With no response the little door slammed shut, and we stood there waiting, for who knows what. The downpour had not slowed a bit, and the hard-falling rain had now thoroughly drenched us all. There was not a dry spot to be found on any of us.

After what seemed to be an eternity, I heard a clanging sound from the other side of the door, and finally it opened. They were letting me in! I turned to look at Donnie, to give him my I-told-you-so glare, and then quickly stepped through the doorway before anything or anyone could stop me. What I had forgotten was that the prison door was cut out of a much larger iron plate that filled the gap between the thick concrete prison walls. The bottom of the door was cut out about eight inches up from the bottom of the plate and required that you take a step over it in order to get in. I did not make the step over.

When Donnie realized I was going down, he tried to grab me, but it was too late. I fell face first into the mud just inside the door. Without thinking, Donnie stepped in to help me up, and Carrie impetuously jumped through the door with him, leaving only Peter still standing outside in the drumming rain. As Donnie pulled me up, I saw the look on Peter's face, realizing that if he didn't move fast, he was about to become a loner outside the prison walls. He hurriedly stepped in, and not a second too soon, because the big red iron door nearly slammed his foot in the door.

There we were, all four of us standing on the inside of the prison walls soaking wet. I literally looked like a muddy, drowned rat.

Did that just really happen? Donnie is in here with me—the very thing he said he would never do! Is there a reason, Lord? Why did You bring him in here? What is about to happen?

Although we were now inside the prison, the guard's attitude toward us did not improve. They treated me as though I was an inconvenience, which I guess I was, but as nice as I tried to be, there were no niceties to be had.

A "Trip" into Prison

After waiting in the guard shack, or whatever that shanty was, we were escorted into a dirt courtyard, now muddied by the tropical downpour that would not relent. Some of the prisoners were randomly scattered about the courtyard in ankle shackles, doing what appeared to be much-needed maintenance work on the dilapidated buildings.

The guard acknowledged only me as he led us up an old wooden staircase, as if my companions did not even exist. No one said it out loud, but our eyes communicated, *I sure hope this rickety thing can hold all our weight.*

At the top of the stairs, we were led down the same long, open-air balcony I had walked down to meet Donaldson the last time I was there. About a third of the way down, we passed an open door in which the guard directed Donnie, Carrie, and Peter to enter and be seated. I intentionally made no eye contact with any of them and was left outside on the balcony alone with the guard.

The guard then led me further down the balcony and in through another open door. I stopped abruptly, because there before me, sitting in an old wooden chair, was Donaldson Samuel, his hands folded in his lap. Immediately, he rose to his feet and said, "Hello, Bonnie; you come back!"

"Yes, Donaldson, I have come back," was all I could muster at that moment.

"It is good you come see me," he said with a cautious smile.

Oh no! What am I doing here? Why did I come again? I should have listened to My Donnie.

Fear crept into my heart and mind as I doubted my persistence in coming back to this place.

"Bonnie, I pray Jesus bring you back again," Donaldson softly stated. And the fear that had suddenly gripped me immediately lost its hold on my heart at the mention of Jesus' name.

"Jesus has brought you here again," he said with full confidence.

"Yes, indeed, Donaldson, Jesus has brought me here once again."

"How you been, Bonnie?"

"I've been fine, very busy, but doing well."

"Busy with your business, Floyd Construction, and talking like you say in your letters?"

"Yes, exactly. And you've been receiving my letters, I take it."

"Oh, yes, I read them every day. How is Mr. Don?"

"Oh, umm, he's doing well. Busy too."

"He no come to Antigua with you?"

Quickly redirecting the conversation, I answered, "Enough about me, Donaldson, how are *you* doing?"

"I'm doing fine, Bonnie. I help around here a lot; I have earned privileges."

"That is very good to hear! And how about Jesus, Donaldson? Are you growing in your Christian faith?"

With a downcast look, he answered, "No, ma'am, I'm not doing too good with dat."

"Why, Donaldson?" I asked with concern.

"I don't read too much my Bible. I work a lot."

At that I was gravely concerned, and I kicked into overdrive.

"Donaldson, you simply have to grow in your faith, and the way to do that is to read your Bible and become more familiar with the Lord!"

"Yes, mon, yes, I know dat."

"Do you remember when we talked a year ago, and I told you I believed your time here in prison needed to be spent getting to know Jesus? If you could do that, then when you are released, you could go back to Barbuda and tell people your story. Your own story of how God saved you and how He wants to save them too!"

"Yes, I remember dat," he slowly answered.

"I know it must be very hard in here, and fifteen years is a very long time, but Donaldson, you have to make the very best use of your time. You need to grow strong in the Lord so you won't fall back into sin when you get out. All this bad that has happened God wants to turn into good, so His Son will be glorified. Just as I said before, I believe one day you will be able to speak to kids on Barbuda about the importance of choosing the right friends and also the consequences of making bad choices. Do you understand what I'm trying to say here?"

"Yes, I du, and I want to du good. I want more God in my life. I will try harder, Bonnie."

"Good, Donaldson, that is very good. I want God's very best for you and . . ."

My train of thought was interrupted as Donaldson began looking with concern over my shoulder. I turned around to see something I had not realized. I thought Donnie, Carrie, and Peter had been put in a different room, but actually we were all in one very large room, which apparently had two separate doors of entry. There, about thirty feet away, across this long room and seated near the wall, sat Peter and Carrie. Walking toward Donaldson and me was Don Floyd with a grimace draped across his face that caused me to fear what he might do next.

Oh, no, Lord, stop him! This cannot be good! Please, God, don't let Donnie do something stupid.

Donnie's face was harsh and blotchy red, his eyes were swollen, and he was sweating profusely. The closer he got, the more concerned I became. I noticed his Adam's apple appeared to have grown in size and was pulsating in his neck. I looked back at Donaldson, and his face was stoic, his eyes locked on the man headed straight for him.

I turned back to Donaldson and said with a trembling voice, "That's my husband, Don."

Donaldson stood unwaveringly and said, "I know he has his eye on me."

I stood up as well, right in front of Donaldson. I looked at Donnie, and shaking my head no, I mouthed, pleading with Donnie, "Don't do this!"

But he wasn't looking at me; his eyes were deadlocked on Donaldson.

Oh, God, You see this going down . . . You've got this, right?

Donnie finally reached us and stood beside me, facing Donaldson. I never saw him even blink, and without hesitation he spoke, "Listen to what my wife has to say. It is truth, and it's important for your future to do all she is encouraging you to do." Donnie stopped talking and swallowed hard, and with an intensity in his eyes I had never seen before, he said, "God is real. If Jesus can forgive me for the things I've done, then I can forgive you . . ." swallowing hard again, "I, I forgive you, Donaldson."

I literally watched an indescribable peace wash over both of the men standing with me. With humility in his voice, Donaldson put out his right hand toward Donnie, "Thank you, sir, thank you. I never went there to kill; I didn't shoot the gun."

"I know, but you were there and have to pay for your mistakes, but you are free in Christ."

And as unexpectedly as he walked up, Donnie turned and walked away, leaving Donaldson and me to say our good-byes.

chapterTwenty-Seven

Farewell, Antigua, Farewell

*S*till in awe and reeling from the day's events, we returned to the cruise ship. We found the perfect spot on deck to debrief and to watch the ship cast off and leave the port.

I could not believe Donnie's account of what went down between him and God while sitting on that bench in the prison. He likened it to the story in the Bible when Jacob wrestled with God. Donnie retold it this way:

It all started with what I would describe as ridiculous and crazy thoughts, but I couldn't get them out of my head. I knew God was guiding me, and He was saying, *Go over there and tell Donaldson that I Am real and that you forgive him!*

I argued with God in my mind, *What? That's crazy! Why would You ask me to do something like that? Donaldson made my in-laws helpless by tying them up, and he beat Bill when he got loose. I don't want to forgive him; I want to see him rot in here!*

It was as if I was fighting in a dream, but it wasn't a dream; I was wide awake. I know my eyes were swollen and red; they must have been bulging out of my head, and when I looked over at Carrie, with resolution in her eyes and a calm confidence in her voice, she said, "Donnie, you know what you have to do!"

I sat there shaking inside; I heard the Lord's voice once more: *Donnie, get up and go over to Donaldson and tell him I am real and that you forgive him.* So I mustered up what little strength I had left after wrestling with God and did what I had to do.

Donnie wrapped up his retelling of his moment with Donaldson, and I sat there in awe. "I'm so proud of you, baby! You told Donaldson that he was free in Christ, and now *you* are free too—free from the bitterness you were holding on to."

"We are all proud of you, buddy. That was a day that will go down in the history books for sure," Peter commented with awe still in his voice.

Unable to stop thinking about my one missed opportunity, I said, "I know it has been an over-the-top amazing day, but I just can't help being sad that I never found Superintendent Gomes. I truly hoped and expected to see him on the dock waiting when we returned to the ship."

Donnie tried to help me feel better, saying, "Well, babe, he most likely never got your message. Otherwise, I know for certain he would have made every effort to see you."

"I know, but he played such an important part in all this. I love that man, and I really wanted to see him." I was still pretty bummed.

The ship horns let out their big blast, letting everyone know we would be departing soon. We all got up from our lounge chairs and headed over to the rail to watch as we spent our last few moments docked at one of the most beautiful places in the world. It was a perfect Kodak moment, so Donnie and I posed so Peter could take our picture. At that moment, Carrie doubtfully said, "You can call me crazy, but is that man way down there on the dock waving and yelling your name, Bonnie?"

I turned to look down, and there before my eyes, dressed in his full Antiguan police regalia was Superintendent Gomes, waving, and yes, I could faintly here him calling my name.

"Donnie! It's Superintendent Gomes. It's actually Superintendent Gomes! I've got to go; I've got to get down there!"

Donnie, ever the voice of reason, then tried to reason with me, "Baby, you'll never make it down there in time. Just stay up here and wave." As soon as it flew out of his mouth he realized how ridiculous that must have sounded to me.

Okay, yeah right, Floyd! I'll just stay up here, stand at the rail and wave. You've got to be kidding me!

I yelled down with the loudest voice I could muster, "Wait for me; I'm coming down!"

I took off like a scalded dog, pushing the elderly out of my way and running over children, trying my best not to cause any casualties along the way. I decided the elevator would be far too slow, because I knew it would stop at every floor on the way down. So I opted for the stairs.

Eleven floors, here I go!

Fortunately Donnie and I had been on an exercise routine prior to the cruise. And while onboard each day, unless we were dressed for dinner, we raced up and down the split stairways that lined either side of the interior of the ship. I knew these stairs, and I was flying down them with the greatest of ease.

Please, God, don't let me trip!

With each passing floor, my heart raced from adrenaline and fear that I would not make it down before they shut the gangway. When I finally made it down, and with the gangway in sight, I heard crewmen shouting, "Stop! You can't go there; we're about to shut it. We're departing!"

I didn't care. The door was still open, and I was going for it! If I got out, and the ship left without me, I didn't know exactly what I would have done, but I really did not care at that point. I barreled past a few crewmembers and made it to the opening. There he was, Superintendent Gomes, just six feet away, and as I lunged forward, two husky crewmembers grabbed both my arms from behind.

"Superintendent Gomes, I came to see you first thing this morning, but you weren't there!" I exclaimed as I tried to wriggle loose.

"I know, Bonnie, they told me. I'm so sorry. I just got your message at five o'clock and came straight here to see you."

"Oh, Superintendent Gomes, I wish they'd let me go."

Turning to the two who were holding me, I begged, "Can't I at least just give him a hug, *please?*"

"No, ma'am, we are truly sorry. We cannot let you leave the ship; the gangway is about to close."

"I was able to see Donaldson again," I shouted out to him, "and Donnie went with me this time. Donnie even forgave him today!" I wanted badly to tell him all the wonderful things we had experienced.

"That is good, my friend, that is very good."

I saw the door begin to close. I looked out at Superintendent Gomes, "I'll write to you, and I'll *never* forget you!"

Then the big door closed tightly. I threw my arms loose of the big hands that held them back and headed for the stairs. With all my might I climbed and I climbed all eleven flights. (It was a whole lot faster going down!) When I made it to the eleventh floor and ran out on the deck, I could barely breathe.

"You made it down, baby. I saw Superintendent Gomes looking into the ship and talking to someone, and I knew it was you. Now you've made it back to the top; and babe, he's right there."

I looked down at the dock and spotted him, and I could see he spotted me too. I saw him waving to me, and I waved back. Then I saw his posture change. He stood straight at attention, clicked his heals together, and raised a stiff right hand to salute me. I knew nothing else to do but salute him back . . . only he could not see the tears streaming down my face.

chapterTwenty-Eight

Setting Myself Up for Success

Fourteen Years Later: October 19, 2010

Dear John Fuller,

I hope and pray this email finds you well. It has been a very long time, about fourteen years since we saw you last. I'm confident you'll remember me, and if not me, certainly my parents, Bill and Kathy Clever, who were murdered off the Island of Barbuda on the yacht *Challenger.*

I know it's been ages since we have communicated. I actually think of you more often than you might believe, so one would wonder why then I haven't been better with my correspondence. Regardless, here I am knocking at your door. Why? Well, after all these years, I am finally writing a book about my parents. Upon my return from Antigua, I was asked by my own church to share the story of my parents' life, tragic death, and the trial experience at a women's luncheon. This was a very large venue with several hundred women in attendance. I will tell you, it scared the living daylights out of me to get up in front of all those women, but I did it! From that one luncheon back in April of 1996, God birthed "Bonnie Floyd Ministries," and I have been speaking all over the United States at retreats, women's conferences, and church services ever since.

Donnie and I still can't believe the change in direction our lives took after Dad and Mom died. Never in a million years did we ever think my speaking would grow into a full-time ministry—one that would allow us to close Floyd Construction and move from California to Texas. Over the years I've developed many different messages, but the story of Dad and Mom is still the heartbeat of my ministry. There is literally never a speaking engagement where I am not asked, "So where's the book?"

After years of questions I am currently in the throes of finishing this long-overdue book. I have spent weeks going through boxes of everything I had accumulated and saved from my parents' life, through to their tragic death and the trial. So many memories . . .

John, I need some help, and I don't know where else to turn. I have questions that need answers. Donnie and I are coming to Antigua in one week and would be so grateful for your assistance in accomplishing the purpose for our trip. I have no idea what became of Marvin Joseph and Melanson Harris. I'm sure they have been hung by now. Donaldson Samuel and I corresponded for a number of years after the trial, and then all of a sudden the letters stopped, and I quit receiving responses from the letters I sent to the prison. Can you help me with any of this? Do you know if Donaldson was released or still in prison? I very much want to meet with him at the prison, or if he's been released, I'm prepared to go to Barbuda to find him.

We are leaving on October 26 and flying to Antigua for a week's stay at the Halcyon Cove Hotel. In addition to finding Donaldson and learning the outcome of the others' fate, I need to come back to refresh my faded memories. My greatest desire is to reconnect with the people who touched my heart and impacted my life. There are three in particular: Superintendent Abel Mac from Her Majesty's High Prison, Ephraim Gomes from the Antigua Police Department, and you, John. There are others, but the three of you are indelibly etched in my mind.

Finding answers to my many questions, reconnecting with you and the others will be so helpful as I write the epilogue for my book. I know I have come out of left field and bombarded you with many questions.

John, I can't believe much has changed in regard to your knowledge of the islands and the influence you have there. I hope to hear from you soon. (To think Donnie and I might just be shaking your hand in person by next week is all very exciting.)

God bless you, John Fuller!

Bonnie (Clever) Floyd

I laid my right hand across the laptop screen and prayed for my last-chance email to make it into the hands of someone who would give it to John. I prayed I would find favor with him after all these years, and he would respond.

I checked my inbox every day, ten times a day, but nothing. After five days, I had given up. I knew an email address on Google for such an influential man was unlikely to be the right one.

On Friday morning, as I was reading my Bible and preparing to write for the whole day, my cell phone rang, interrupting me. My first thought was, *Nope, I'm not answering.* When I looked at the screen on my Blackberry and it read "Unknown Name, Unknown Number," I seconded my first notion and said out loud, "Nope, I'm not picking up the phone." I was not going to let anything keep me from writing that day, *period!* And with that flakey thought, I hit the green answer button and said, "Hello?"

A familiar voice on the other end said, "Bonnie? John Fuller."

I jumped out of my red recliner and cried, "You called; you really called! I've checked my emails every day, and I had just about given up."

"Well, I've been ill and out the office and just got your email. I didn't even finish reading it before I rang you. So you're coming to Antigua next week, yes?"

"Yes, I am, and John, I've prayed every day you would contact me."

"Yeah, yeah, I'm sure you have; you're that way. I haven't forgotten this about you, Bonnie Floyd."

I quickly thought to myself, *Okay, Bonnie settle down, lower your octaves. Don't be too over the top, or he'll back away, and you'll blow this connection.*

I could not believe I had just said that to myself. I loathe being told to settle down, and when Dad would say "lower your octaves" to me as a kid, it made me want to crawl under the nearest rock.

John did not seem fazed by my excitement at all; as a matter of fact, I could tell by the tone of his voice that he was amused with me. I knew I had found favor with John many years ago, even though he often gave me a bad time about my faith in Jesus. I still had and cherished the broken piece of pottery he had given me the night The Boys and I had dinner at his tree-house all those years ago. God gave me a love for this unique and wonderful man, who would not rest until justice for my parents was served. Shortly after I met him, he won my heart, and eventually I think I won his too.

After briefly going over a few things I wanted to accomplish on my trip to Antigua, it was decided I would ring John from the Halcyon after we arrived and got settled. With only four days left until we took flight for Antigua, I was finally filled with excitement, joy, and confidence that this long-overdue trip was going to be a success.

READY, SET, GO!

The alarm went off at five o'clock the morning before we left; I still had so much to do. I rolled over and picked up my Blackberry from the nightstand and scrolled through the emails that had come in during the night. My heart skipped a beat when I found one from Dave Marshall at Scotland Yard.

As if God had not done enough with John Fuller to set me up for success, He sent me another response to one of my cry-for-help emails. I lay there in bed reading his email with tears running down the sides of my face. The paragraph that struck me most read (in his British way of speaking):

Scan this code for A Detective's Perspective

> It is great to hear from you again—I talked about you only a few months ago when I took a church service that included my testimony highlighting how our encounter was key in God putting me back on the straight and narrow—the prodigal returning! I read bits from the letter you sent to me and which I still keep.[1]

A few years after I had returned home from the trial, I remember receiving somewhat of a confession letter from Dave. In the letter he told me he was a Christian, and though he had strayed from his faith in Christ, the whole time in Antigua he knew I was speaking truth. It had been many years since I'd had any contact with Dave, so the email from him was a glorious reminder of how God had used our tragedy to bring one of His sheep, which had strayed off the path, back into the flock.

I had never been more ready for a trip in my whole life. I thought back to a day a few months prior when Kimberly called and insisted a trip to Antigua was necessary for my book's success. I remember bristling at the thought, but not because I did not want to go back. All I could think about was the time it would add to finishing my book and how I had lost touch with everyone I knew there, not to mention the cost. All of it just overwhelmed me. Now, with less than twenty-four hours before my feet would be on Antiguan soil, I was physically, spiritually, and emotionally ready.

Physically, our clothes were ironed and packed, which is a rarity for me, since I'm usually throwing things into the suitcase at the eleventh hour before a trip.

Spiritually, a countless number of family and friends were covering us in prayer. I had asked the Lord to prepare Donnie and me for what we were about to encounter, and most significantly, I told Him I was willing to do *anything* He asked of me.

Emotionally I was anxious yet excited but striving to keep it all in check. I was nervous about seeing Donaldson again after having no contact for over ten years. I had to trust what I knew about him from years past, rather than fear the unknown. I was concerned that what I was going there to accomplish would only lead to more unanswered questions. I chose to trust God completely and knew that He would never lead me on a wild goose chase.

Yes, I was ready. *Let's go!*

We boarded the plane for Antigua at 5:15 a.m. Not knowing for sure if we would have Internet service once we got there, I made my last post on Facebook as soon as I was seated:

My Donnie and I are off to Antigua—the place where it all happened, the place where my parents were killed, and the place where my life changed forever! Going to refresh faded memories and reconnect with those I met there. Doors on the plane are shut. Cell phones off. Up, up, and away—we are off on a big God adventure!

chapterTwenty-Nine

Back to Where It All Began

$\mathcal{D}$onnie hates the middle seat on planes. Who doesn't? But as I knew we were about to come into view of the beautiful Island of Antigua, it was time for Donnie to give up the window seat. Willingly, he obliged.

There it was! I couldn't believe my eyes. I almost had to pinch myself to believe I had actually made it back. I wasn't sure what direction we were flying in from until I saw it. I was amazed at how familiar the island was to me. I knew immediately we had come in from the northeast when I saw Dickenson Bay, which had been my home away from home in 1996. It continued to puzzle me how the one place on earth that I should detest had become a place I longed to be. I had come to love this place for so many reasons, and the emotions running through me as I looked out at the island reminded me of what it feels like to "come home."

When we landed, I barely recognized the airport. It looked as if the *Extreme Home Makeover* team had paid the Island of Antigua a visit. No more foam green pigeon-holed concrete walls for this airport. They were now enclosed to accommodate air conditioning and had been painted a light terra cotta color. It was much larger than before, and the most impressive change was the process of getting through customs. Friendly greeters nicely dressed in uniforms were there to assist travelers through customs and answer any questions they might have. The whole process was a breeze; we had our luggage packed in a taxi and were on our way to the Halcyon in less than an hour.

As we journeyed by taxi to our hotel, I admit I felt I had lost all familiarity of the island. I did not recognize anything until we arrived at the Halcyon and pulled up to the security gate. I remembered the little one-man security shack and the heavy iron gate, which is more like a big arm that stretches across the road. In order to raise and lower it, the well-dressed guard had to put his whole body weight into it, crumpling his uniform as he created sweat beads on his brow.

As we drove down the hill leading to the main entrance of the Halcyon Cove Hotel, it all came back to me. We walked inside the open-air lobby to the reception desk where we were greeted by Normalyn. The beautiful, sweet woman immediately welcomed us and familiarized us with the hotel and the week's planned activities. Her smile warmed the room, and her eyes were kind and caring; I knew instantly I was going to love her. I must have asked Normalyn a hundred questions that first day. She never once seemed a bit bothered; she made me feel at peace, which was just what I needed.

A Shocking Call

I wanted to call John the second I arrived, but remembering to keep my excitement in check, I chose to get completely settled into our room before I rang him.

Our room was in the absolute perfect poolside location, right next to where I had been sandwiched between my British brothers. The minute I walked into the room, that wonderful familiar smell hit my nostrils, and I just stood there breathing it in. I was back. Yes, I was back, and at that moment I was certain I was standing in the center of God's will.

We unpacked, took a short stroll around the grounds, and did a little reminiscing about The Boys, who were definitely going to be thought of and greatly missed on this trip. I left Donnie *suffering* on the beach, soaking up the sun and relaxing, while I slipped away to call John.

I had to make the call from the lobby, because all the room phones were out of service and would not be repaired until later in the day. Ideally, I would have liked a little more privacy for this call that I was anxious to make, but that wasn't an option. John answered on the third ring.

"Hi, John, this is Bonnie."

Without hesitation, he replied, "Well, you certainly didn't waste any time calling."

"You said for me to call you after we got settled here at the Halcyon, and that's exactly what I did," I smiled as I answered.

"So what are your plans for your stay here on the island?" he asked.

As I stood there, leaning against the reception desk, I immediately became frustrated with having to strain to hear him over the lobby noise, I thought, *Are you kidding me, John? Did you read my email? Did you pay attention when we talked on the phone? I have made no plans; I am counting on you to help me make them!*

"I was hoping you were going to help me with that."

"Yes, well I was at the prison yesterday, and I saw Mel. I told him you were on the island and wanted to see him, and he said he wants to meet with you."

At that moment my mind went in six different directions, and thoughts were swirling in my head. Mel? Who's Mel? Oh, Donaldson must still be in prison . . . *Mel? Why is he calling Donaldson "Mel"?* I began to slowly pronounce his whole name in sections *Don–nald–son Sam–u–el,* trying desperately to get Mel out of his name. It wasn't happening, so I said, "Who's Mel?"

Matter-of-factly, as if I should know who he was talking about, John said, "Mel. Melanson Harris. When I was at the prison yesterday, I saw him. I told him the daughter of the American couple on the boat was here and that you wanted to see him."

"*Wait! What? Who?* Melanson? I thought he was dead! Didn't those men hang?" My head was spinning. I couldn't have heard him correctly. The lobby noise was deafening, but when I looked out into the lobby, nobody was there.

"No, Bonnie, they were never hung. They are both still in prison. There was a spoke put in the wheel, you might say, of capital punishment several years back. It caused a stay on all capital punishment throughout the Caribbean islands."

"Uh, okay, well, I didn't know anything about that 'spoke in the wheel,' but John, I didn't tell you I wanted to see *Melanson*. I came here to find *Donaldson*."

"Oh, yes! That's right! You did say you were looking for Donaldson, didn't you? I did locate him for you. He has served his sentence and is back on Barbuda. As for Mel, you certainly don't have to meet with him. You're the one driving this boat, not me!"

With a newfound clarity of mind, I said, "Yes, John, I am driving the boat, but that doesn't mean I may not turn the helm over to you every once in a while."

I knew without a doubt that the One who was ultimately at the helm of this trip back to Antigua was God, and if He so deemed for me to meet with Melanson, then that is exactly what I was going to do.

With that thought, and giving myself no time to question it, I said, "John, there has been so much prayer put into this trip that I am not going to refute anything immediately. If it is God's will for me to meet with Melanson, and since you have already made the arrangements for that to happen, then I am willing to go. Now for the main reason I have come to Antigua, what about my seeing Donaldson?"

John was no longer pondering my visit to Antigua. I believe he knew right then I had a purpose for this trip, and I was intent on making sure it happened.

Our conversation ended with the rest of our week perfectly planned out:

Wednesday: John would pick us up at the Halcyon to have dinner with him and his wife, Sarah.

Thursday: John would set a time for me to meet with Melanson at the prison.

Friday: We would go over to Barbuda to see Donaldson.

I walked away from the lobby feeling confident for about two minutes about the plans we had just made, and then reality set in. The thought of going to meet with Melanson brought fear and uncertainty, but the thought of going to see Donaldson again after so many years brought peace and excitement. Could any two thoughts be more conflicting? The gamut of emotions I was being hit with was overwhelming. All I really wanted to do was reason this out and decide what wisdom was telling me.

Donnie looked up with anticipation and hesitation. I began to tell him all that had transpired between John and me. It was actually difficult for me to repeat to Donnie all that I just heard as I was still having a hard time fully comprehending it myself! After a long pause, he looked at me and said, "I don't think I ever truly believed they were dead." He paused again and then much to my amazement said, "As for Melanson, if this is what God has set forth for us to do, then we'll do it, but we will just let that one play out on its own."

I fully expected a completely different reaction, but I could not have been more wrong. I realized then that Donnie had purposed in his heart not to be a hindrance and not to allow his feelings and emotions to get in the way of whatever God had sent us there to do, even if what He was asking of us went far beyond what we could have imagined.

I was absolutely dying to call Kimberly, my trusted friend who had lived all of this with me over the years, but I wanted to wait until the phone in our room was working. Donnie and I decided to take a walk on our old familiar beach to watch the sun set. It was as breathtaking as the first time

I had experienced a Caribbean sunset—absolutely beautiful! Afterward we headed to the Arawack Terrace for our first dinner back at the Halcyon.

I love Caribbean food. Oh, who am I kidding? I love all food, but when a food's taste and smell brings back memories, it makes the meal all the better. I was especially looking forward to topping the meal off with some of my favorite liquid fire, Susie's Hot Sauce—*kapow!*

After dinner we stopped by the reception desk to confirm that the room phones were indeed repaired and working. Instead we received the cold, hard reminder that we were in a third-world country, and no matter how nice, angry, or persistent you became, things were done in their time, not yours. The room phones would not be working until the following afternoon. That meant I would be making the call from the reception desk again, except by that time "Karaoke Night" was in full swing at the lobby cocktail lounge—a chaotic backdrop to a phone call I was desperate to make.

Normalyn was more than accommodating in helping me make the call to Kimberly. I was disappointed when I heard her sweet voice in a recorded message instead of in person. I sighed, my heart desperately wanting to connect with my friend.

When we left for Antigua, I was uncertain what our Internet capabilities would be once we got there. Much to my delight, we found that we had full access and online privileges.

I decided to log on to my Facebook account to see if anyone had responded to my last post before leaving the United States. I was amazed to see how many people were praying for and encouraging me online. Suddenly an instant message from Kim's oldest daughter, Johannah, popped up on my screen.

"Hi, Auntie Bonnie! Are you and Uncle Donnie safe in Antigua?"

I typed furiously to let her know I desperately needed to speak with her mom. Immediately she was on a mission to make the connection happen, and that she did! We messaged back and forth at lightning speed.

"I found Mom. What do I tell her to do?"

"Tell her to call the Halcyon ASAP!" as I typed out the phone number and waited for her response.

"She's calling and can't get through! Now what, Auntie Bonnie?"

"Tell her I'll try calling her again!"

Finally I heard my friend's voice on the other end of the phone. Peace washed over me. *Now if I can only hear her over the hideous sounding wannabes singing karaoke in the bar.*

I have to say, Kimberly Noelle is the more conservative one in our friendship. She is quieter and more reserved; I am boisterous and demonstrative. Consequently I was surprised by her enthusiastic and excited reaction to the arrangements made for me to see Melanson instead of Donaldson; this spoke volumes of encouragement to me. She said,

> Of course you need to go see him, this has God written all over it! I know this is not what you expected, and you don't think you're prepared for this, but Bon, you are! I wish I could be with you right now, but I am here for you, and you are not walking through any of this alone. Donnie is right by your side, I am only a phone call away, and as soon as we hang up, I'll be making a bunch of calls to let everyone know so they can pray. You can do this! God has prepared you for such a time as this, Bon!

A Tree House Dinner

Donnie and I were up early the next morning, excited to go to the Fullers' for dinner that evening. We decided to take our daily quiet time with the Lord down to the beach. So, after a great breakfast at the Arawack Terrace, we were beach-bound with our Bibles. I just knew God was going to speak to me as I spent time in His Word that day. I was definitely looking for His direction in this face-to-face meeting with Melanson, especially knowing that I was going to Barbuda to find Donaldson on Friday.

As I sat on the beach that morning, I opened my Bible to scan through it, stopping here and there, reading and meditating on several different passages. Donnie was next to me reading as well, and after what seemed to be a short time he looked over at me and said, "Babe, can I read something to you?" He sat up in his lounge chair and began to read. As he did I sat up in my lounge chair astounded. *My God never fails me!*

The words Donnie read penetrated my mind and my soul as I heard the Lord speak loud and clear:

> Seek the LORD while He may be found,
> Call upon Him while He is near.
> Let the wicked forsake his way,
> And the unrighteous man his thoughts;
> Let him return to the LORD,
> And He will have mercy on him;
> And to our God,
> For He will abundantly pardon.
>
> "For My thoughts are not your thoughts,
> Nor are your ways My ways," says the LORD.
> "For as the heavens are higher than the earth,
> So are My ways higher than your ways,
> And My thoughts than your thoughts." (Isaiah 55:6–9)

"For He will abundantly pardon. For My thoughts are not your thoughts, nor My ways your ways" Are you kidding me? Could there be another passage in the entire Bible more perfect for us today than this one?

There are no coincidences with God, and there is no way Donnie "just happened" to turn to that passage. We both desperately needed to hear from the Lord that morning, and He faithfully responded to our need.

God had abundantly pardoned Donaldson, and going to the prison to see Melanson was definitely *not* our thought or our way. We both knew now beyond a shadow of a doubt that this was no mistake. *This has God written all over it!* I sat satisfied with the message God had given us; it filled my day with contentment. I was ready to do whatever He asked of me.

To say we were both looking forward to dinner with John and Sarah that evening would be an understatement. When John pulled up to the Halcyon, I knew immediately it was him. He looked great, and other than just a few more wrinkles, he was as handsome as ever. We sat in the open lobby catching up for a bit before we headed to the Fuller tree house. John first wanted to tell me he had contacted Johnny DeSouza on Barbuda so he could meet us Friday to see Donaldson. I was thrilled with that news and assumingly asked, "So Donaldson wants to see me?"

"Well, I have no idea, I haven't talked to him, but of course he'll see you. Why wouldn't he?"

Did he just ask me why wouldn't he? I could rattle off about twenty reasons from the top of my head why he wouldn't want to meet with me! His letters had stopped coming ten years ago! There must be a reason he quit wanting to have contact with me.

I calmly replied, "Great! I'll make the arrangements first thing tomorrow to get over to Barbuda on Friday."

"Yes, do that," John said, and then proceeded to tell me he had confirmed my going to the prison to see Melanson for the next day at two o'clock in the afternoon.

I was eager to find out about the illness that had taken John out of the office for a few weeks. He threw his hand around in the air as if to brush me off when I questioned him. This hand gesture was one I had become very familiar with back in 1996; he always responded that way when I asked questions in regard to the trial he didn't think I should know or when I made references about the Lord. I knew all too well he did not want to talk about it, and that concerned me.

With a little persistence John finally opened up and let us know that he had been one very sick man; it was his heart. Not only did he suffer from a heart attack, but when the doctor on a neighboring island attempted to put a stent in, there were complications, and John's heart began to fail. The procedure was aborted, and John was airlifted to a hospital in Florida where they saved his life.

By looking at John we would have never known he had come so close to dying just weeks before. Once again God was showing me that He was the One at the helm of the trip. We had originally planned our trip to Antigua for September but some unforeseen plans had forced us to change the date. If we had come in September, John would have been in a hospital in Florida. It had become evident in just one short day on the island how very much we needed John to make this trip a success by accomplishing all we set out to do.

To say I love the Fullers' house would be a huge understatement. The Bible refers to there being mansions in heaven; I believe my mansion is going to look a whole lot like that tree house. Now I fully realize the location of this house is in the Caribbean, and building something like it in Texas would not be prudent. However, when we get to heaven, the weather will be perfect every day forever. So a tree house mansion would be a most appropriate structure to hope for in the kingdom of heaven!

Sarah Fuller is one of the loveliest ladies you will ever encounter. She is beautiful inside and out. What I love about Sarah is how she loves John. You can see it in her eyes, and you can hear it in her voice. I had not seen Sarah for almost fifteen years, yet when I walked into her home, I felt as though we were long lost friends. She was the easiest person to talk to, whether she was explaining to me the current state of political affairs on the island or talking with me about the Lord. I could have spent the rest of our trip with the Fullers and I never tired of that wonderful and kind lady.

John is equally as wonderful to me in a much different way. I have no doubt John Fuller cares a great deal about me, and I know for certain he loves his island. For those reasons he hated what happened to Dad, Mom, Criddy, and Tom, and for as long as I've known him he has longed to see justice served. I know John takes jabs at me quite a bit regarding my Christianity, but I also know he can quote more Scripture word for word than most devout Christians I know. Donnie and I have found him to be a loyal friend. We believe he would do absolutely anything for us, and he has. So regardless of how he comes across on the outside, God has shown me John through the filter of His eyes, and what I see is one amazing man.

Over dinner we discussed family, politics, religion, and of course why we had returned to Antigua. John reiterated to Donnie what he had said earlier to me about the visit to see Melanson the next day: "I say you go tomorrow and get the whole damn thing over with!"

To that My Donnie said, *"Amen!"*

I became far more apprehensive about the unexpected trip to the prison when I learned at dinner that Melanson didn't tell John he *wanted* to meet with me; he said he *would* meet with me. There is a huge difference in a person wanting to meet and a person who is willing to meet.

I kept going over in my mind, *Does this change anything? Does this mean I don't need to meet with him?*

I'd love to say that is exactly what it meant, but I know my Lord better than that. I prayed with everything for God to ordain my steps and to open and close doors. I was willing to do anything He asked of me. Because of that, I knew the exchange between John and Melanson could not be a mistake. Though the information could confuse my mind, I knew I was well covered, sheltered, and protected with prayer by so many; God would not allow me to be "set up."

One hesitation for me was that Melanson is a *halfwit*. That is the term they use around the islands to refer to a person whose "family tree doesn't fork." I learned that about him in the days of the trial. The fact that someone who is as dumb as a stick could overtake my father is something I have always had a very hard time comprehending.

How would I know if he was grasping what I would tell him, or if he even cared? What exactly would I say? What should I not say? Could I believe anything he said to me?

All I knew for certain was that God would be faithful to give me exactly what I would need, when I needed it.

Back to the Red Iron Door

The next day our newfound friend and taxi driver, Johnny Lake, took us to the prison. I knew we were getting close as I began to recognize local landmarks I remembered from years ago.

As we pulled up, my eyes locked onto the all-too-familiar thick, red iron door. Why they chose to paint it red I will never know, but red is certainly the appropriate color for a door that leads you in and out of that hellhole.

John arrived promptly at two o'clock, and we approached the iron door together. John reached up and gave the big brass knocker a hard rap. As was the custom, we stood staring into the eight-by-eight-inch horizontally barred cutout in the door waiting for a guard to slide it open. Finally the obscure door slid to the side, and the guard gruffly commanded, "State your name and your purpose." In annoyance John answered, "You know who I am; open the door!"

The female guard, clearly annoyed by John, slammed the little door shut and took her sweet time in opening the red iron door, proving just who was in charge there. With legs stationed a foot apart and arms firmly folded, she stood like a rock blocking the entrance. John proceeded to tell her that he had brought us to see Melanson and that he has permission from the superintendent to do so.

She looked him dead in the eye, with no hesitation, and said, "No!"

"Don't tell me no; do you know who I am?" John retorted.

She further explained her answer in relaying to John that the superintendent was out sick, and she would need to check to see if he left orders to let us enter. She then moved to shut the door in front of John. However, before she could even step back to slam the door, John reached in and swiftly moved her aside; he had made his way inside the prison. Before she could get the door shut, John looked back and said to us, "Hold tight."

We stood waiting at the crimson iron door for what seemed to be an hour, but was probably only twenty minutes. When it finally opened, John stepped out, and with a very satisfied look on the female guard's face, she slammed the door shut. The look on John's face said everything; they were not going to let us enter. John asked me if I wanted to try again on a different day. I knew if I hesitated at all he'd pull the plug, so I quickly answered, "Yes, sir! If you're willing to try again, than so am I."

It was decided to make the next attempt on Saturday, since the next day we were scheduled to visit Barbuda.

chapter Thirty

The Reunion

$\mathcal{W}$hen I attempted to make reservations on the Barbuda Express, I was told two things. One, reservations were not necessary; you just show up at St. John's Harbour and buy the tickets the morning of departure. Two, the boat departed at 8:30 a.m. As it turned out neither was true. The boat departed at 9:15 a.m., and on that particular day reservations were most definitely needed. Because we had arrived so early for the 8:30 departure, we were the first in line, and it was a good thing we were.

Ivonne, the ticket saleswoman, told us it was unlikely we would make it on the Express that day, because a large group of forty young children were taking a trip to Barbuda. My heart sank.

I was as nervous as a cat on a hot tin roof, praying, hoping, begging God to make a way for us to be among the passengers. When I was about to have a nervous breakdown from worry, I realized I had done all I could to find favor with Ivonne, and the trip was in God's hands. All I could do from there was keep praying that His will would be done, stop worrying, and leave it to Him.

Finally, I saw Ivonne writing our names on the manifest, and I knew we had made it. Within a few minutes, we received our tattered, recycled boarding passes, and we wasted no time climbing aboard.

Donnie wanted to sit where the seating was padded, which happened to be in the middle of the boat. I emphatically opposed. Since I had been a little girl, my favorite place on any boat was the bow, and I was headed straight to it. I claimed my spot on the bench that backed up to the bow. Above the bench seat was a wide ledge with a big open window. I knew I wanted to get up there and sit right in that window with my face to the wind, just as I had done as a child. I had to play it right though and be careful. If I climbed up there too soon, I would surely attract the attention of the forty youngsters onboard, and they would start climbing to sit there with me, and that would blow my opportunity for certain.

When we were just outside the harbor, one of the deckhands came through the window and looked down at me. I asked in the nicest way I could, "Are ya going to let me ride up there?"

His reply, "You gonna fall out?"

With extreme confidence and a wink I said, "Of course not!"

As I climbed up on the ledge and up to the window, the sea air hit my face, and I took in the deepest breath I could. I slowly let it out and then literally got lost in my thoughts.

I could hardly control my excitement of seeing Donaldson again. *What will it be like? Will he want to see me? What will we say?* Then the anticipation turned to a sick feeling of guilt. *This is so weird, to be this eager to see the one who bound and gagged Dad and Mom.*

But no matter what I told myself, I could not keep the excitement from welling up. My head was reeling with questions and concerns. *Will Johnny DeSouza be there to meet us? What on earth will we do if he isn't?*

The Reunion

Barbuda

I remembered that when the boat pulled up to the dock, there were no buildings, no taxis, nothing. If our prearranged transportation did not come, we were sunk. Johnny was to be waiting for us, and we were counting on him.

My erratic thoughts continued. *What if Johnny is there, but he wasn't able to find Donaldson?* That would be highly unlikely on that small, remote island, but yes, I went there in my mind.

What if he did find Donaldson, but he doesn't want to see me? What if Donaldson's heart has hardened toward God after so many years in prison? What if too much time has passed with no communication, and we don't really have the friendship I thought we had? Had I told my story over and over so many times, and made more of it than what was really there?

Donnie walked over to check on me, and I tried to convey the fury of thoughts racing through my mind. He carefully cautioned me not to set myself up for disappointment. His concern was that this visit might not hold the same magnitude for Donaldson as it did for us. He reminded me that through our ministry we keep the memory of my friendship with Donaldson fresh in our minds. What happened years ago might be just a faded memory to him.

As we pulled up to the worn, hurricane-battered dock, I scanned the road that ran behind the dock where the prearranged transportation generally stood waiting. No Johnny. Donnie asked, "Baby, are you sure he's not one of those standing on the road?"

Oh yes, I was most certain; I remembered exactly what he looked like. He was tall and thin, with a somewhat distinguished look, which was a rarity in Barbuda. From where I stood all I saw was a short, big-bellied man, a beach bum tour guide with dreadlocks, and a few taxi drivers, but no Johnny.

Just then, out from behind an old, large fishing boat strolled Johnny DeSouza. I noticed him scanning the boat for me. I was much easier to spot, since Donnie and I, along with two guys from Colorado, were the only white Americans onboard. I wanted to wave furiously at him but refrained. However I almost wiped out several other passengers as I disembarked. Once I reached the dock, I slowed my pace so as not to overwhelm our old friend.

Like most Antiguans and Barbudans, Johnny was low key, not easily excited or prone to show outward emotion. Someone as gregarious as I am often makes those with that type of inconspicuous personality take a step back. As I walked over to him, I casually asked, "Johnny?"

With a nod he replied, "Yes, ma'am."

"Do you remember me?" I asked.

"Yes, yes, of course I do."

"How have you been, Johnny?"

"Doing well, had some ups and downs with my health, but I'm fine now."

I really did care a great deal about how Johnny was doing, but I have to admit that all I wanted to do was blurt out the question that was burning inside me.

"Johnny, did you find Donaldson?"

"Yes, yes, I did."

"Well, does he want to see me?"

"Yes, yes, he said he did."

"Okay, great, when?" I asked calmly, holding back my enthusiasm.

"I'm taking you to him now. He's waiting for you."

Ahhh! I screamed within my head.

A Revelation

Johnny was employed by Codrington Lagoon National Park and drove a very nice truck, for which we were thankful. We had ridden on those primitive island dirt roads one too many times in vehicles that made the ride that much more tumultuous. This time the dirt roads of Barbuda were somewhat more tolerable. As we drove we talked about Donaldson.

Johnny told us he was doing well and had been in no trouble since getting out of prison. He was working for his cousin who owned K. B. Supplies, a construction supply business. His cousin gave him the second chance he desperately needed after getting out of prison. It wasn't until later that I realized how much of a second chance Donaldson really needed.

I asked him if he knew anything about Melanson, and he shared more with us than anyone else ever had. He said, "Mel wasn't a bad boy growing up, but when he was teenager he left the island to live with family in New York. He set out to get an education and make a better life for himself than the island could offer him. Unfortunately the exact opposite occurred; Melanson got involved with gangs and drugs and eventually found himself in trouble with the law. Before he was convicted of the crimes he committed, he was extradited back to Barbuda. With his return he brought back all he had *learned* while on the streets of New York."

I asked him this question, "Johnny, Mel is slow in the mind, yes?"

"Yes, yes he is."

"Was he always that way? I mean before New York and the drugs?"

"No, he seemed to be a normal kid. It was the smoking marijuana and the drugs that messed up his mind. I heard he's preachin' in the jail now. He found Jesus."

I almost broke my neck turning around to the backseat to see the look on Donnie's face. I really don't think shock and awe would be an understatement. I could not believe my ears.

"We're here," Johnny said.

When we pulled up to the business, I noticed right away that it was a well-kept place that spanned quite a bit of land. Several white buildings were scattered over the property, one of which appeared to be someone's home.

Johnny hit the horn with three quick honks, and we waited. No one appeared and my blood pressure started to rise again. Johnny pulled down the road a bit and hit the horn a second time. Again we waited. Finally, from around one of the smaller white buildings close to the road appeared a man about Donaldson's height but much thinner, wearing a bright yellow T-shirt, khaki pants, and clear safety glasses.

Johnny said in a quiet voice, "That's Donaldson."

I looked directly into his eyes as he approached the truck, and I knew at once it was Donaldson. I remembered his jaw line to be fuller and squarer, but it was him. Yes, indeed, Donaldson was once again standing right before my eyes! What do I do now?

I called out from inside the truck, "Donaldson?"

And he replied in his deep voice, "Yes, Bonnie, it's me."

I fumbled with the door handle and couldn't exit that truck fast enough. We stood there, not more than three feet apart, together again after so many years. Not a word was spoken, but when I made the slightest move, he reached forward with both arms outstretched cautiously offering me a hug. I reciprocated. At that moment all my doubts, fears, and concerns were washed away. At one point he pulled back, looked at me, and said, "Why you stop writing me, Bonnie?"

In disbelief I replied, "Oh Donaldson, I didn't stop writing you; you stopped writing me!"

"No, ma'am, I kept writing you, and when no letters came from you, I stop writing too."

I thought my heart would break right then and there. We spent the next few moments thinking through how the letters ceased being delivered on both ends. We finally concluded that it all tied into Superintendent Mac's retirement. Without him in that position, we no longer had an advocate within the Antigua prison system. However none of that mattered now because there we were standing together. The past was the past, and we had found each other again. This time we did not have to depend on or go through a prison to stay connected.

For the first few minutes Donaldson and I were engrossed in our conversation, even though both of us were very aware of Donnie standing less than a foot away. The best way to describe My Donnie at that moment would be to visualize him with a line drawn right down the middle of his body. One half represented my bodyguard, and the other half represented a man who was taken in by the moment, having completely dropped his guard.

Donaldson turned to Donnie, reached out with his right hand and said, "Mr. Don, how are you?"

At that point I was praying that the tender side of Don Floyd would shine through. Without hesitation Donnie reached out his hand to accept Donaldson's handshake. Donaldson cautiously leaned his right shoulder in for one of those man-type hugs, and to my relief, Donnie responded positively. I could not help but think at that moment that it was all so much more than Donnie bargained for when he signed up to marry me.

We had a lot to catch up on. When I explained to Donaldson about my book, he seemed to be genuinely pleased that my story would be told and was willing to help me in any way he could. Donaldson invited us to the porch that was attached to the outside of his cousin's house. He quickly dusted off and pulled up white plastic chairs for us to sit; and thus began our much-needed visit.

I began with the first question I had planned to ask him. I had imagined that day a hundred times. I knew precisely every question I wanted to ask him and the order in which I would ask them. I still could not believe I was sitting there with him, my heart so full of joy, peace, and contentment.

"Donaldson, what was it like for you in prison, and how did you hold up in there?"

"It was okay. I did what I was supposed to do, I made no trouble, and I served my time."

"When did you get out?"

Without one bit of hesitation, as though it happened yesterday, he answered, "February 27, 2009. I was twenty-three when I went in, and today I am thirty-eight." He didn't expound on that fact, but we clearly read between the lines; essentially, he had lost fifteen years of his life in prison.

Donaldson seemed to know his dates. They had become very important to him, and he remembered them vividly.

I remembered during the trial the day Donaldson had become so upset and told Melanson's lawyer, "Stop confusing me! I know days. I don't know dates!"

It was good to see that he had become more self-assured.

"So how are you doing now, and how is your walk with Jesus?"

"I'm doing good now, but when I got out of prison it was difficult. My family had much shame and was hard on me. I couldn't take it no more, so I left Barbuda and took the boat back to Antigua."

I could see it was hard for him to talk about his past and those hard days of shame. He wanted to change the subject, and when he did, he looked up at me, no longer downcast from his thoughts of the past, but with excitement, to tell me something personal he was proud of. It reminded me of when I met him for the first time. At the end of that first encounter, he looked up at me with excitement and proclaimed, "I know how to write!"

This time his announcement was not much different, but another way for us to connect. He proudly stated, "I make music, Bonnie!"

"You do?"

"Yes, I write songs about my life and about God. I wrote a song called 'God Is Watching.' I know you would like it. I made music and wrote songs in prison. When I went back to Antigua after prison, I go there to make my music. I made a CD."

"You have a CD! May I have one?"

"Yes, yes, I'll give you more than one. Some people say my music no good, not Christian."

"Well, why would they say that? Do you say bad words?"

"No, no, nothin' like that. People say my music too harsh."

After more questions about his music, it was Donnie who realized what he was trying to tell me that I just was not getting. It was not the words or content, it was the actual music. The music Donaldson had written was rap! Religious people on Barbuda are very traditional, and rap music was certainly not acceptable to them.

We shared with him that our church at home, Genesis Metro Church, worshiped with a full band, complete with lead and rhythm guitars, bass guitar, keyboard, and drums. Donnie told him, "There are many people who don't like it and think it is wrong to have a full band at church, but we love it! As long as your content glorifies the Lord, don't let anyone tell you it's wrong or that it's not Christian."

Scan this code for informa-tion on Genesis Metro Church

He understood what Donnie was telling him, and he really liked the idea that we rocked out in worship at our church.

"Donaldson, can I write you now that you are here on Barbuda?"

"Yes, yes, and you can call me too!"

"Really?"

"Yes." And with that familiar proud announcement look on his face he declared, "I have a cell phone!" He quickly retrieved it from his front pocket and said, "I just got it, but I don't know to use it real good yet."

Donnie chuckled, saying, "Donaldson, I've had mine for a few years, and I still don't know how to use it real good."

I carefully considered all the mental notes I had made of questions I wanted to ask Donaldson. I realized I had asked him earlier about his walk with the Lord, but I never got an answer. I asked again and this time he answered; for the second time that day the man almost broke my heart.

"Well, Bonnie, not too good, not too good."

"Why?"

"Because of what I did, it makes me feel uncomfortable every day. Every day I feel bad for what I did, so I can't feel comfortable."

"Donaldson, when we first met, we talked a lot about Jesus."

"Yes, yes, we did."

"When we prayed that day, was that the first time you had asked Jesus into your heart?"

"Yes, ma'am, and I asked him before that to help me when I escape from the prison with the five guys. When we getting caught, the police had guns and grenades, and I called out to God to help me. A voice tell me to drop and roll, and I did, and it saved me. I believe that was God. I talk to God every day. I tell God every day I'm sorry for what I did. But I can't forget. I can't feel comfortable with it."

I said, "Donaldson, do you believe you are a Christian?"

"Yes, yes, I do, but I don't feel good."

"Why?"

"Because of what I did, I can't forget."

"Donaldson, if you have asked Jesus into your heart, then you can come to a place where you're able to feel forgiven every day. The Bible says in the book of Romans that if you confess with your mouth, 'Jesus is Lord,' and believe in your heart that God raised Him from the dead, you will be saved. Anyone who trusts in Him will never be put to shame. Never means never, Donaldson!

"The Bible also tells us that when we ask for forgiveness, our sins are as far removed as the east is from the west. Do you know what that means?"

Intently listening he replied, "Yes, forever."

"That's right, forever! Why then do you think you need to keep asking for forgiveness?"

"Because I don't feel comfortable about it, Bonnie. I can't stop asking every day. I have to keep asking for me to feel comfortable."

"Okay, I understand, I really do. So, if you feel you need to ask every day, then ask, but not because you don't think you're forgiven, because you are. It is important that you understand that. If you don't believe completely that you are forgiven, then in essence you are calling God a liar."

I knew then Donaldson needed to spend more time reading his Bible, and I committed in my heart to encourage him in that in the future.

"Bonnie, I can't believe you and Don are sitting here with me. When Johnny come by this morning, he ask if I remember you. I tell him yes, and he tell me you're coming to see me." Donaldson then raised his hand and pointed to the corner of his eye and said, "I got a tear right here."

I already knew by then he was as glad to see me as I was to see him, but that was God just putting the icing on my cake.

During our conversation he spoke often of his mother, but never his father, so I asked about him, and Donaldson told me his dad lived in the United States and had for some time. He could not remember in which state he lived, but he told us that he was a Christian and was about to be made a deacon at his church.

"Where does your mom live, Donaldson; is it far from here?"

"She lives right down the road."

"Is there a chance I would be able to meet her?"

"I'll take you to her."

"Oh, I would like that very much. What is her name?"

"Juliet Harris. She lives with my stepfather. He's a good man."

I asked him if his mother knew about me, or would it take some explaining, and he said, "Oh, she knows all about you coming to the prison to see me and the letters." He told me he still had every one of my letters and the books I sent him, and that they were at his house. I told him that I had saved all his letters as well, and at that he smiled.

I wanted him to know and understand I hadn't tired of writing him; I hadn't had a change of heart or given up on him.

"How long you stay, Bonnie?"

"We are on Barbuda only for today; we will return to Antigua on the boat this afternoon." I could see he was disappointed, but he chose to focus on the now, and I was relieved. The last thing I wanted was to disappoint him.

FINAL QUESTIONS, GOD'S ANSWERS

I went back through my mental list of questions and already knew there was only one question left I had not asked. My heart was pounding. *Am I ready for this? Do I really want to know? Is it right or fair for me to even ask him? I have to know.*

"Donaldson, can I ask you about that night on the boat?"

Looking down at the ground, he said, "I don't like to talk about that night, Bonnie, but I will deny you nothing. What you want to know?"

"Did my dad say anything?"

"No, not much; he was a thinking man."

Yes, he certainly was a "thinking man" . . . I've never described him that way, but what a perfect description of him.

I'd asked the question, it was out there, and I wanted to pry him open like a can. Even if Dad didn't say much, I wanted to know each word that came out of his mouth, but I felt I was to leave it alone. What I could not leave alone, however, was what I asked him next. It was clear throughout the trial that Donaldson never pulled the trigger or even held the shotgun. All through the depositions and the trial Marvin had consistently denied having anything to do with the murders at all. Melanson habitually lied, changing his story every time he opened his mouth.

I so badly wanted the full, honest story. I wanted to know what happened, how it happened, and the order of events as they unfolded on the boat.

When I had met with Donaldson back in 1996 and 1997, it never occurred to me to ask those questions. During those visits all God had put on my heart was his soul and his salvation—period. But this time it was very different; I knew this time I would not leave until I knew the truth of what happened that dreadful night.

"What happened when my dad got away?"

He just looked at me and said not a word.

"Did he get far?"

"No, ma'am, he did not get too far."

I wanted details, and Donaldson wasn't offering them.

"Who caught him, Donaldson, do you remember?" I probed.

"Yes, I remember. It was Melanson. Your dad got his hands loose."

I looked over at Donnie, and I could tell, though he wanted to know as well, he thought I was pushing him too hard.

When I looked back at Donaldson, I saw the pain in his face that my questions were causing him; I also saw compassion. The compassion was for me, and I knew I needed to stop.

This is not what you came here for, Bonnie. I heard the Lord speak loud and clear.

There was just one more question I had to ask. One more thing I thought I absolutely needed to know.

"Donaldson, who killed my parents?"

He looked up at me with eyes asking why I wanted to know that and then lowered them slowly to the ground. The words trailed out, and he began retelling the events of that evening.

"I was up on deck and heard the gunfire. When I heard it, I thought, *No, we're not supposed to shoot no one.* I climbed down below. Marvin had shot the young one [Tom]. I yelled, 'Why you shoot the gun?'

"Marvin looked at me, said, 'No witnesses.'

"Then Marvin handed me the shotgun and yell at me to do the same, I tell Marvin, 'No! I shoot no one. You said we shoot no one.'"

Donaldson struggled telling me the first part, and as he went on, he became almost inaudible, but I heard him. He told me that Marvin handed Melanson the gun, and he aimed at my precious mom. She was praying, calling on the name of Jesus, and as her Catholic faith had taught her, she was crossing herself when Melanson pulled the trigger. My dad, who I deeply loved as no other, took the next bullet to the chest. The last to go down was Criddy, their captain.

There it was, I knew for certain how it all went down. I had waited fifteen years for that information. It did not make me feel any better or any worse. I thought I needed it for closure, but I already had closure. God had given me the peace I needed many years ago. And once peace invades your heart, perfect healing occurs. I had perfect peace in my spirit; it was just my flesh crying out for something that does not satisfy.

Looking back, I realized for the first time I had asked every question I had in my mind to ask, but in the end God controlled the answers I received. He knew what I could handle, and He knew what I couldn't. I'll never know the last few words my dad spoke that night, and I'll never ask that question again. I know my Lord, and I know He knows what's best for me. If it were His will for me to know my dad's final words, I have no doubt Donaldson would have told me.

Here is what I do know. I do not doubt my father's salvation; God showed me the day I walked out into the waters of Low Bay. I stood in those waves shaking my fist in the air at my dad, telling him he had better have kept his promise to me. God strongly reminded me in those gut-wrenching moments that my dad's promise meant absolutely nothing if my Father in heaven didn't keep His. The Bible clearly promises, "All who call upon the name of the Lord God will be saved" (Acts 2:21 NIV). And I stand in that; I believe it, I trust it.

Meeting Donaldson's Mother

The intensity of the conversation slowly became easier, and we decided it was time to go down the road to see Juliet, but not before we stopped to capture a few moments on camera. It was a gorgeous day on Barbuda. The sun was brightly shining down on us, and the sky could not have been any bluer than it was. Donaldson wanted Donnie to take our picture together with his landscape creations as the backdrop for the photo. We stood in front of a beautiful flowerbed that Donaldson had built.

He draped his long arm around my shoulders, and there we stood together, waving at the camera. It had been thirteen years and nine months since we had last seen each other, and nothing had changed between us. But just as the words of the old saying go, "Absence makes the heart grow fonder," and my heart was swelling. I was continually amazed and reminded that God's ways are not our ways, and He truly works in mysterious ways.

There was a freedom with this visit that was different from the other two; I contemplated why and realized I was talking to a free man. Jesus paid, on the cross, the ultimate price for Donaldson's sins, and he had accepted Christ's love. He was spiritually free. And now he was a man who had paid his debt to society and the worldly penalty for his sin, so he was physically free as well. Donaldson was no longer the man who bound and gagged my parents; he was now my forgiven brother in Christ.

I had wanted to walk with Donaldson to meet his mother, but Johnny would have no part of that. He was driving us, mostly because John Fuller asked him to take care of us, and that's exactly what this honorable man intended to do. As we took the short drive to Juliet's house, Johnny told us he had made arrangements for a boat to take us over to Low Bay. I was humbled by Johnny's commitment to meet our every need.

We pulled up to Juliet's house, and Donaldson jumped out of the truck, opening my door for me before Johnny came to a full stop. You could see the excitement on his face as he stretched his hand out toward his mom's house. The house was painted a very bright yellow. I noticed the front door and all the windows had wooden, working shutters—a stark reminder that hurricanes are a serious threat to that little island. Only ten named storms have actually hit or brushed Barbuda in the last sixty years, but it had been just two months since Hurricane Earl came through and left his devastating mark on the newly built luxury hotel on the beach of Low Bay. Surprisingly the rest of the island weathered out Earl with little damage.

Donaldson led the way up onto the porch, and an older man dressed in a white T-shirt and a green baseball cap came to the door. Before a word could be spoken, a tall woman in a bright, white sundress trimmed with gold piping appeared just inside the doorway. Her head was crowned with an adorable wide brimmed straw hat, and when Donaldson introduced me, her face lit up in disbelief.

Meeting Juliet was important, because when Donaldson told me of the shame he had brought on her and the rest of his family, I wanted her to see for herself that I had truly forgiven Donaldson.

It was apparent within just a few minutes that Juliet knew Jesus. She could quote the Bible like nobody's business. The scriptures she rattled off were all on the subject of forgiveness. She was stunned that we had traveled all the way to Barbuda from the States just to see her son. She said Donaldson had told her all about me and that he showed her the letters. She never came right out and said it, but I knew she had her doubts about me. She wondered if I had really forgiven her son, or maybe I had changed my mind. If I was for real, why did I stop writing for ten years?

All I hoped for was that this unexpected visitor standing on her porch would refresh her faith in Jesus and bring complete reconciliation to the relationship between her and her son. We spent the next hour visiting with this sweet woman. I could sense through our short time with Juliet that she was a genuine person and had passed much of her character on to her son.

We posed for another photo before saying our good-byes, and Donaldson said something that caught my attention, "Yes, yes, let's take a family picture together." I thought about it for a minute and then dismissed it. Surely he wasn't indicating me as *family*.

It wasn't until we headed back to the truck that I realized Johnny never got out; nor had he when we were with Donaldson. I felt a twinge of guilt for walking away from the truck and forgetting all about him, but he didn't. He was perfectly happy to serve us in any way he could, and we were grateful.

Donaldson went back to work while we made our visit to Low Bay, planning to meet with him once more upon returning.

The Reunion

BACK TO LOW BAY

When we pulled up to the lagoon there was a man named Pat Richardson waiting to take us over to Low Bay. He had a fiberglass utility boat with a good-sized outboard on it, so we made it across the lagoon in no time. Pat was another friendly islander who was more than happy to interrupt his day to take us across the lagoon. He spoke to us about the *Challenger* murders and that he vividly remembered the details of those days. He reiterated, as we had heard many times before, that the tragedy had brought much shame to his island for many years.

Pat also told wonderful stories about the lagoon and the days before the luxury hotel, Lighthouse Bay, moved in and bought the peninsula. The peninsula is a very narrow strip of land that separates the lagoon from Low Bay and the Caribbean Sea. The lagoon, to our surprise, is only eight feet at its deepest point. Lobster diving was a popular hunting sport at one time, and once they had the lobsters, the divers would row over to Low Bay and barbeque right there on the beach. Pat's tales made the tropical locale come alive as we envisioned its lively history. My mind totally went there and imagined cutting that live lobster in half and laying it on the grill and watching it sizzle to mouthwatering perfection. *I wonder if they had butter?*

We pulled up to a small dock that was next to a long, beautifully constructed, covered pier. Pat jumped onto the dock and spoke to the attendant from the resort who was on guard that day. He granted us permission to roam the beach and take pictures as long as we kept the hurricane-damaged hotel out of the photos. We were delighted he was so accommodating.

Before we knew it we were shaking the welcoming hand of Mo Sallah, the general manager of Lighthouse Bay Resort. Mo was not familiar with the *Challenger* murders and was not thrilled to hear about them. A story such as that was not good press. I assured him that my heart was to tell the story of a beautiful place where, unfortunately, something very bad and unusual had happened.

Unlike Johnny, Pat stuck pretty close to us but gave me space when he sensed I needed it. I stood on the sands of Low Bay once again, this time with My Donnie by my side. He was as awestruck by the natural beauty of the beach and bay as anyone is the first time they see it. Even with the secluded resort erected there, the tranquil beauty had been extremely well preserved.

The sand was whiter than I remembered, with only a hint of pink. When I mentioned that to Pat, he said it was because of the storm surge from the hurricane. He assured me that in a matter of time the beach would return to its natural pink luster.

I wondered how I would feel this time compared to when I was here with the Williamses. I was less emotional, and the sea did not beckon me, but it still mesmerized me. All I wanted to do was stare out into the bay where *Challenger* had been moored in the soft waves and look around at what they saw that day. I wanted to take in the peace and serenity they must have felt in that glorious location. They lived their last day on earth doing the very thing they both loved the most. Mom said it herself in the last journal she ever wrote, "Oh, to be sailing again!"

I really miss them. I thought about how I would love for God to allow Dad to appear on the beach right at that moment and let us spend just five minutes together. In a split second everything I wanted to tell him about the last sixteen years flashed before my eyes, and I knew five minutes would never be enough time. I reconsidered what I would say to him if given five minutes now, and it was simple. All I wanted to do was look into his familiar beautiful blue eyes—the same blue eyes I see every time I look into the mirror—hold his hands, and tell him how very much I still loved him. And then I would ask him what it was like to know Jesus face to face.

New Meaning to Family

When we reached the dock back across the lagoon, our faithful friend Johnny was waiting to take us back to Donaldson. We said good-bye to Pat, and we headed back.

When we arrived back at K. B. Supply where Donaldson worked, he was excitedly waiting for us outside. I jumped out of the truck and followed him as he motioned me into the office. We walked through the door and over to the front desk where Donaldson called out, "Come, Thomas, you must come and meet my family!" I stood there stunned. There was no dismissing it this time, he had said it again—*family.* "You must come and meet my family."

Thomas is Donaldson's cousin, who also works at K. B. Supply, and when he came from the back office to meet me, he seemed a little taken aback by my enthusiasm to meet him. "Wow, you're certainly full of energy; where do you get all your joy?" he laughed.

My first thought, of course, was to tell him it was Jesus, but I decided to tell him my excitement was from being able to reunite with Donaldson after all these years. After meeting Donnie, the light bulb turned on in his head, and he realized who we were. "You are the Americans' daughter, aren't you?"

We stood in the office and talked for a long time. Thomas was also a Christian, and much like Juliet, he knew the Bible very well. He also quoted quite a few scriptures on forgiveness, and then with a look of true amazement, said, "I know what the Bible says about forgiving people, and I have heard stories of people who forgave the impossible, but not until today have I ever met anyone who has really done it. You two are real; you are modern-day people living out what the Scriptures tell us to do. Because of meeting you today, I have seen a new kind of faith—one that inspires me to try harder to live out what I read in the Bible."

For Donnie and me there is no greater compliment, no bigger fulfillment than to be told our lives in Christ have inspired someone else's faith.

As we stood there talking with Thomas, I looked over at Donaldson. He seemed perfectly content to just stand there on the sideline of our conversation with Thomas, but I was not. I had come to see Donaldson and knew my time with him was running short. I knew he had brought us here to show us something special, so I asked what it was he was eager to reveal.

Excitedly, Donaldson handed me five copies of his CD. The CDs carried no label, and he had handwritten the song titles for me on a piece of binder paper. He also gave me two photographs of himself. He wanted me to have pictures of himself clean shaven and better dressed than he was today. He apologized for the way he was dressed, and he told me he only learned of my coming that morning after he had arrived at work.

He brought out every one of my letters, but only to show me that he had kept them. As I looked down at my letters from so long ago, I noticed how well kept they were, but also how the creases in them had worn thin from being opened and closed, opened and closed.

I overheard Thomas telling Donnie that Marvin Joseph had somehow managed to call him from prison, requesting that Thomas send him some books. The books, Thomas said, were evil. Donnie asked him what he meant by evil, and he answered, "Demonic, cult stuff."

"You didn't send him the books did you?" Donnie demanded.

Thomas assured him that he didn't, and their conversation went on about Marvin, but I turned back to Donaldson.

"You don't get calls from him, do you, Donaldson?"

"Yes, ma'am, I do, but I don't send him the books he asks for either."

"Donaldson, please don't take calls from Marvin. He is evil, and it will only bring harm to you if you do."

I asked him how Marvin would even have access to a phone. He wasn't sure, but he guessed that someone probably slipped it to him in his cell. He then told me something very disturbing. He said that while he was still in prison, he knew that Marvin had asked someone on the outside for pigeons.

"Pigeons! Why on earth did he want pigeons?" I blurted out.

My mind went crazy, and in a split second thought, *Oh no! He is planning his escape and wants pigeons to write little notes to attach to their feet and send to people in the outside world!*

My thoughts of Marvin planning his escape were quickly dashed when Donaldson informed me that he wanted the pigeons so he could break their necks and do things with their blood. I stood there in shock and dismay, my face plastered with my horror and disgust. All I could muster at that point was a plea to Donaldson to never have anything to do with Marvin. He readily made me that promise.

I knew the time had come to say good-bye, and the lump in my throat was forming rather nicely. Donnie asked for us to gather and pray before we left, and without hesitation the four of us joined hands to pray. Donnie's prayer ended in unison with an emphatic "Amen!" I turned and hugged Thomas good-bye and then Donaldson several times.

As we were walking out the door, I looked back for one last glance at Donaldson, and he said these parting words: "Bonnie, when we were praying, in my mind I see you and me together talking and telling our story."

I stood there in awe and reminiscent of my leaving him the first day we met fifteen years before. He had walked toward the door of Superintendent Mac's office, stopped in the doorway and turned back. With the brightness of the sun shining in behind him, all I was able see was his silhouette, but I heard what he said, "You come back?" My heart wrenched that day knowing I would most likely never return, but I said to him with all the confidence I could muster that I never thought in a million years I would be there in the first place, but if he prayed and I prayed, one day maybe I'd return. He nodded and then obediently put his hands behind his back and stood as the guard shackled and chained him and led him back to his prison cell.

What a stark contrast to fifteen years ago. Donaldson was walking away from me on his own this time, to his home, not led away shackled and chained. However, it wasn't only his walking away that contrasted the past; it was also his parting words. I honestly believed I would never return when he asked me if I'd ever come back, but I did . . . twice. This time I honestly believed his parting words would come to pass, because I had heard them before. My Kimberly has been telling me for years that she has seen in her mind Donaldson and me on stage together telling our story.

AN AMAZING RETURN TRIP

What was sure to be an uneventful trip back to Antigua on the Barbuda Express was once again anything but that.

Donnie, a.k.a. "Mr. Friendly" (one of the things I love most about him), sparked up a conversation with Greg, the captain/owner of the Barbuda Express. As most conversations on this trip had gone, Greg asked us, "So what brings you to Antigua and Barbuda?"

Donnie briefly shared our story, and suddenly Greg's face lit up. "I knew Criddy—he and I were very good friends!"

Criddy! Captain Greg knew Criddy! Will this trip ever stop astonishing me?

I turned my reflective thoughts from the day to face the captain and simply said, "Are you kidding me?"

Greg met Criddy in Bequia, St. Vincent, in the Grenadine Islands in the spring of 1989. Criddy had been backpacking with his girlfriend, Sue, and looking for a ride up to Antigua for Sailing Week, so Greg invited them to sail up with him.

As their friendship progressed, Greg wrote excellent references for Criddy, which eventually led him to becoming captain of Peter Ogden's Computacenter *Challenger*.

When the Barbuda Express returned to the dock in St. John's Harbour, Lake was there waiting for us in his taxi. In just a few days we had grown accustomed to his faithfulness to be there for us whenever we needed him. It had been a long, emotional day, and we were ready to get back to the Halcyon and relax. We passed by the front desk to be greeted by the sweet receptionist, Normalyn, who seemed to be waiting for our return. She was eager to know how it all went and if we had found Donaldson. She was thrilled to hear all had gone as well as it had.

I went to bed and woke up thinking about the possibility of seeing Melanson. I wondered if what Johnny said was true about his "finding Jesus"; I really hoped it was after meeting with Donaldson. From the trial we all had a pretty good idea it was Melanson who shot Dad and Mom, but with all the lying that oozed from his mouth during his testimony, there was room for serious doubt.

What on earth was I going to say to him? I went over the possible conversation in my head a thousand times, and no scenario seemed to play out quite right. I made the decision that I would say nothing at all. I would wait on him to speak first; I had full confidence my God would give me the words I would need.

I expected to hear from John first thing that day about our going to the prison. I was met with disappointment to learn John was not able to get us in; it would have to wait until Monday.

Sure . . . great . . . Monday it is, John! No problem, I'm just going insane here. I mean, what's two more days, forty-eight hours of anxiety going to hurt me? I brought plenty of my high blood pressure pills with me; I'll just take extra!

The Antiguan independence holiday would take place over the weekend to provide plenty of distraction to keep my mind off of this ominous task.

INDEPENDENCE DAY

The following day was Sunday, and it was Independence Day on Antigua. It's a day that means a great deal to the people of the island. Antigua and Barbuda gained their independence from England in 1981, so that momentous occasion was still fresh in the minds of many islanders. Their independence meant as much to them as ours does to us, maybe even more so, because the entire island shuts down to celebrate.

Never wanting to miss out on a party, we jumped into Lake's taxi and hit the streets of St. John's where the main event takes place. I was still having a mouthwatering hankering for the barbequed lobster that Pat, our Barbuda escort, had told us about, so I was thrilled to find lobsters on the grill at every stand. And yes, oh yes, there was butter!

Willing but Will It Happen?

By nine o'clock Monday morning, I was antsy to speak with John and could not wait another minute to make the call.

"You don't waste any time do you?"

I let him know I had mustered up all the courage I had to even take this step, and I was indeed ready to go. "John, I certainly do not wish to waste another moment!"

He chuckled at my persistence and promised to ring back as soon as he had an answer from the prison.

Are you kidding me? More waiting? This man is killing me, and I swear he likes it!

Much to my surprise John did call right back only to tell us today would not work; it would have to be Wednesday.

Breathe Bonnie, just breathe. God is in control of this; not you and not John!

The only problem with Wednesday was we were scheduled to leave on Tuesday, but I certainly didn't tell John that. This was the very reason I made my flight arrangements with the flexibility to change them if needed. One call to American Airlines and it was done. God was reminding me once again that He was the One at the helm of this ship.

We were actually delighted to have an extra, unexpected day to enjoy paradise, and we made the very best of it!

Wednesday morning had arrived, and it was "make it or break it day." Our flight was scheduled to depart at three-forty in the afternoon, and we had made the decision that no matter what happened we were not going to change it.

I was to call John at nine o'clock in the morning, and as promised I did just that.

"I'll ring you back," he quickly answered. *Click!*

Our bags were packed and sitting at the door. We paced the floor, desperately waiting once again for the phone to ring with news that I would or would not be going to Her Majesty's High Prison to meet with Melanson Harris. By ten o'clock I was agitated and anxious; we decided we could not keep this pacing up all day; waiting for that blasted phone to ring was more than our nerves could handle on this last day.

I looked over at Donnie; I saw his furrowed brow and the strain on his face and knew the battle in his mind had returned. He had been having a hard time with the notion of going to see Melanson, and even so, he never once insinuated that he wouldn't go or that he would try to stop me. He had been nothing but a constant source of loving support.

At 10:15 a.m. I was through waiting! I walked over to my suitcase, threw it on the bed, flung it open and grabbed my bathing suit. "I'm going to the beach," I declared to Donnie. I refused to waste our last day pacing around the hotel room. Donnie stayed back to make arrangements to have all calls forwarded to the Carib Bar.

We had made some friends while at the Halcyon, and I scanned the beach looking for any sign of them. I didn't want to wait for this news alone. Once I found them, I filled them in on the status of things and stretched out on a lounge chair and let the Caribbean sun warm my face.

Forty minutes later, we heard Donnie's voice, "I have news." The seven of us sprang up in our row of lounge chairs like a choreographed line from the Radio City Rockettes and in unison said, *"Well?"*

He stood there quiet, as if enjoying the captive audience he was holding; he had our full attention. He slowly and painstakingly announced, "We're not going."

I swear you could have heard a sand crab crawl. We all sat there with our mouths wide open catching sandflies. I was dumbfounded; I couldn't believe it, I just could not believe it! Donnie told us that when he was up at the front desk the phone rang, and it was John calling. He said John was angry about the whole thing and found it to be absurd that they would not let us in to see Melanson. John is one who is in and out of that prison all the time; they know very well who he is. With the superintendent being out ill, the guards were exercising an authority they don't often get to use, and they apparently liked it. My guess is John will see to it they regret their excessive use of authority.

For us it was clear that the guards were not the ones who had kept us out that day. We knew full well who was in control the entire time, and although we were willing to walk through it, God shut the red iron door to the prison.

chapterThirty-One

Home

Lake pulled his taxi right up to the American Airlines check-in counter, and in the midst of all the hustle and bustle, I almost missed a great surprise. There in all his greatness stood John Fuller, patiently waiting to be noticed. I almost started crying, but like my dad, that would only have made him feel uncomfortable. So I held back the tears. I wish he knew how much I loved and appreciated all he did for us. If you asked him, he would tell you he had done nothing at all, but it wasn't just what he had done for me; it was his presence in my life for which I was so grateful.

Donnie found our seats on the plane and didn't consider sitting anywhere but the middle. He knew my name was written all over that window seat. As we taxied out onto the runway, I wondered when I might return. The circumstances that had brought me to this place all three times had been orchestrated by God, so why would I expect anything less than His perfect will for the future. Maybe the next time I see Donaldson won't be in Antigua or Barbuda; maybe he will be coming to Texas to see me.

As we took off and headed for home, I strained to see Antigua for as long as I could, looking to the northwest, hoping I might catch a glimpse of Barbuda, but it never came into view. I looked over at Donnie, who was out like a light, which was nothing new for him. It is a regular occurrence for Donnie to look over at me at touchdown and ask, "Are we taking off?" But I knew this time my poor Donnie was emotionally exhausted and had slipped into at least a three-hour sleep coma.

Alone with my thoughts I began to replay the entire trip in my head: *Why didn't I get into the prison? Why did I have to go through all that to end up not being allowed in?*

I don't feel in any way the potential for me to meet Melanson was a mistake. I think God was asking, *Do you trust Me?* I wanted to pull the plug after the first and second attempts, and I easily could have, but I had to let God close the door, not me. I know myself all too well—pulling the plug would have been a temporary fix to my fear. Once I was home I would have begun to question whether or not I had missed an opportunity that God had given me, and I knew I could not live with that. Just as fire refines gold as it heats up, so I felt tried and refined as I had passed through my own version of the fire.

This whole experience offered me a new understanding of what it means to truly forgive. In some cases God calls us to offer forgiveness face to face, and other times it may be simply before the Lord. Regardless of the circumstance we cannot harbor unforgiveness in our hearts, because in the same way God forgave us we must forgive others.

Home Sweet Home

As hard as it was to leave Antigua, it was so good to see the millions of lights that illuminated the Dallas skyline as we flew into DFW Airport late that night. After living here for over ten years, Texas had certainly become home to us.

"Home, sweet home" is what we both said when we finally laid our weary heads upon our pillows. I reached for my Blackberry to set my alarm, and Donnie said, "Don't do it, babe. You don't have to get up at six o'clock every day of your life. Just go to sleep, and if you wake up at six, fine, but if not, just sleep. Okay?"

Reluctantly I set my phone back on the nightstand and fell sound asleep.

His Redeemer Lives!

October 26, 2010: It was six o'clock in the morning on what seemed to be a normal, cold, fall morning in Celina, Texas. Then the phone rang. It was Donnie's cell phone; he reached for it and said, "It's a 268 number; I don't know who that is. I'm not answering."

I lay there for a second, then sat straight up in bed shouting, "Answer it, answer it; that's a Barbuda number!"

Donnie answered, and I clearly heard a very familiar voice coming through the phone. Donnie quietly chuckled and said, "Well, we are fine, Donaldson. How are you?"

I lay back in the bed with a huge grin on my face and joy in my heart. I heard Donaldson say the reason for his call was to be sure we made it home safely. It wasn't a normal cold, fall morning in Celina after all. It was a great and awe-inspiring fall morning, because Donaldson had called just to check on us.

I anxiously awaited my turn to talk, but even with all that was going on in my head, I couldn't help but realize whose phone he had dialed—Donnie's. *He has my number, because I gave him three of my business cards, and Donnie gave him one of his, yet he called Donnie.* Once again Donaldson was showing me integrity and respect. Just as he prepared himself to meet me by dowsing himself with Brut cologne, he was doing it now by calling Donnie first and asking permission to speak to me.

When the phone was finally passed to me, I thought there was nothing left to say. He and Donnie had already discussed it all until Donaldson said to me, "Bonnie, all the island is talking about how you come see me."

Apparently it wasn't only his mother who needed to know that my forgiveness was real and sincere, but so did the people of Barbuda.

My return to Antigua in search of Donaldson was immeasurably more than I could have asked or imagined.

I found him, yes. What I didn't know was that God had planned the trip to show an entire island community that through His Son, Jesus Christ, Donaldson had been forgiven and that his Redeemer lives!

Epilogue

His Redeemer Lives!

To this day I can still see the intensity in his blue eyes and the assurance on his face when he said, "Bean, I promise you, if I ever get into a position where I fear for my life, I will call on the name of Jesus, but I have never been, nor will I ever be in a position where I am not in total control."

I had replayed that conversation in my mind a million times, even before Dad and Mom had died. Dad had made it clear that he believed in God, but I knew that believing alone was not enough. We must confess with our mouths, "Jesus is Lord," and believe in our hearts that God raised Him from the dead. "For it is with your heart that you believe and are justified, and it is with your mouth that you confess and are saved" (Romans 10:9–10).

I often wondered what it would take, with my dad's confident assurance about himself, for God to get his attention and show him that no man can always be in total control. I always thought it would take God speaking to him in an audible voice or giving him a burning bush experience like Moses, but all it took was a simple roll of black tape.

Just the thought of being bound and gagged for hours is something I can't and don't want to imagine. But that seeming act of torture bought my dad time, time to consider Jesus and time for Dad to contemplate his promise to me. In my life my dad made me very few promises, but the ones he made, he always kept.

However, Dad's keeping his promise is meaningless if God does not keep His. But we have the blessed assurance that He does! "For [God] who promised is faithful" (Hebrews 10:23) and bound Himself with an oath, so that those who received the promise could be perfectly sure that He would never change His mind (Hebrews 6:17).

William Norman Clever was bound and gagged with black tape before he breathed his last breath and stepped into heaven. If you have yet to receive "the promise," please do not be deceived into thinking that you, too, may have the opportunity to be bound and gagged before you die so you have time to call on the name of Jesus.

God promises you, "Everyone who calls on the name of the Lord will be saved" (Romans 10:13 NIV). And God is bound to His promise.

Notes

CHAPTER 12

1. Leppard, David. The Sunday Times, UK, February 6, 1994.

CHAPTER 15

1. Graham, David. "When killers came to a rich man's playground." The Independent UK, January 30, 1996.

CHAPTER 28

1. Email from John Fuller on 28 October 2010. Used with permission.

About the Author

Bonnie L. Floyd. *Real, relatable,* and *refreshing* are words often used to describe Bonnie Floyd. Perhaps it is because she could easily be a next door neighbor to any of us. *Bound to a Promise* is a true story of tragedy and redemption that unexpectedly resulted in the opportunity to share that story with others and, ultimately, the birth of Bonnie Floyd Ministries in 1996.

Bonnie has taken her contagious zeal for the Lord and her authentic love for people to various conferences, retreats, and churches throughout the United States and beyond. Her powerful and dynamic messages bring the Scriptures to life for audiences of all ages and offer useful and practical ways to apply them to everyday living.

For several years Bonnie served in various capacities with Women of Faith and is currently an administrator for Barry and Sheila Walsh. More importantly, she has a deep love and respect for God's Word that is born out of her service as a teacher and small group leader for more than twenty-three years.

Bonnie has been married to "her Donnie" since 1987. Both California natives, they now make their home in Celina, Texas—a home that provides a perfect setting to share Bonnie's passion for cooking by entertaining family and friends. They make their church home at Genesis Metro Church in Frisco, Texas, where Bonnie, who was ordained as a minister of the gospel in 2010, is an active member in women's ministries.

Scan this code for more information about Bonnie Floyd Ministries

Bonnie Floyd
MINISTRIES

REAL. RELATABLE. REFRESHING.

Bonnie has an authentic love for God's people.
You will always find Bonnie out among them
following her passion for leading others
into a deeper relationship with Christ.

For more information on her ministry or to book Bonnie
for a retreat or speaking engagement visit her website at:

www.bonniefloyd.com

*Scan this code for
information about
Bonnie Floyd
Ministries*